DAVID LLOYD
The Autobiography

DAVID LLOYD

The Autobiography

DAVID LLOYD with ALAN LEE

CollinsWillow

An Imprint of HarperCollins*Publishers*

First published in 2000
by CollinsWillow
an imprint of HarperCollins*Publishers*
London

© David Lloyd 2000

1 3 5 7 9 8 6 4 2

A CIP catalogue record for this book is available from the British Library

ISBN 0 00 218952 6

Set in Postscript Linotype Sabon
Typeset by Rowland Phototypesetting Ltd, Bury St Edmunds, Suffolk
Printed and bound in Great Britain by Clays Ltd, St Ives plc

Photographic acknowledgments
All photographs supplied by David Lloyd with the exception of the following:
Allsport pp 8 (bottom), 10 (top and centre right), 11 (bottom), 16 (centre right);
Patrick Eagar pp 6 (both), 7 both, 8 (centre). 9 (bottom), 12 (bottom), 14 (all), 15
(all except centre right); **Empics** pp 10 (centre left), 12 (centre); **Lancashire Evening
Telegraph** pp 4 (bottom right), 5 (top and bottom left); **Graham Morris** pp 8 (top),
9 (top), 12 (top); **PA Photos** pp 9 (centre), 11 (top left and right),
16 (top and centre left).

To my family,
children Sarah, Graham, Steven and Ben,
and my lovely grandchildren
Sam, James, Jasmine and Joseph

Contents

Acknowledgments

Cricket has been so good to me and any sportsman is always indebted to the many people who have helped, encouraged and inspired along the way. I am no different and would like to thank everyone – coaches, colleagues, family and especially my Dad – for their understanding and support throughout my career. I have enjoyed, tremendously, going back through my scrapbooks, which prompted the memories to come flooding back.

Finally, Alan Lee has been a good friend over the years and I'm grateful to him for capturing me as I am, and I would like to thank him for all his time and efforts on my behalf with this book.

Introduction

I might have been a plumber and I once worked briefly in a brewery. Other than these fleeting diversions, all my working life has been spent in the game of cricket, which makes me one of the luckiest men alive. Whatever may be said about me – and people have said plenty down the years – nobody could justifiably question my passion for cricket or my knowledge of it. I know the game back to front and if I was born to do anything, it was to talk about cricket. A good job, then, that in my early fifties I have found myself with a comfortable seat behind a microphone for Sky Sports, indulging myself and getting well paid for it. I have to pinch myself some days, just to make sure it has all worked out this well.

It did not always look so rosy. Life has offered a few slings and arrows along the way, some of them of my own making. Always, there has been cricket to console me, because it is a game that offers so many different outlets to enjoy. I know – I seem to have sampled almost all of them in the 40-odd years since I took my first steps towards a playing career on my home town ground at Accrington in north Lancashire.

Since then, I have played at the highest level, captaining my county and touring Australia with England. I have been a county umpire and a coach to every level of player from primary schools to the England team; I have spoken on the game on the after-dinner circuit and I have commentated for radio and television. True, nothing can quite compare with playing the game well, but nobody can do that forever. I am one of the fortunate few who has found new niches in cricket and enjoyed them all.

Of course, it has not all been sunshine and roses. How could it be, when I spent five years leading a Lancashire team packed with strong, assertive characters and more than three years coaching England, encountering the backwoods resistance of the counties to progress, trying to change some entrenched habits among players and administrators, beating my head against solid walls? But no matter what was thrown at me as England coach, it did not sour me, even on the blackest days when my efforts and enthusiasm were being undermined; I am glad I did the job. Glad, too, that I came out with my positive nature intact.

In coaching, as with captaincy, I found that the best times were those I spent with the players, preparing for the games and then playing them. The toughest times were those in between, when politics reared its head. Every sport has its internal politics and cricket has a web as complex as any. It was never my scene, never interested me, even when I discovered there were those in the web who might wish to do me down. Probably, I suffered for my innocence in this sphere. Certainly, I would have made a very poor politician.

In times of trouble, I have always had people to turn to, some less obvious than others. In latter years, if things were tough on an England tour, I would unburden myself to a man named Dennis Callow. Dennis is a cheese-maker from Leicestershire, whose proudest boast is that Tesco – run at the time by Lord Ian MacLaurin, now the boss of English cricket – bought 5,000 Stiltons off him one Christmas. 'I told them they had under-ordered,' he said. 'They came back for another 2,000.' I like a man with that optimistic outlook and Dennis was good for me. I met him one winter when he was just part of a supporters' group and we became firm friends. He was my sounding board, my hidden mentor and confidante, a kind of father figure.

My own Dad, God bless him, is as devoted as ever, living alone in his bungalow just up the road from Accrington Cricket Club. Dad could be a double of that nice, short-sighted fellow in *Last of the Summer Wine*; his life is simple, his tastes as straight-forward as his strict Methodist beliefs would suggest. He was never much good at cricket himself but his encouragement for me, and subsequently for my sons, has been immense. More than that, his loving attention to scrapbooks through the years has made the writing of this book easier than it would otherwise have been.

I knew the time would come to put everything down on paper, commit it to history, and the time announced itself when I moved out of coaching and into commentary. I look on from a different perch now but my views and my beliefs are unaltered. So, too, my loyalties and friendships. I cannot think of an enemy I made among the players during my time with England and I look back now with pride and pleasure at some of the careers I might just have helped along, Nasser Hussain prominent among them.

I wanted Hussain in my team when I took over the side and he rewarded me with a double-century against Australia – ironi-cally, on the same Edgbaston ground where I made my own 200 for England 23 years earlier. In 1999, I wanted him to open the batting in the World Cup and he took that on willingly, too. Now, as England captain, he is confirming his maturity and per-sonality; in South Africa last winter, even amid defeat, he was terrific, and that gives me more pleasure than I can say.

England must stick with Hussain, and with the new coach, Duncan Fletcher. They might need four or five years to bring about the necessary improvements – the very improvements I had identified in my own time – and they deserve a long run of loyalty from their bosses, from the media and from the public. I will continue to say so from my own, privileged seat, where I can now pronounce on world cricketing affairs and think back, as I frequently do, to the modest back street where it all began.

CHAPTER ONE

Number 134 Water Street

These days, Accrington is a town with no heart, a random community divided by a hectic trunk road linking the motorways that ring Manchester. It can be a rough place, too; rough enough for me to call it 'The Wild West'. Come late evening, turning-out time, it can feel intimidating. The mills, for so long the main source of employment, are long gone and, in the modern way, nothing has replaced them to bind the locality together. So Accrington has become part of the urban sprawl round a major city, and is subject to all the attendant social ills. It is not much of a town and it is no longer my home, yet it retains a fond place in my heart, for it was once my whole world.

In Water Street, where I was born on 18 March 1947, the cobbles on which I once batted undefeated for 23 weeks against a long-suffering school pal have long since been ripped up, along with all evidence of the outside toilets that were once shared by several families, mine included. The back-to-back cottages, archetypal north-country in their time, were condemned by the council years ago but the original structures still stand, tarted up considerably now. The shops that surrounded and provided for us have gone, too, and Water Street is quite a civilised residential area as it slopes steeply down towards the busy town centre. In my mind, though, it is still as it was half-a-century ago, when cars were rarer than power-cuts, every winter seemed to bring thick snowdrifts and the cobbles outside our house could be Old Trafford one day and Wembley the next. A street of dreams, and some of them even came true.

I was an only child and the great regret of my mum was that I was born a boy. I was not keenly aware of this at the time, of course, but I know it now, not least because, as some squirmingly embarrassing old family photographs show, she used to clothe me as a girl, in dresses and tight frilly coats, and grow my hair long and curly. She even gave me a pram to push around, and a doll to look after. Apparently, I was to have been called Gwyneth. Heaven knows what would have become of me if I hadn't discovered sport . . . not that I had far to look for it.

Dad was absorbed in amateur sport, you see, especially football, which he had played for 25 years as a full-back in the town leagues before hurling himself into a series of jobs as secretary or manager of various local teams. He'd been a useful player, I'm told, if only at a modest level; more importantly he was a terrific organiser and it was his example that set me off on the sporting trail. The pride he felt in my achievements he kept to himself and his scrapbooks, of which there are many. Dad still lives in Accrington, though since Mum died he has been in a more functional bungalow, 500 yards from the cricket field, with a talkative budgerigar called Peter for company. Every time I visit he seems to have started a new book of cuttings or photographs, his private record of family progress, yet he is a quiet and undemonstrative man, one who keeps his strong opinions to himself. We never had the kind of father-son relationship that could be called close or confiding – I wouldn't seek to discuss problems with him and, in latter years, I have gone out of my way to keep them from him – but I did not lack for support and I can see his involvement all over again now as he charts every development in the cricketing careers of my sons, Graham and Ben.

I always knew we were poor. There was no resentment in me,

no sense of deprivation or the social rage we hear so much about nowadays. We just got on with it, made the best of our lot, and in general we were happy enough. Mine was a caring upbringing, by parents who would protect family above all else, but in common with most of those around us we had no money to speak of. Mum worked in one of the weaving mills that were dotted around the area in those years and I have a vivid memory of the deafening noise of the place on the days when I would finish school and then walk to meet her from work. It always struck me as an intimidating environment and, even if the industry had not been rendered obsolete, I would have needed a blindfold and a hard shove to get me working there.

Dad had worked for some years in a foundry but it made him unhappy, and he spent the second half of his working life as an operating theatre technician at the local hospital. As a boy, though, I did not recognise the word 'operating' and I thought he worked at the local cinema, doing something impressively technical behind the film screen.

Mum was the dominant figure in our house. Her family, the Aspins, are still well-known around Accrington today and, in my childhood, there was a clannish element to them that was not lightly crossed. If you kicked them once, they were likely to kick you twice, and twice as hard. Strength of numbers had something to do with this: Mum, Mary Jane Aspin, was one of 13 children, seven boys and six girls, and I guess they each had to develop a personality pretty darned quick to be heard at all. Mum had no difficulty in this regard and when she became Mrs Dave Lloyd she ruled the roost at 134 Water Street. All the money that came into the house went straight to Mum, who gave Dad £1 a week to spend. Knowing him, he probably put that in the church collection.

An example of the parental pecking order came through religion, which was a powerful theme to my upbringing. Dad has always been devout; his bungalow today contains any number of

17

strategically-placed crosses and he remains a pillar of Cambridge Street Methodist church, one block up the hill from Water Street. Dad has a good singing voice – always has had it seems – and one of his abiding pleasures in life is to go around local hospitals and old people's homes and sing his repertoire of hymns. He's done this for nigh on half a century now and although he's not far off 90 himself he still likes to think of it as singing 'to the old folk'. He is an act in demand, too, judged by the list of bookings, some of them many months ahead, which he keeps pinned up in his kitchen.

The point here, though, is that Dad, despite his strong beliefs and strict doctrines, never pressed religion on me, but Mum, who was not very religious, did. He practised his religion in his own introspective way and it was only much later that I realised this had impacted severely on my youth. As far as I know, for instance, Dad has never touched a drink in his life – no, not even at Christmas, when if Mum made a sherry trifle, she would always have to make a separate one just for Dad, free of alcohol. I never stepped foot in a pub until I was 18 and, out of respect for Dad, I would never have a drink in his company.

Dad and I would go to the Methodist church two or even three times each Sunday; Mum never went but she'd give me what for if I dared to skip it. In fact, she would think nothing of hitting me with her frying pan, an act of corporal punishment that would have the social services department foaming at the mouth now but which I accepted as a salutary part of growing up.

Kids expected to get a belt if they were naughty in those days – or, at least, the kids round our way did. The actual whacking was seldom as hard to take as the humiliation that went with it. If I'd done something wrong, for instance, the whole street would know about it because I'd be sent round to bring a belt from my Uncle Harry's house, five doors down. Uncle Harry – one of many aunts, uncles and cousins who congregated in a street that seemed to be damned near full of our family – was secretary of the local Working Men's Club, a naval man whose most memorable habit was to chew tobacco and spit it into the fireplace, something I always observed with a kind of fascinated horror. But Uncle Harry also had a thick sailor's belt and I regularly had to suffer the indignity of asking to borrow it just so Mum – always Mum, not Dad – could give me a good whack. Then, I would have to trail sorely back down the street to return it.

The Working Men's Club was a focal point for the community, not least because so few families around us had a television. I remember the night when one of our neighbours became the first to own a TV and everyone in the street crowded into their front room to goggle at this speckled black-and-white picture as an object of desire, a miracle of its age. It was almost as exciting as getting our first inside toilet, though we had to wait a good bit longer for that . . .

I only recently found out that the Lloyd family was originally Welsh. This might have seemed apparent from the name but it had never occurred to me. I just assumed we were Lancastrians to the roots. In fact, my great-grandfather was from Cardiff and he moved up to Shrewsbury in search of work; subsequent generations shifted a little further north and lost all trace of the Welsh accents but it might help explain why I've always had a feeling for Wales, felt comfortable there and often chosen it for holidays. We occasionally went there as a family but, in general, our outings – always by buses and trains – would involve staying at Methodist guest houses, though there was also the treat of a trip to the Heysham Towers holiday camp in Morecambe. We had just arrived on such a holiday in July of 1963 when Dad read a paragraph in the *Daily Express* saying that Lancashire had taken me on their books. So, in a state of high excitement, we abandoned the holiday and took the bus straight home again.

All of which seemed a distant dream in 1956, when I took my

first, hesitant sporting steps as a nine-year-old at Peel Park Junior School, adjacent to the old Accrington Stanley ground. I ended up as captain of both cricket and football and we did all right. At football, indeed, we did rather better than that. In my last year at the school, just up the hill from Water Street, we played 11 other schools and beat them all, scoring 63 goals without conceding one. I played left-half but we were so superior to most of the opposition I spent most of the games as an extra attacker and scored hat-tricks in four consecutive games. I wouldn't have remembered this but one of the earliest and dustiest of Dad's scrapbooks supplied the information, together with a faded cutting from the local Accrington newspaper reporting the achievements of Peel Park and adding that 'in recognition, Mrs Dave Lloyd, mother of the team captain, has promised to supply the lads with a slap-up supper'. This meant pie-and-peas and was a forerunner of many such social suppers Mum was to cook in succeeding years for football teams, usually run by Dad and featuring me in some prominent position.

The 'family' theme was one that Dad loved to foster within his teams. It would be a curiosity now for a local football side to gather regularly at the manager's house, certainly without alcohol involved, but in the 1950s these evenings were social highlights, apparently enjoyed as much by the drinkers in the team as those who religiously abstained. Mum's pie-and-peas were a neighbourhood legend, and not just to the champions of the Accrington Schools football league.

Some years earlier, Dad had given up playing for one of the most successful football clubs in the area to join a struggling side called Cedar Swifts. This was typical of him. Winning every week with an obviously superior team evidently held no charms; he would rather be at the helm of a crew that starts in the shallows and strikes out to conquer the deeper waters. Cedar Swifts were perfect for him and he took them through various levels of Accrington football, described variously in the admiring local rag as 'team manager, trainer and general administrator'. It did not stop there, either. The Swifts only had 12 players on their books and when two were unavailable one rare Saturday, including the only goalkeeper, Dad went between the sticks. Another week, I recall, the referee didn't turn up, so Dad took on the whistle and later praised the sportsmanship of both teams to the local reporter present.

They must have loved Dad in the offices of the *Accrington Observer* because he was always on to them with snippets of local football news. They haven't forgotten him to this day and, quite recently, he was made the subject of a weekly feature they run called 'Observations', in which they interview a well-known local person on life in the vicinity. Dad can be both crotchety and eccentric in his advancing years and, for some reason, he interpreted it all as a quiz, a series of cunning trick questions, which made much of the outcome a hoot. 'What's the most important thing in your wardrobe?' he was asked. 'My coat-hangers,' he responded gravely.

Cedar Swifts had the characteristic Lloyd social side to it, which meant that I was drawn into the club long before I was old enough to play. I would always be around when the players called in and, more often than not, I would go along to watch them on Saturdays. Their goalkeeper was Peter Westwell, who was to become chairman of the Lancashire League and – by representing their resistance to change obsolete traditions and accept a Premier League in the county – partly responsible for their conflict with everything that should happen at the grass-roots of English cricket. My boyhood memory of Peter is altogether more favourable, as he was the man who introduced me to Accrington Cricket Club and even generously paid my first year's subscription as a junior member. I don't suppose I was suitably grateful at the time, as I wasn't overkeen on cricket at the age of ten, but it was not long before my bicycle wheels were more familiar with the potholed track that leads from

Thorneyholme Road into the cricket ground than with any other piece of land in Accrington.

The town cricket ground is not a thing of beauty. Imagine a village green, perfectly manicured, with a church on one corner and a pub on the other . . . and you have got precisely the wrong idea. Like most Lancashire club grounds, Accrington is well-maintained but functional. No frills. It does, though, have an atmosphere, which was enhanced several times over in the days when the big local derbies might attract crowds of more than 2,000 on a Saturday afternoon. Everyone paid to come through the gate, and an extra 6d to sit in the enclosure outside the white-painted clubhouse, but there were always a few who liked to watch from the other side of the hedge at the top end of the ground. This would enrage the old boy who did the public address announcements and he would often pick out such characters and try to embarrass them, bellowing things like: 'The man in the red shirt by the tree, I know you haven't paid.' Unfortunately, he invariably chose to make these announcements just as a bowler was charging in.

I was 13 when I started my club cricket, playing for the 3rd XI, and if I wasn't hooked by then I never would be, because the Accrington professional that year was Wes Hall. It was to be another three seasons before Wes came fully to the eyes of an English audience with the 1963 West Indies touring side but he was already well embarked on his Test career and already a spectacular sight with a ball in his hands. He came round to our house a few times, probably even sampled Mum's pie-and-peas, and he took sufficient interest in me to make me feel important. The Accrington ground was scarcely big enough to accommodate his run-up and he literally pushed off from the sightscreen, a daunting sight for any visiting club batsman with a job to go to on the Monday morning.

By this time, of course, I had moved on to secondary school after making no more than an average job of my 11-plus examination. In those days, social divisions were made at 11; to pass or fail that exam meant the difference, to many, between a white and blue collar, an office job or a life on the factory floor. I was a borderline case and, as such, I went to Accrington Secondary Technical School, which theoretically trained its pupils to be skilled craftsmen. The drawback for me was that I was useless with my hands, which made it just about the worst school I could attend. As my sport developed, I became steadily more paranoid about protecting my hands and I worried constantly about hitting them with a hammer or burning them during some experiment. It frightened me to take part in many of the activities that were fundamental to the curriculum of a technical school.

On the other hand, the place did me no harm at all in the broader aspect of educating the person. It was a small school, with only 200 boys, and it actually had a decent tradition of supplying good cricketers – Jack Simmons had just left when I joined. Discipline was also instructively regimented: haircuts had to be trim and short, uniform worn smartly and shoes shining. If anything wasn't right, you were sent straight home, and as I knew what would await me there for such a transgression, I made certain things were right.

I was no stranger to discipline, so the strict school regime held no terrors. My home life was sheltered. Boring, it would be called now, though it never seemed so to me at the time. Even as my teen years progressed and friends began to go to dances and parties, I would be kept on a tighter rein. The church youth club was about the extent of my social horizons and, even then, I had to be in by a certain time, and that meant early. It was beyond my wildest dreams to go anywhere near a pub, so I only knew of Accrington's murkier side by reputation. It was probably a rough-edged town, even then, and many boys of my age and acquaintance were involved in scraps every weekend. That side of things passed me by, because my orbit was simply school, church and sport. At first, despite the urgings of Peter Westwell and the inspiration of Wes Hall, the sport of my choice was football.

Accrington was not a bad place for a would-be footballer. It might not seem so now, for it has been without a Football League side since 1963, but I could go and watch Accrington Stanley as a boy and I did so week after week. So too, it seemed, did most of the neighbourhood. The ground was 500 yards up the hill from home and, half-an-hour before kick-off on a Saturday, the street would be full of people. These were crowds of a like I'd not known anywhere else, nor would for some time to come, and the atmosphere of the match made a big impression on me. Watching football, of course, was different back then. Because I was so small, we'd walk through the turnstiles each Saturday with a house brick for me to stand on. Can you imagine the response if you tried that now? Occasionally, we'd sit in front of the wall behind the goal, not only in danger of a thump in the face from the heavy, leather-and-laced ball of the day but also in open contravention of all the spectator restrictions that apply nowadays. No-one ever ran on the pitch, though. It just never occurred.

I would come to play for Stanley in their non-league days but as I crept into my teens it was the 'family' teams that gave me a start in the game. Dad was into the running of two teams by now. In addition to Cedar Swifts, who were doing very nicely thank-you in ever more exalted divisions, he had helped to found the Cambridge Street Methodists, essentially a church side. I started playing for them at the age of 14 but it was some years later that we entered the All-England Methodist Cup and won it. We had a crack team by then, including my Lancashire cricketing team-mate David Hughes, a centre-forward and quite brilliant in the air. The national final, by coincidence, was played on the Accrington ground.

I played some seasons for Cedar Swifts, too, and we certainly won more games than we lost. Dad still reminisces about how I started out as the club mascot and I know he was proud of the progress I made. His comments in the scrapbooks were not exactly one-eyed, though. If I fouled up, he would say so on paper, if not to my face. '26 January . . . David played well, though he did earn a black mark from me for putting a corner behind – no excuse for this,' is a typically terse entry.

Once Accrington Stanley had been bailed out of financial crisis by the SOS (Save Our Stanley) public appeal, I began to play centre-forward for them, though I was always more of a provider than a goalscorer. Briefly, I played for two other Lancashire Combination sides, Rossendale United and Great Harwood, regularly coming away with some vivid bruises as illustration of what a physical league it was. Just once or twice, I remember playing left wing for Great Harwood with Jack Simmons at centre-forward. As you might imagine, Jack took no prisoners – he was very much the old-fashioned striker, fond of route one and thinking nothing of bundling the goalkeeper into the net if he came between him and the ball. He was good, though, and held a number of league goalscoring records before being forced to pack up when he broke his leg for the third time.

I was luckier than that. No serious football injuries came my way. It was just the threat of them that made me pull back from the game. I played on into my mid-20s and took a few risks to do so, because my Lancashire contract meant there was no way I should have been playing football once April had started. This, however, was the month when leagues and cups were decided and there were several illicit evenings when I would dash back from Old Trafford to play in a floodlit football game, usually under an assumed name as a token defence against prying eyes from Lancashire. It wasn't very satisfactory, because I didn't dare get injured so I found myself pulling out of the 50-50 tackles I once relished.

I had never viewed it as a direct choice between cricket and football, it never struck me as starkly as that, but the fact is I could have pursued an opportunity with Burnley and, cricket having taken over in my priorities, I chose not to do so. Burnley were the premier club in the area. Jimmy McIlroy was the coach, Ralph Coates and Willie Morgan were the players of the moment and their approach made me a figure of envy among my pals.

Harry Potts, who seemed to manage the club forever, actually came to our house to sign me on schoolboy forms as a 15-year-old – and was probably plied with some of my Mum's pie-and-peas – and they thought enough of me to give me a run of games in their 'B' team. I played on the left-wing, then at left-half, and did all right considering my age and lack of experience, but everything was flying at me at once now, and although as a teenager you cope with any amount of sport, decisions were being taken almost subconsciously.

My week was cluttered. On Tuesday evenings after school, I'd do two hours' football training at Turf Moor, then come back to Peel Park for indoor cricket training with the school. Thursdays were the same, only in reverse order, and when Saturday came around, I'd be at Old Trafford for cricket coaching at 9.30 in the morning, then bus back home to play football for Cedar Swifts in the afternoon. Inevitably, the homework got a bit neglected.

In time, the football training got neglected, too, as cricket took me over. Burnley lost interest in me, as I must have appeared to lose interest in them, and the door to one glamorous career was quietly closed. In fact, as the time came for me to take GCE O-levels and leave school, advanced education never being a genuine option, I was not aware of any attractive doors creaking open.

I did manage to pass three O-levels, which was one or two more than might confidently have been predicted. I got English okay, and Woodwork, largely because I enjoyed the theory of it even though I hated the practical side. Somehow, I also managed an adequate grade in Technical Drawing, which surprised no-one more than my teacher. 'How the hell you passed, I'll never know,' he said on the day I left, shaking his head uncharitably.

The idea of technical schools is that you emerge into a trade apprenticeship, perhaps as a carpenter or joiner. I was slated to be a plumber. Don't ask me why, because I have no idea, but it was there in black and white: D Lloyd to start plumbing apprenticeship with Accrington Council. It was then, in the summer of 1963, that we went on holiday to Heysham Towers and Dad's eagle eye chanced upon that paragraph in the *Daily Express*.

CHAPTER TWO

From Accrington to the Lancashire League

I did not instantly become famous and I certainly didn't get rich. The net impact of being taken on the staff at Old Trafford was that Lancashire paid me £6 a week instead of the £7 a week I'd been getting for turning up each day of that summer to bowl to the members in the nets. There's nothing like bringing a kid back down to earth . . .

The money meant nothing, though, against the excitement, the fulfilment and, not to be underestimated, the relief of knowing I no longer had to go through the charade of starting a plumbing apprenticeship. Instead, with Lancashire experimentally following a lead set by professional football clubs, I was to be an apprentice county cricketer – the last, as it turned out.

It was not headline news. I might have made a mild stir in the sporting consciousness of Accrington but nobody would have heard of me outside our corner of north Lancs. The surprise was that Lancashire's approach made the national press at all, but once it did so it was no surprise that Dad spotted it. Thursday 25 July 1963 was the day that changed both my career plans and the family vacation plans, bringing us back from the holiday camp as fast as public transport could carry us – which was painfully slow.

Accrington to Morecambe is a simple journey nowadays. By car, around the northern motorways, it takes little more than half-an-hour. But in 1963 we had no car and there were no such motorways. The trip back involved three buses and a lot of fretful hanging around. It seemed endless. Once we made it back to Water Street, though, the letter from Geoffrey Howard, Lancashire's secretary, was awaiting us as confirmation of the offer. Two weeks later, the details were complete and I joined the ground staff immediately. 'Wonderful news,' Dad wrote in his scrapbook. 'Mum and I are very proud today.' I was pretty pleased with myself, too.

There had been a good deal of talk that summer about me being taken on but I did not want to believe it until it actually happened. Coming from my background, with such limited career options, it hardly need be said how much it meant, even if one or two of the immediate effects were negative. I took a pay cut and, for a time, I was prevented from playing for Accrington because I had become a professional. This was clearly crazy and self-defeating, both for the league and for inexperienced individuals like myself, but it was a while before anything was done. Essentially, I was banned from playing for my home town club, on the ground where I had grown up, my only 'crime' being to have absorbed the lessons learned there well enough to graduate to another tier. It is a shockingly ingrained insularity that makes such rules and I cannot help reflecting on the benefits of the Australian system, which promotes the opposite philosophy, encouraging first-class and even Test cricketers to maintain their affiliations and return to play for their clubs whenever available.

Accrington had brought me along intelligently and there are many at the club to whom I shall always be grateful. Whatever cricket I was getting through school – and some of that was at decent representative level – nothing prepared me for the step up to county standard quite like the League. At 16, I was opening the batting in the first XI against some fast and fierce overseas professionals. It was a terrific grounding.

Lancashire, of course, had also been monitoring my progress

in schools cricket, not least because I played some games in the best of shop windows, at Old Trafford. Bob Cunliffe, the PE master at the Technical School, had thought I was capable enough to go for Lancashire Schools trials and I quickly found out I was as good as anyone around. It was not, though, my batting that got me noticed but my left-arm slow bowling – chinamen and googlies that kids of my age found pretty hard to fathom.

We had a decent county team. Frank Hayes was involved, making plenty of runs, and our best fast bowler was Bill Taylor, who went on to play for Notts. We had another batter, an opener called Alan Thomas, who was the best player in England by a mile at his age. All of us thought that he would be the one to make the grade, but after one year with Lancashire he decided that county cricket wasn't for him and packed it in. This may have been a statement on the English system and its peculiar demands that permit no productive life outside the game. Certainly, Alan Thomas has not been the only player of potentially enormous ability to be lost to cricket in this way.

I could be forgiven if such profound thoughts never troubled me at the time, for this was a period of intense personal excitement. Unlike Thomas, I had no inclination for any career outside sport and Lancashire were giving me the chance to live out my daydreams. The county knew a bit about what I could do from the winter coaching sessions and they made their interest plain by asking me along in my holidays. I went every day – the £7 a week was to cover expenses – and played some matches for the Club and Ground side, an amalgam of young hopefuls and club members. These games were played on the back field at Old Trafford which no longer exists, having gradually given way to a branch of B & Q, three office blocks, a car park and an indoor school. Such land sales were sadly essential, simply to keep the county club afloat, but, long-term, they did nothing for the facilities. The Old Trafford square these days is hopelessly tired because it has to accommodate every game played on the ground. Peter Marron, the groundsman, does his best but the surface is just worn out. When I signed up, all fixtures other than 1st XI games were played on the back field, which was kept in such pristine order by Bert Flack and his groundstaff that nobody minded.

It was vast back then. There was room for a dozen nets and they were constantly in use. My main duties involved bowling for hour after hour, sometimes to the county players but just as often to the members who, in those days, used Old Trafford for more than mere spectating. Many of them were affluent men, prominent in local society, such as Lord Winstanley, who captained the Club and Ground, and R A Boddington from the brewery family. Then there was a man called Peter Kershaw. I can still picture him now, striding out to bat in the nets clad in his white cardigan, with leather buttons like miniature footballs. He regularly put half-a-crown on his middle stump and stood, French cricket style, in front of all three. I would try my damndest to spin it round his legs, giving the ball a tremendous rip, and just occasionally I would succeed and claim the half-crown. Unwittingly, Peter Kershaw was teaching me how to spin it big.

My bowling would eventually desert me, a case of the 'yips' familiar to plenty of spinners, but it was responsible for the early recognition that came my way, while my batting took very much longer to develop. I bowled regularly for Accrington's 3rd XI in 1960 as a 13-year-old, and when I stepped up to the 2nd XI the next summer it was principally as a bowler. I took plenty of wickets, too, including five against both Todmorden and Bacup. It was doing my confidence a power of good.

More than anything, I was growing to love the cricket club and would spend every spare moment there. I had gone through the starstruck stage, when I used the Lancashire League handbook and its pictures of the club professionals to collect autographs, and now I had the competitive spirit. I wanted to be in amongst them, scoring runs and taking wickets. I wanted to play cricket every day of the week and, by and large, so I did.

There were club nets on two evenings a week and Under-18's practice another night. There were some midweek evening fixtures, too, and then when the school holidays arrived at last I would cycle to the ground every day. We lads would have a running battle with the groundsman, Frank Nash, who could be stern and protective about his square, but it was big enough to absorb a great deal of cricket and he let a few of us on to practice if he was in a good mood. I especially remember a lad called Ian Birtwistle, who bowled very slow swingers. He's only recently retired, having taken something like 1,000 wickets in the league, whereas my life sometimes seems to have described a couple of complete circles since those holidays we spent together.

The Accrington club is far enough out of town to lose something of the social element that binds many clubs in the locality. Other than on match days, people did not use the place for its bar, or for any facilities other than the pitch and the nets. This is not to suggest there was anything disparate about the team – there could never be, with a league rule stipulating that every player had to live within five miles of his club headquarters. This, though, did not mean that every decent cricketer in the area came to our club, because if you lived in the centre of Accrington you were qualified for nine different league clubs.

When I started, this was great for stimulating local rivalries but as time has passed, and transport and travel have become so much simpler, the congestion of clubs has lost its virtue. Accrington cannot hope to sustain so many clubs in an age when people have so many alternative interests. It was all very well in the 1950s, even the 1960s, when clubs tended to play only on Saturdays and it was established that whole families would devote the day to cricket, mother making the teas and the kids playing around the boundary. In the main, that doesn't happen anymore, but those responsible for administering league cricket in the county have kept their heads buried deep in the sand. There has been talk of amalgamating the Lancashire League and Central Lancashire League, which in my view would be advantageous to all, but everyone is scared of losing what they know. So they continue with the absurd situation in which Accrington, Rishton, Enfield and Church, for instance, all play in the same league, their grounds separated by drives of about five minutes. It is all too parochial, a statement that could apply equally to so much else that is wrong with the game in this country.

Spectator numbers have also decreased dramatically. Accrington would regularly draw up to 1,000 for their league games when I was in my teens. Briefly, such crowds were recreated in the mid-1980s, when I was back at the club after retiring from Lancashire – this, though, was almost exclusively down to one man. Vivian Richards' highly publicised decision to play a season for Rishton, at a time when he was the casualty of the strife at Somerset, gave the league an injection of adrenalin and Accrington reaped much of the benefit. By luck, we were drawn to play Rishton at home, soon after Viv made his debut. Through more good fortune, the sun shone brightly and the crowds flocked in, a throwback to 30 years earlier. The place was humming with 2,500 inside, most of them drawn by the quaintness of seeing the world's best batsman playing in their own backyard. We filled it again when we drew Rishton at home in the league cup and the money we made from those two days helped pay for some improvements, like the new clubhouse roof to replace the leaking original. This was one of the priorities I had set when I went back, along with improving the seats around the place by importing some unwanted ones from Old Trafford, and generally sprucing the place up with trees and flowers. I transplanted a few trees from my own back garden and they are still doing fine on the far side of the ground, helping form a protective screen against the adjoining railway. And I enlisted Dad's support on the gardening front, which appealed to him greatly.

Dad has always been happiest when he is doing something. It was the same when I was a boy and he would forever be coming up with home improvement schemes. When we got an inside bath and toilet at last, he had it built in what was once my bedroom, then put up a partition; so the joy of not having to go outside to use the toilet was partly offset by being unable to swing a cat in my own room. He did something similar downstairs, putting up another partition to separate the hall from the parlour – the famous 'front room' of so many households of that time. We never went in there. 'We must keep it nice for special visitors,' he said. But we never had any, so the room stayed empty.

Dad hates being idle, so gardening is good therapy. He has dozens of tubs and pots full of plants outside his bungalow, mostly raised on bricks or planks to protect them from the neighbourhood cats that raise his ire, and until recently he made regular, loyal visits to the cricket field to tend the flower-beds, a losing battle against the mindless vandalism that routinely wrecked his handiwork.

Nowadays, Accrington are lucky to get 100 people through the gate on a Saturday and they also make far less on the social side than clubs such as Haslingden, who not only get plenty of spectator support but maximise it with a thriving bar and restaurant. Everything was different when I began playing, and I don't think I say this entirely through the inevitable rose-tinted spectacles. If we did not thrive like some clubs as a social centre, we certainly thrived on the field, where a succession of good professionals and some staunch backup from the locals brought consistent results and enviable support.

The professionals were of great use in helping to shape my game. I was an avid listener, considering no moment wasted in the company of these playing gods, nor having any of that modern mix of cynicism and embarrassment that seems to afflict kids today when it comes to learning anything from the older generation. The only pro of that period who did not help advance me was Bob Simpson; he charged two shillings for each coaching session and we couldn't afford it.

The Indian slow bowler, S K Girdari, succeeded Wes Hall at the club and stayed in the area for years, working as a male nurse in Lancaster. 'Girdy' was far from being one of the best players to grace the league but he was a good coach and a great help to me as I developed from the small and timid figure that set out in 3rd XI cricket. I wore shorts when I first played in the leagues, which is some indication of the family finances. When I was chosen for Lancashire Schools, I had to borrow bat, pads and gloves from the team bag because we just couldn't afford new kit, and I still clearly remember the day Dad took me to Gibson Sports shop in Accrington to buy my first bat. It was, in its way, a solemn induction ceremony and the pride with which I chose the Stuart Surridge Ken Barrington Coil Spring, then took it home to treat it from the jar of linseed oil that we kept in the toilet, was a bit like a mother taking her first baby home.

Time clouds the mind and I guess Accrington had its un-savoury side then, just as it does now. It was the era of teddy boys, who tended to use bike chains to help out in their scraps, and Saturday night was usually the night for fighting. I knew this from hearsay, from the lurid tales spun by schoolmates and from what I picked up at the club. I had no first-hand knowledge, because I never mixed with such types or at such a time. My life revolved around church and cricket and my weekend activities were conducted almost entirely in the presence of Dad, who would whisk me home immediately cricket was over on a Saturday evening.

Rishton were the opposition when I made my debut for the Accrington first team in July of 1962. For a 15-year-old, it was a torrid baptism – batting at number eight, I went in on a hat-trick. I successfully saw that off but made only one before getting bowled. As was usually the case at that time, I fared better with the ball – much better. My six overs, in fact, brought me three for 24, including a wicket with my second ball in league cricket. As proof of the variety of cricket I was playing at the time, I turned out for the Under-18s against Church two evenings later and made 71 not out, my highest score to date, then travelled south to Basingstoke on the Wednesday to represent North of England Schoolboys against the South. I would have played every day given the chance, and there were spells when I damned near did so. I had that schoolboy's dread of the season ending, which might have helped excuse my one 'duck' of the year coming in my last game for Accrington seconds.

Two entries in Dad's scrapbooks are testimony to the progress I made that summer and the disparity between my batting and bowling prowess. I'd been sent by the school on a coaching course at Lilleshall and emerged with a report that read: 'A most promising bowler. He will also make runs if he learns to make a firmer distinction between attack and defence.' Later that summer, after spending a fortnight at Old Trafford – 'everything free, plus £1 a week pocket money' – I was specifically mentioned as a likely candidate when the *Manchester Evening News* ran a story about Lancashire's idea to take on apprentices. 'In an attempt to beat the serious cricketing blight at Old Trafford,' it began gloomily, 'Lancashire are considering introducing an apprentice professional scheme.'

And so they did, but it was another year, almost to the day, before D Lloyd left school and became eligible. By then, I had played another football season and, if only in the subconscious, relegated it to second place in my sporting affections. This must have been the case, because I still have a telegram sent to me in April of 1963 that would have had most boys of my age leaping to give a positive answer. 'Please ring Burnley 777, reverse charge,' it read. 'Would like you if possible to play tomorrow.' It was signed H Potts, Burnley FC, and was a last-minute invitation to make my debut for the Burnley 'B' team, but I turned it down because the Lancashire Cricket Federation had selected me for an Under-19 trials day at Bolton and I preferred to take up that opportunity. In the event, this was also denied to me as my designated lift to Bolton failed to materialise, so I spent the day stewing in frustration while my places in cricket trials and football team were left unfilled.

Burnley did choose me again for the 'B' team the following week but I think the die was cast. I knew then that I wanted to play cricket for Lancashire and that no other sport was going to get in the way. From that day on, football came a poor second.

When the new Lancashire League season started, I was put straight in the first XI, and now it was as an opening batsman. A sign of changing times, of a changing cricketer. Nothing spectacular, though. First game, I blocked relentlessly for more than an hour and made 13. This was to be the pattern of things for a while. They would moan in the local paper that I couldn't hit it off the square and they'd be right, but nobody at the club complained, or tried to change me, because they knew they were developing a player. If I managed 20, and batted a good while against a decent pro, I'd done well. I'd also done a lot to boost my confidence, which was growing anyway from playing regularly with a decent bunch of players who knew how to treat a young player.

It was a real cross-section of local society in that side. A fellow called Linden Dewhurst was the captain, and very much the father figure; there were two brothers, Frank and Derek Rushton, and a quick leg-spinner called Eddie Robinson. He died in 1999 but would have walked into any modern county team because he could do what they are all crying out for. He was a great character, too, making everyone laugh at will. Then there was Russ Cuddihy, who played both football and cricket for the town and later became chairman of the cricket club. He was a real hard man – no-one would mess with him – but a real friend to us all.

Our wicket-keeper was Jack Collier, another who is still around the town, and I remember him for two things. He used to put raw steak inside his gloves to protect his hands when he kept wicket to Wes Hall. And he had this habit of coming up behind you when you'd just got out, rubbing your shoulders in a comforting way and saying: 'Eee, you were going so well today, I'd backed you for 50.' You'd got one.

Some terrific cricketers were playing in the leagues in those days. Everton Weekes and Clyde Walcott had been among the pros before I started, but I did play a bit with Eddie Barlow, the South African. Eddie became a good pal in later years but he gave me a backhanded incentive back then by saying openly that I would never make it to county level. Anything like that tends to spur you on if you've got something about you. One of the quickest bowlers in the league was the West Indian, Chester Watson. He played for Church and, one year, took 140 wickets at about five runs apiece. I saw him in Jamaica a couple of years back and he still looks no more than 28.

It was good cricket, hard and competitive if, at times, too negative. Teams would be inclined to bat on too long, killing games rather than risk losing, and it was this attitude, of course, which hastened the advent of overs cricket at club level. You soon learned which teams would play it the right way, though, and you also learned which ones it was best to miss. This was still the time of the Wakes Weeks, the annual factory holidays that were staggered among the mill towns. At Accrington, we would always hope that our wakes week – and the exodus to Morecambe – coincided with a fixture against Chester Watson and Church. We were usually disappointed.

CHAPTER THREE

Two Noughts and an Unhappy Eighteenth

I made nought in my first innings for Lancashire. For good measure, I made another nought in the second innings. As I was also implicated in a run out, dropped an important catch and the team lost to Middlesex by nine wickets, it was not exactly the debut of my dreams. Fair to say there were moments in it when I heartily wished Old Trafford would swallow me whole.

Strange to relate, I had felt so ready for the big day I was bursting out of my boots. An unworldly teenager I may have been but nerves were not to blame for such a start and I don't recall feeling overawed. The fact remains that my only positive contribution to a sorry three days for Lancashire was to take two wickets and even that was nothing to feel proud of, as they came pretty expensive and I bowled like a drain.

It was the middle of June 1965, and I was not far past my 18th birthday. I had already played a lot of cricket, at a variety of levels, but the urgency with which Lancashire promoted me – and the anticipation that surrounded it – had as much to do with the parlous fortunes of the county as my own rapid development. Lancashire were in trouble and, because of it, they clung desperately to the promise of fresh blood.

Most of the problems passed over my head, to be honest. They just didn't mean much to a teenager whose only interest was in playing the game, rather than its internal politics. There was an atmosphere about the place that surprised me but, of course, I had nothing to compare it with. For all I knew, it was natural for there to be an 'Upstairs, Downstairs' divide, in which the young players were expected to be cringingly subordinate to their seniors. For all I knew, the 'Dogs' Home', as our below stairs dressing-room was labelled, was the fate of the juniors at every club. Similarly, the jealousies and acrimony of the time had no real impact on me. I probably thought such conflict was commonplace in county cricket, though I did know that for a big, well-supported club like Lancashire, the record of our first XI in the early 1960s was neither commonplace nor acceptable. In four consecutive years, from 1962 to 1965, we finished 16th, 15th, 14th and 13th of the 17 first-class sides. It was hardly a startling rate of improvement and it led to a number of high-profile casualties, much media hair-tearing and a highly unusual attempt to secure a new captain through an advertisement in *The Times*.

The upheaval was at its most intense during 1964, my first summer on the staff. Not only did we lose our secretary, Geoffrey Howard moving south to Surrey and being replaced by a rugby league man in Jack Wood, we also lost an entire committee and discarded several senior players in pretty unpleasant circumstances. My memories of it all are sketchy at best and I don't suppose I had a clear idea of what was going on at the time but the upshot was that the club dispensed with Peter Marner and Geoff Clayton because, so their statement read, 'their retention was not in the best interests of the playing staff or the club' – diplomatic code for a dressing-room revolt with which the committee lost patience. Jack Dyson was also sacked – 'not up to the required standard' said the committee – and Ken Grieves was fired as captain. Whatever the motives and merits of this clear-out, it did not sit happily with the members, who called a special general meeting and threw out the committee en bloc.

Lancashire had always been accustomed to success, or at least the prospect of success, and this spell in the doldrums had come hard. The club had not won the championship since 1950 – and still haven't to this day, come to that – and the promise of finishing runners-up to Yorkshire in 1960 had come to nothing. Everyone, from members up to chairman, was frustrated and I guess there had to be some fall-out.

Maybe I gained more than most from it all. Certainly, the anxiety to uncover young talent, untainted by the sourness and failures of the recent past, was very strong and, for that reason, my cause was probably championed by some influential voices at the club. I made my championship debut before I'd even received my 2nd XI cap, which says plenty about the impatience levels. I had given them some reason for such faith, though, and clearly I'd attracted the right kind of reports in the months since I signed my apprentice forms and waved a cheerful farewell to a career in plumbing.

The first county coach I encountered was Charlie Hallows, who always seemed a hard taskmaster to me but apparently was leniency itself compared to his predecessor. T S 'Stan' Worthington had been Lancashire coach for 11 years up to 1962, so I was regaled with endless stories about him when I joined the following year. Some were so elaborate and colourful that I hardly knew whether to believe them, but the legend of Stan lives on even now among those Lancastrians with long memories, despite the fact he has been dead more than a quarter of a century.

Stan had spent his playing years at Derbyshire, and a curious career it had been. He started out as a number 11 and ended up making a Test century against India at The Oval and opening the batting for England in Australia. When he moved into the coach's job at Old Trafford, so it is said, he ruled with a rod of iron. The players of the time were frankly frightened of him and, from the pictures they paint, I'm not surprised.

His trademarks were blazer and cravat, trilby and cigarette

holder. A figure from the sepia-edged past, then, but plainly not one to trifle with. Along with Cyril Washbrook, the club captain during the 1950s, Stan's unchallenged authority was based on dominance and fear. Often, he would arrive at games unannounced and determinedly unseen, intent on viewing players 'in the raw'. I'm told he used to hide behind bushes as he watched but – if you can believe it – that his presence was invariably given away by the sight of his trilby peeping over the undergrowth. It is a good anecdote, anyway.

That trilby became a magnet to the more mischievous players, though in order to indulge any prankish ideas they needed the Dutch courage of plentiful alcohol. A chance arose during the turbulent months of discord between players and committee, when the likes of Marner and Clayton, maybe even Tommy Greenhough, a leg-spinner with an awkward, rocking run-up but a delivery that is pure Anil Kumble, were doing 'jankers' in the second team. They were in the wilds of North Shields, for a Minor Counties fixture against Northumberland, and, as was the custom for such matches, they were staying in a guest house rather than a hotel. I imagine there was a deal of moaning about it all.

Stan had appeared at the game and, one evening, his trilby appeared on the hat-stand in the hall of this typically Victorian guest house. For a group of players just back from a local pub, this was too good a chance to spurn. An impromptu game of rugby ensued, in which Stan's hat was drop-kicked up and down the hallway until it bore more resemblance to a rag. All present then staggered to bed in high spirits, a buoyant mood that was significantly deflated by breakfast time the following morning. The lads, in fact, were eating their cornflakes with deliberately downcast eyes when Stan marched into the dining-room and cleared his throat ominously.

'Last evening,' he began, 'I believe there was a game of rugby in the hallway, featuring my hat. This evening, you will all have another opportunity to play rugby with my hat – only this time my bloody head will be underneath it.' With this withering challenge he stalked out, leaving a roomful of cricketers with appetites abruptly lost.

Young players will invariably lack respect for their coach, in the same way that pupils lack respect for their teacher. It's simply a generation thing. In my case, it was many years later before I appreciated how good a player Charlie Hallows had been. To me, his memories and tales simply came from another era, while I was impatient to be getting on in mine. I never thought of him as anything other than a good coach, yet in the 1920s and 30s he had been part of a Lancashire side that brought the club its most sustained period of success. Charlie would tell us of travelling to places like Somerset and only booking into the hotel for one night because they knew the game would be won in a day and a half. If we won the toss, he said, only the first five would routinely stop at the ground – the rest would sometimes go to the pictures. And, oh yes, there was always a crate of ale in the dressing-room, steadily imbibed during these one-sided games. It was all a long way from the Lancashire of the 1960s, languishing near the foot of the championship with a win of any kind precious and elusive, and everyone at each other's throats.

Only a few weeks remained of the 1963 season when I joined but it was time enough to make my debut for the county seconds against Cumberland. Jack Bond, who was to become such a central figure in my county career, was in our side that week, along with two more stalwarts-to-be, Ken Shuttleworth and Jim Cumbes. I don't recall making any runs but my bowling, still my principal suit in those days, carried me through. I was bowling orthodox rather than wrist-spin by then and I took six wickets in the match, enough to make me believe that batsmen at this level might be as vulnerable to left-arm spin as they seemed to be in the clubs and schools.

The apprenticeship scheme meant that I was employed year-round by the county and, all too soon, it was winter. Football filled my weekends but the midweek work was largely practical. There were no other apprentices but there was an elderly joiner called Tom Mound, and between us we built the little timber stand that stood at the nursery end for years. Some good, after all, had come of those endless reluctant woodwork classes at school. In fact, they gave me a start in other areas, too, because part of the deal was regular attendance at Accrington College of Further Education, where carpentry and joinery were the curriculum.

The club had a full-time maintenance staff, including a painter and decorator and a joiner, but Tom and I might be seconded to anyone during the winter weeks. Some of it was plain labouring, but as the stage was Old Trafford, it was labouring with love. It was varied enough and I was just pleased to be part of Lancashire, but as I still didn't have a car the days were long. Mum and Dad both left for work early, so Water Street was a hive of activity long before dawn in the coldest months, with my journey to Old Trafford, by bus and train, starting soon after 6 am. Like any teenager, I'm sure I had mornings when the last thing I wanted was to leave my bed, but I'm equally certain I never begrudged a moment I spent at Old Trafford.

The following season could not come around soon enough for me. I had no lofty expectations – Dad's grounded attitude made sure of that – but after a couple of Club and Ground games went well I found myself being picked regularly for the county 2nd XI. Over Whit weekend, I played in what was known as the Rosebuds match, against Yorkshire seconds, and our captain that day was Bob Bennett, who went on to become chairman of Lancashire and tour manager of England during my time as national coach. As he also chaired the England management committee, he was essentially my boss but, back in 1964, I was concerned only with when he would bring me on to bowl and what number he'd put me into bat.

My sheltered and relatively strict upbringing made me pretty circumspect in the dressing-room at first. The politeness I'd needed at home transmitted to my behaviour at the club and made me one of the more timid types. It didn't last. It couldn't, or my life would not have been worth living. I was a good listener, so inquisitive and eager to learn that I probably made a bloody nuisance of myself, and I quickly discovered that with 28 players on the staff you had to develop a personality in order to be noticed. Show signs of weakness and you'd be trodden on by those upstairs. I speak from bitter experience here.

The seasons I had spent borrowing and begging kit meant that I was both grateful and protective when I finally came to possess enough of my own. The sensitive seniors would understand this but Peter Marner thought he would have a bit of fun at my expense. He picked up the treasured new bat that had cost £4 11s from the sports shop in Accrington, threw it on the floor of the Old Trafford dressing-room and trod on it. 'You'll be able to get your oil in there now,' he chuckled. It need hardly be said that I didn't see the funny side.

Home life continued much as before. I still went to church with Dad, maybe twice every Sunday, and it was not simply through a sense of obligation. The Christian faith may have been bred into me but I took it on willingly enough and I have maintained it ever since despite scarcely attending church at all after my 21st birthday, a prolonged absence for which my partial excuse is a dreadful singing voice.

Dad watched me play every weekend, and as many midweek days as he could get off work, and he filled in his notes and scrapbooks meticulously. Looking back at his entries for 1964, I marvel at how much cricket I was able to play – everything from Accrington Under-18s upwards – and at the bald fact that a lad who was destined to go in first for England against Lillee and Thomson had a batting average of 6.5 in his first season for Lancashire seconds.

It could only get better and, thankfully, it did. First, though, I had another winter to get through, which meant football for Rossendale United and Cambridge Street Methodists, along with some altered duties back at Old Trafford. For this close season, I was based mostly in the ticket office, which meant I came under the wing of an elderly couple called Wilf and Winnie Black.

The Lancashire of the 1960s was just a cottage industry compared to now, run on a Victorian shoestring. There was no shop, indeed no club merchandise to speak of, and certainly no computers. The odd, old-fashioned typewriter was the solitary concession to technology in an office where almost everything was written by hand. Wilf and Winnie were very sweet to work for and just a typical pair of clerks. Alongside them a woman called Edna Bownass printed scorecards in season, and other club mailings, on an ancient Caxton press, but my duties involved answering correspondence and entering the payment of subscriptions and ticket applications on the cards that corresponded to each member, then re-filing them in the big tray files of the time. Just secretarial work, really.

As the spring of 1965 dawned, things were looking up all round. A request from the county, to the effect that I should be allowed to play for Accrington when available, was agreed by the Lancashire League. Better still, I began to go in at the top of the order for the club, which helped my batting no end, and because I was now the club professional I even profited from the traditional match day collections around the ground.

Lancashire took note, too, and when the county 2nd XI season began in mid-May they felt it was time to find out if I could bat more productively up the order than I had managed lower down. 'A wonderful start to the season,' Dad wrote proudly after our first match against Leicestershire seconds. 'Batted no. 5 and went in at 29 for three, stayed in throughout and finished 55 not out, then bowled 14-8-25-4. In the second innings he bowled better still with 31-13-58-7 and at one stage had four wickets for no runs. To say the least, this is a wonderful performance for a youngster . . . easily David's best game with any team.' Less partial judges were quite impressed, too. In the *Daily Express*, one of the papers that covered Lancashire on a daily basis in those days, Derek Hodgson thought it was already time for graduation day. 'The attack must have another spinner and if Sonny Ramadhin has lost his penetration then the 18-year-old David Lloyd, a slow left-hander, must be promoted. He took 11 for 83 in the midweek win over Leicestershire seconds.'

That single performance probably did more than any other to hasten my progress. It wasn't just that I took wickets – I'd done that before – but I showed I could hold my own with the bat. With the first team in a transitional phase after the purges of the previous year, there was a willingness to experiment that undoubtedly counted in my favour. So, too, did the press coverage that continued to come my way. Dad's daily monitoring of the *Daily Express* bore fruit again at the end of May. Beneath the headline 'STATHAM KEEPS HIS SPIN ACE WAITING' the item read: 'The left-arm spin bowler English cricket is seeking will appear in the championship in the middle of June, probably against Derbyshire at Buxton. His name is David Lloyd, he is 18 years old and he will be playing for Lancashire. These extravagant claims for the future of a boy who has developed the difficult art of spin bowling are made not by me but by experienced and knowledgeable officials at Old Trafford. Lloyd, they say, has not only control of flight and length beyond his years but spins the ball, can bat and is a good fielder.'

It makes me squirm now to read words that strayed so far to the pretentious, yet as far as the headline prediction was concerned, the *Express* was wrong. I was kept waiting less than another fortnight. I did, indeed, play against Derbyshire at Buxton but I made my debut two games earlier.

On Saturday morning, 12 June, I reported to Old Trafford quite unprepared for what was to come. I had read and heard a good deal of speculation about how soon I might play but there was no indication I was even under consideration for the game against Middlesex. It was such a non-starter that I had gone to the ground without my own kit and Dad had made no plans to attend.

Lancashire, though, had lost six of their first eight championship games, the last of them narrowly, to Hampshire, only the previous evening. It was a case of something having to be done to stop the rot and the selectors decided to drop Geoff Pullar, the number three batsman, and Tommy Greenhough. When Brian Statham pulled out with a groin injury, three new players had to fill the gaps and the names announced were Harry Pilling, Peter Lever and myself.

Dad was at work that Saturday morning but after I had recovered from the shock of selection and got myself changed, I phoned him. It was ten minutes before start of play by then but we had won the toss and I would not be batting until number seven. I knew he would need no persuasion to get there and, before lunch, he and Mum were in position in the ground. Sitting with them were Susan Wallwork, the girl I would later marry, and her parents. The five of them saw me make my entrance at 140 for five and take my leave, a fruitlessly long time later, bowled by Fred Titmus for nought.

Geoff Pullar had given me plenty of advice before I went into bat, just as he would do on numerous occasions in the weeks and months to come. In hindsight, I was obviously being groomed to succeed him, and I'm sure he was far more aware of this than I was, but he offered help genuinely and in the right spirit. Against Titmus, he told me, always get well forward but play with the bat in front of the pad to avoid the ricochet catches to close fielders. I followed the code faithfully and it succeeded inasmuch as I did not give my wicket away lightly. I was in so long and pushed forward so relentlessly that I needed a salt tablet for a bout of cramp, but Titmus got me eventually. Second time around, I was out to the off-spinner Don Bick, again for nought, caught behind by John Murray. We subsided to a meek defeat but this did not dampen Dad's scrapbook ardour as he wrote of 'very proud Mum and Dad' and of 'tears and lumps in the throat'.

There were telegrams, including one from my old school and another from the lads at the Accrington club. And there was a mixed press. One paper said I had made 'a useful start', qualifying this by adding: 'True, he achieved a pair as a batsman but many great cricketers have suffered this fate at the start of their career'. John Kay, the censorious voice of the *Manchester Evening News*, was not convinced. 'I am all for giving youngsters their chance but there is a clear case to be made out for introducing them gradually – not throwing several of them in together at the deep end. To pitch 18-year-old David Lloyd into the fray without Statham at the helm was, I fear, carrying things too far . . . it might have upset a promising player's confidence in himself.'

But I don't think it did. Of course, it was mortifying to get out twice without scoring and I wasn't wildly happy to drop the Middlesex nightwatchman, Bick, at the start of the second day – especially as he went on to make 55. I knew I didn't bowl at my best, either, but I was swept along by the adrenalin of the moment, the sheer, unexpected pleasure of being there.

I was dropped for the next game, though, and in all the circumstances I couldn't feel any surprise. I'd travelled with the side, the Tuesday night journey from Manchester to Tunbridge Wells giving me an immediate taste of the quirks of the fixture-list, but Statham was fit again and I had to content myself with 12th man duties.

Peter Lever batted number seven in that game, which indicates what a long tail we had in those days, and another batting collapse led to another rethink. I was brought back for the Saturday start at Buxton – in this instance, I think, more for my batting than bowling. As someone whose first-class average was nought, I was now confronted with the formidable Derbyshire pace attack of Les Jackson and Harold Rhodes, helped by a wet pitch. It was 47 for five when I walked out to bat but I came through this examination with more distinction than my first.

I made 19 out of our miserable 88 all out, then enjoyed the party as Statham and Ken Higgs plundered the conditions to dismiss Derbyshire for 61. Second innings, I'd got to 15 out of 123 for nine when the rain returned to wash out what might have been a rare Lancashire win. I'd done okay and, now, my confidence was certainly high. They won't drop me again, I thought. But they didn't have the chance.

There was a week before the next scheduled first-team fixture but there was no rest for me and nor would I have sought one. The second-team had a couple of games in the north-east and, in the second of them, against Durham University, I broke a finger. It was the first disruptive injury I'd suffered playing cricket and it could hardly have come at a worse moment. Three weeks out was the decision, so I fretted with frustration as four championship games took place without me. Every lost day, at that age, seemed painful.

They were not entirely idle weeks, though, and at the end of them my name was in the papers for a different reason. I had asked Susan Wallwork to marry me and on 17 July, our engagement was announced. It was to be almost another three years – until 30 March 1968 – before we tied the knot but we both came from traditional families and long engagements were nothing unusual in the 1960s. We were both only 18 and knew little of life, I guess, but we had grown up together, living in the same street and going to the same junior school and the same church. Her family were a step up from mine and her father had risen to town mayor – he was Alderman Wilfred Wallwork when we got engaged – but that mattered to neither of us. Susan, who followed cricket even before we started going out, worked as a shorthand typist at a factory in Accrington. She'd been my first proper girlfriend and I saw no reason to doubt we would always be together. That I was wrong is no reflection on her and she remains a sweet person and a stalwart mother to our children.

I celebrated our news by making three against Glamorgan. Jeff Jones, the best left-arm quick bowler of the time, got me out, and did so again in the second innings, though not before I'd blocked through more than an hour for 14 in a losing cause. The club responded by giving me my second XI cap, which qualified me for a minor pay rise but was much more a recognition of progress.

My appearances were spasmodic during the rest of that season but I did play in my first Roses match, at Sheffield, and contrived to mark it with my second pair – caught Close bowled Wilson in both innings. Again, I batted a fair while – fully half-an-hour in the second innings, and gained some satisfaction from surviving my first encounter with the legend that was F S Trueman. But still, I didn't get a run and we were well beaten again.

Yorkshire were to finish only fourth that year but they would resume normal business by taking the title in each of the next three seasons and, like all teams who grow accustomed to winning, they developed a sheen of superiority that would have opponents cowering before a game had even begun. That side of the late 1960s, with Boycott, Sharpe, Close, Illingworth and Trueman as its focus, was as good as any I have seen in county cricket – and they knew it.

I ended that first, half-season of championship cricket with 202 runs and 17 wickets but my best performance came in the last game of the year, against the touring South Africans. Four wickets came as a relief after some initially rough treatment from a tall left-hander. I had watched him from the field during the first morning and thought he looked vulnerable around leg-stump. When Brian Statham brought me on for the mandatory single over of spin before lunch, I duly attacked that area and saw my plan exploded as this chap – utterly unknown to me – hit every ball to the square-leg boundary. As I trailed off with the unflattering figures of 1-0-24-0, I asked one of the senior players who this batsman was. 'He's called Graeme Pollock,' came the answer. 'He'll never make a decent player. Much too free.'

On the last day of that tourist match, as we were bowled out in familiar fashion for only 117, I was last out for 42. I was no longer just a promising bowler. I had taken my first tentative steps as a county player, I was engaged and now I owned my first car – a blue Mini with 48,000 miles on the clock, my pride and joy. In all senses, I was on the road.

CHAPTER FOUR

Jack Bond and his Merry Men

Wisden was cautious in its assessment of my prospects. The 1966 almanac, reflecting on my initial forays into the first-class game, offered the sober judgement that I was 'a useful batsman as well as a left-arm spinner of distinct possibilities'. Lancashire were equally sparing, never short of encouragement but intent that I should not acquire ideas above my station. For three seasons after my championship debut, I was seldom sure of my place in the first team and when I was finally given my county cap, in July of 1968, it inflated my annual salary to a heady £950. It was enough to get by on, but it certainly fell short of giving me a comfortable cushion on which to start married life, when I wed Susan Wallwork immediately after my 21st birthday.

These were frustrating years for me. My impatient mind was telling me I was ready to push on, to establish myself as a county cricketer and then cast aspiring eyes further upwards. But my results were telling me I still had a great deal to learn. Lancashire had not been wrong to push me forward as an 18-year-old – not in my view they hadn't, anyroad – but they were not getting an instant return on their gamble either.

They were not short of perseverance, playing me in the first team virtually throughout 1966, yet I was to spend much of the following summer back with the seconds. In large measure, I guess this was due to the decline of the skill that got me noticed in the first place. My spin bowling ceased to work for me, first regressing into something flatter and less guileful and then, through lack of returns brought about by something akin to nervous paralysis, gradually disappearing from my game. I got the yips. Golfers know of it, many of them, and for some reason it snares spin bowlers too. It can be a misery, the very anticipation of bowling – or, for the golfer, putting – striking fear in the heart until you would really rather not do it at all. By the time I became a capped player, I was virtually a specialist batsman, and not especially sorry about it.

Many were surprised, though, because there had been some fanciful forecasts of my future as an all-rounder. At the time, I'd been delighted to read them, too. We were playing on uncovered pitches at Old Trafford, something I would love to see restored to the English game. There is a paranoia about it now. It is a commercial no-go area, for fear that the game would forever be condemned to the pavilion. In fact, it didn't work like that at all. Sure, we occasionally played in conditions that might now be deemed unplayable but this was extremely rare. Maybe three times a year we encountered a really wet pitch, and probably one or two of those would behave impeccably, but the wider variance of conditions did a great deal for techniques with both bat and ball.

Leaving the wickets uncovered once a game had started was a matter of individual choice at that time – and our club stated that they were doing it specifically to encourage spin bowling. As Sonny Ramadhin, a marvellous man from whom I learned a good deal, had now moved full time into the leagues, this meant Tommy Greenhough, Ken Howard and me. Lancashire believed they had an unusual prospect in D Lloyd and they were investing in it.

The press caught the mood of optimism. Even John Kay, who was known in his long tenure at the *Manchester Evening News* for having a sharp edge to his pen, wrote some gratifying lines about the young Lloyd. 'I believe he could become Lancashire's best all-rounder since Len Hopwood did the double way back in the thirties', he wrote. I'd never heard of Len Hopwood but it sounded impressive, anyway.

I had my moments in that first full summer. One day, in particular. In the first week of July, with the team running on empty after a string of defeats, I took seven for 38 at Lydney. Gloucestershire, needing only 193 to inflict yet another loss on the Red Rose, were dismissed for 132 and I was a hero for a day. In the context of what had gone before, and what was still to come, it was a fleeting cause for celebration. 'It was a tremendous performance', said the *Daily Mail*, 'and makes his previous total for the season of only nine wickets at a cost of more than 40 runs each look bewildering.' They had a good point there, but the *Accrington Observer* did not bother with such trivia. 'It will probably be only a matter of time before he makes his Test debut', they trumpeted. And they were right, in a sense. It was a matter of eight years, almost to the day.

It didn't help me that the week after my bowling had made headlines at Lydney I suffered another injury, this one careless and freakish. It came, believe it or not, from cleaning my bat, a labour of love for me and one I undertook with the relish and regularity an obsessive housewife might reserve for polishing the silver. I was using a razor blade, which slipped and cut my hand badly enough to put me out for a fortnight.

I was fit in time to get a few runs and wickets in a rain-ruined Roses match but 1966 was to end with Lancashire showing no discernible improvement and D Lloyd having lost a little of his media lustre. John Kay, who was nothing if not close to the club, posed some uncomfortable points in his *Manchester Evening News* column: 'Something must be done and I will start the ball rolling by asking what plans has the committee for bridging the ever-widening gap between the experienced players and the young raw recruits? There are talented youngsters at Old Trafford but is the best use being made of them? Two questions: WHO is responsible for the lost form of the left-hand spinner with the ball? WHY is Lloyd now a medium-pace swinger instead of a slow spinner?' Dad had written his own, curt caption to this piece – 'John Kay talking out of his hat' – and I badly wanted him to be right. Yet as I spent most of the following summer in the second XI, with my bowling steadily becoming a secondary and subsiding skill, I had to come to terms with a change of emphasis.

Charlie Hallows had always championed my cause and I thought a lot of him for it. In fact, I would happily indulge his eccentric coaching methods, which sometimes involved teaching me to come down the pitch against spin bowling by stealth, rather than like a bull at a gate, by placing a pad on my head and insisting it should stay there – a sporting version of a deportment class. When the season began, Mr Hallows gave a public explanation of my demotion. 'We think Lloyd is potentially a first-team player of uncommon talent,' he said in that way that always precedes a significant 'but'. 'Last season, through no fault of his own, his bowling opportunities were restricted and he was not used as often as he should have been. We want to develop his spinning and in the early weeks of the season he can do that better with the second team.'

It was a sugaring of the pill, no doubt, but through the early weeks of the summer there seemed no great determination to get me bowling long spells. Instead, I was pushed up to open the batting in second-team cricket and, as if finding my true identity, began to make a go of it. It did my confidence a power of good, too, and when the call came to return to the senior team for much of the second half of the season, I batted with a good deal more conviction.

Many people considered I had become an enigma when barely out of my teens and James Lawton, in the *Daily Express*, wrote:

'David Lloyd, the 20-year-old all-rounder Lancashire hailed as a great, then almost forgot, is ending this season of lost opportunity in a blaze of full employment.' My bowling, though, did not escape some harsh criticism. I made a half-century against Northants but failed to take wickets on a wet pitch. The *Guardian* reporter hung me out to dry. 'Lloyd, lacking experience, could neither bowl a length, maintain direction, nor make the ball lift or turn with any real venom.' If I had a bad day then, it was not the only one. Of the 21 first-class wickets I managed in the first-team that season, eight were taken against the amateurs of Scotland. The all-rounder status I had enjoyed through my teens was soon to be scrubbed from the CV.

Confinement in the second-team was not without its benefits. For one thing, the first team was still a struggling side, the merits of its bowling frequently undermined by poor batting. David Green was an exception to this, and a shining light in the dressing-room, where, not least because Brian Statham was so essentially quiet, he held court with wit and wicked humour. I had learned that, as a younger player, it was wise not to get into conversation with him, but rewarding to listen. His mickey-taking of those around him was unceasing, without meaning them any harm at all, and his opening partner, Geoff Pullar, came in for more stick than most – Sir Noddington Pullsworth was one of the kinder nicknames he coined for him. Peter Lever was called Peter Pimple and Ken Shuttleworth, who was not the brightest, Ken Dull. I developed a lot of my own sense of humour from 'Greeny' and, looking back, I think our dressing-room in the mid-1960s would have been a dour and perhaps dispirited place without him.

The club was changing only slowly and the juniors in the downstairs dressing-room were forced by circumstances to get along together and develop as a gelled unit. The likes of John Sullivan, Harry Pilling, Ken Snellgrove, Peter Lever, Ken Shuttleworth and myself grew up together and became very close, which certainly enhanced the spirit and understanding when we all came together in the first XI.

That was not far off, either, for wholesale changes were looming. Brain Statham had been holding the fort for three seasons, captaining through his own peerless playing example rather than any inspirational skills in management or motivation. He had told the committee he should do the job because he recognised the precarious period the club was going through and knew that his reputation and record commanded respect. Even in the autumn of his career, he knew he had something to offer. It was the right move on a short-term basis and despite the lack of any real progress in team performance, Statham attracted no criticism during his time in charge.

He never said much and he never bothered with nets, but nobody seemed to mind. He was that good. If he had been away on tour with England, we would never see him at Old Trafford until the season was about to start. We might have our first game on a Saturday and Brian would stroll in on Friday morning, ask how we all were, pin the team up on the board, take off his sweater and away we would go.

Of course, this would not do now – there would be howls of derision, calls for heads to roll – but expectations were difference in the 1960s. Brian was a very special bowler, commanding a consistency of line and length and a control of movement for which our game has howled in vain these past years, but in the way he prepared, relative to modern professionalism, he was neither better nor worse than any other top player.

The stringent demands of health and fitness simply did not apply back then. The best example I can muster of what passed for the routine of professional sportsmen was the constant presence on the team lunch tables of bottles of Watneys Red Barrel. Few were left undrunk and this practice continued for some years. I vividly remember my first Test match in 1974, at Lord's. I was not out at lunchtime and instead of an energy drink or a pint of milk, I drank a shandy. Do that today and I would be condemned forever as an alcoholic who couldn't get through a day without a drink, but nobody thought anything of it in those days.

There was nothing like the fitness training players undergo now, or the variety of pre-season preparation. We would do a lot of nets – usually two hours in the morning and another two hours after lunch – and the concession to something different would be an occasional game of football on the back field, in which the senior players would, by custom, grab one of us lads and sit on him to general mirth and merriment.

This was not the only aspect of cricketing life that was very different from what is accepted now. Travel was another thing. Some teams still used the trains, though increasingly few, and I certainly did all my journeys by car. Traffic was not the problem it is now, but time hung heavy. These were the infant days of motorways and even the M6 was not complete – to get to all points from Birmingham southwards, we had to leave the half-built motorway at Cannock and crawl across the A5 to link up with the M1. Southern trips were such an adventure that the fixtures would often be grouped together, giving us a fortnight or so away, but we would still regularly get into our next venue at 2 am on the morning of the match.

Cars were still a luxury rather than an exception, as the heavily sponsored youngsters of today regard them, and it was usually a case of making do. John Prescott would have been proud of our lift-sharing. There were seldom fewer than three or four to a car and I vividly remember one journey back to Manchester from a southern trip in Tommy Greenhough's Ford Anglia. There were five of us – two in the front, three in the back and, just to add to the creature comforts, a kit-case (or 'coffin' as they are known) across the knees of the back-seat trio.

Tommy was not the most confident of drivers and we knew something was wrong when we saw the signs for Sheffield. He'd taken the A1 rather than the M1 and entirely missed his turning cross-country. We ended up having to cross the Pennines via the infamous Snake Pass – the M62 was not even a Roses dream – and it took absolutely hours, at the end of which our driver was a nervous, exhausted wreck.

Lancashire made the inevitable captaincy change at the start of the 1968 season, but they did not replace Statham with another household name. Far from it. Instead, they installed a man who was never sure of a first-team place on playing ability alone. If this sounds cock-eyed, forget it, for it turned out to be one of the shrewdest decisions the club ever made and the precursor to years when we could once again hold our heads high.

Jack Bond was not a player who would ever put pounds on the turnstile receipts. He was as likely to bat number ten as anywhere and he did not bowl. His career batting average was only in the mid-20s and he might have faded from the game prematurely but for Lancashire's foresight in putting him in charge. As a captain, he was little short of a sensation and in five years in the job, he lifted the Gillette Cup three times and the newly formed John Player League twice.

Jack's virtues were many. He was utterly unselfish, for one thing, and would use his wicket in whatever way each game dictated. If we needed to block out, he would go in and do it; if we needed a sacrificial slogger, he'd put himself forward for that too. The team ethic burned strongly within him and he so obviously cared, not just about results but about the people achieving them.

He was a sold churchman, a strict Methodist in every sense bar the shunning of alcohol, an area in which he cheerfully and regularly failed. He was skilful in the handling of doubtful characters and he encouraged players to express themselves, to do the basic things properly but always to enjoy it. He was not a stern disciplinarian in the sense of laying down the rules and curfews but he set the right examples and, in some ways, he was another father figure like Statham. Jack could offer more, though, because he was starting with a clean sheet of paper, complete freedom to mould a new team his way, and at his disposal he had a group of young blokes who had come through the ranks together, were bursting to do well and would communally run through a brick wall for him.

Success in any job is all about being in the right place at the right time and Jack was lucky here, too, for the start of the Sunday League offered a challenge that was right up our street. Most of us had come through the leagues and were accustomed to playing overs cricket on a single afternoon. While certain other counties floundered in the environment, or failed to identify its potential, we took to it immediately. A lot of that was down to Jack, for working tirelessly to improve our fielding, sharpening our motivation and generally making the most of our advantages. We were flying high at 40-overs cricket before many other sides had worked out how to play it.

There was a spot of feeling our way to be undertaken first, though. In 1968, as we set off under this new stewardship, nothing changed immediately, either for the team or yours truly. Well, one thing had changed – since March, I was a married man and had moved out of Water Street into nearby Ascot Way. At 21, I now had responsibilities; but I still had no first-team place.

I knew it could not be delayed much longer after a second-team game against Northants at Old Trafford towards the end of May. I scored runs in both innings, going in first, and took a few wickets. As the senior side was not setting the world alight, I awaited the call, which came in time for the Roses match at the start of June. A week later, I made my maiden first-class century against Cambridge University (main bowlers Roger Knight and David Acfield) and things really didn't look back.

I was still getting stick from the regulars at Old Trafford for slow scoring but I silenced that in a run-chase against Middlesex. We needed about 50 from the last seven overs to register our first win of the season and I made sure we got them, surprising myself with the ferocity of my hitting. 'Lloyd the lash', they called me in the *Daily Mirror*. Suddenly, things looked up all round and between 18 June and the end of the season we won eight games to finish sixth in the table. I narrowly failed to reach 1,000 runs for the first time but finished top of Lancashire's first-class averages. Most important, I had found a niche. I was going in first, and that's how it would stay.

We had a blip in the championship the following year but maybe that was because our efforts were focused on the new competition that was to become so much our domain. We relished the Sunday League because we were young, we could field and we knew how to pace a run-chase. We also had some cricketers whose talents were ideally suited to it, none better than Farokh Engineer and Clive Lloyd.

Overseas players have been a perennial issue for debate in the past 30 years but we won the pools with our two. Farokh and Clive, who started with us in 1969, settled so happily they began to feel like Mancunians. The proof is that they are still there now, and everybody in town knows and likes them.

They both had an early problem or two, as you might expect. With Farokh, it was the road system that mystified him. He lived on the south side of Manchester and the only journey he was confident about was the one to Old Trafford. He conquered the M6, so he pointed his car in the right direction when we were playing down south, but crossing the Pennines to Leeds completely defeated him. It took him four hours.

If Clive had been a different sort of bloke, he might easily have packed his bags and gone home after a few weeks with us. Lancashire had housed him in the centre of Manchester and the address, Unit Two Sauna, should have revealed to them the type of place they were renting. Apparently, they remained oblivious and Clive found himself sleeping on a euphemistically called 'massage bed'. It was an abysmal way to treat anyone, let alone a man with the personality and the talent of Clive.

He was extremely thin back then, an image that his size today may seek to contradict, and not only did he hit the ball miles but he was a great fielder and a useful swing bowler. When we reached – and won – our third successive Gillette final, against Warwickshire in 1972, Clive opened the bowling and raced through his overs before they knew he'd been on. He was a warm and genuine fellow to have around, and an amusing one, too. He would pick up phrases and keep repeating them in that deep, resonant Guyanese voice. 'Okey-bloody-dokey' was one of his favourites and we heard it endlessly.

Clive played only a few games in 1969 before leaving us to join the West Indies tour party. But he made an instant impression and helped us start impressively before some big and enthusiastic Sunday crowds. This was a culture shock to most county professionals, who tended to enjoy their Sunday golf and lunch and felt a bit piqued at having to turn out in games many regarded as trivial, but we loved it from the start.

Farokh was not only a world-class wicket-keeper but a versatile batsman anywhere in the top six. He became my Sunday opening partner and could play explosively, while I got on with doing things more steadily. In sharp contrast to Clive, who put in hours in the nets, Farokh never practised – he was just a complete natural.

John Sullivan was another key man. He went in at number five and whacked it mercilessly. Then he'd bowl eight overs of little dibblers that would regularly tease out two or three for nothing. In Lever and Shuttleworth we had not only a pair of high-class opening bowlers but two terrific athletes in the outfield. David Hughes was another who stood out in overs cricket, bowling his left-arm spin meanly and batting with a flourish. He became the engine-room of the team along with a man who could be described as many things, but never as a natural athlete.

Jack Simmons was 27, and a qualified draughtsman with Lancashire County Council, before he came full-time into county cricket, but it's fair to say he made up for lost time. He's still doing so, in fact, because he now chairs the Lancashire committee and the club, plainly, is his life. He's got a business head on his broad shoulders – he earned such good money in league cricket in the mid-1960s that the county couldn't afford to keep him – and has never been short of a bob or two but he was a brilliant team member and a complete one-off. The stories of his eating habits are legion. They are also all true.

I took him home once, after a day's play, and he asked to be dropped at a chippy called Jack's, 500 yards from his home. Once he'd brought his fish and chips, he sat down on the wall outside to eat them. It was raining, he lived a block or so away and I was still there waiting to chauffeur him, so I asked what seemed the natural question. 'Why don't you take them home, Jack, eat them in your own kitchen?' He looked alarmed. 'If I take these home, Jackie'll not make me any supper,' he said.

At Blackpool one year, Jack booked a table in a local fish restaurant. The curious thing was that he didn't book it for dinner but for lunch – on a playing day. I've seldom seen him move so fast as when the bails were lifted for the interval – he was away in his car, with a couple of other players in tow, and I'm told he demolished two specials, pudding, chips and peas with fish on top, and still got back for the first ball of the afternoon.

Occasionally, he didn't even make it. Southport always put on home-made gooseberry and cherry pies for pudding at lunchtime and when the bell went for us to take the field one day, he'd just started on a full one. For an over, we fielded with ten. Then Jack emerged from the tent licking his lips, the cat that got the cream.

He'd often stand at slip with a biscuit in his top pocket, just to keep him going, and he once justified eating two huge apple pies by saying: 'They said I was to eat a lot of fruit.' Unsurprisingly, he was a very poor pre-season trainer, especially when it came to the five-mile run that would often complete our session in those days. He was once spotted climbing down from a lorry at the gates of Old Trafford, having tailed himself off from the rest of us and convinced the driver he was lost. Another day, he set off for the run with a copy of the *Manchester Evening News* under his arm, open at the property pages. He explained, as if it was the most natural thing in the world, that he meant to stop off on the way to view a couple of houses he might buy to rent out to the younger players.

With Jack, life was never dull, never short of a story. But he was a damned fine cricketer, never mind his size, and he was to play a critical role in the most successful years of my county career.

CHAPTER FIVE

Captain of Lancs

Lancashire took time and trouble grooming me to become county captain but nothing could adequately have prepared me for the circumstances in which I started the job. We were playing at an army camp in Germany and, when the time came to walk to the middle and toss up, my options were limited by the fact that only one other Lancashire player was on the ground.

This was end of season, 1972, and a typical situation of boys on tour, or men behaving badly. For reasons that now escape me, the club had decided that we should have a September trip overseas but, instead of dispatching us to somewhere glamorous – Montego Bay, for instance – we went to Moenchengladbach for a week. It was great fun but I ended up being very glad it wasn't a fortnight.

Unbeknown to most people, even to many in our dressing-room, Jack Bond had made up his mind to stand down at the end of the 1972 season and it was decided at the start of that year that I would succeed him. The club's idea was that I should spend as much time with Jack as possible that summer, to learn from his methods, and this was no hardship as the two of us got along famously. It did not go down well with everyone, though. Even Jack Simmons, one of my greatest pals, was among those who began to think I was tagging along after the captain to curry favour when it came to naming a new captain – they were all unaware that the decision had already been taken.

Once it was out of the bag, such misapprehensions were cleared. Nobody seemed surprised at the committee choice and the handover was smooth and unopposed. When I was put in charge of the first game on the German jaunt, however, it was not quite the sinecure it may have sounded. You have to remember that we had just won the Gillette Cup for the third year running and that the competitive edge of the season had given way to a yen for some good nights out and a spot of fun. Supervising a group of cricketers in this mood is akin to keeping control at St Trinians.

I could see the way things were heading on our first evening at the camp. Our accommodation was anything but palatial – we shared rooms in spartan, military housing blocks in the compound – but the compensatory factor of this odd venue became apparent when we gathered that night in the Officers' mess. There were 18 of us on tour and, as often happens in such a large group, there was a tendency to hang back from the bar when we made our entrance. Fortunately, Jack Wood, the club secretary, was designated tour manager and he did the right thing by stepping forward to say the first round was on him. The majority ordered German beer but some were more adventurous and I distinctly remember one of the lads calling for a Parfait d'Amour. I don't think he'd any idea what it might taste like but the manager was buying and it looked an attractive bottle on the row of optics. Jack asked the barman to tot up the damage and, to general amazement, it came to two and sixpence. After a brief, stunned silence, someone yelled 'get 'em in again, then', and the tone of the evening was duly set.

Jack Bond had decided by now that he wouldn't play in the opening fixture and I was intent on taking my responsibilities with due seriousness. Hence, after only a couple of beers too many, I left the rebel-rousers in the mess and retired to my room, where I produced a notebook and started noting down fielding positions for each intended bowler.

Such diligence came to naught in the morning. Edward Slinger, later to become a judge and a senior member of the county committee, turned up on time but we had the changing room to ourselves. I won the toss and had no option but to bat first, then sprint back to try and wake the dead. As I stared up at a row of tightly closed curtains, it was clearly not going to be a simple matter and hammering on the doors brought a number of fierce and unprintable replies from the darkness within. The good-time boys, like John Sullivan and Harry Pilling, were especially vitriolic about my prospects of getting them out of bed and onto the field. But gradually, reluctantly and in various states of desperate hangovers, they appeared.

Things did not improve. Any thought that this was to be a gentle social game against some barely competent hosts was dispelled by the sight of the opposition opening bowler marking out his run-up. Corporal Williams was a West Indian and, in traditional style, he was extremely quick and eager to impress. The playing surface was a mat laid on concrete, which was more conducive to the Corporal's needs than the blurred reactions of our batsmen, and the upshot was a rout that did not get my captaincy career off to the most dignified start.

Jack Bond found it all highly amusing, as in retrospect it was. His legacy, though, was a strong one and when I took on the job in earnest for the summer of 1973 I had under me a team that had become accustomed to success – at least in the modern environment of one-day cricket. This was fine in one sense, and greatly to Jack's credit, but it did make him a difficult act to follow. I had learned a good deal from him and respected him immensely, a feeling that was to dissipate a shade some years later when he came back to the club as team manager.

It is fair to say we had a tricky period in our relationship then. It was partly down to me, because I was coming towards the end as a player and had undoubtedly adopted some of the cynical, dissatisfied ways of players close to retirement. Some of it, though, was Jack's doing. He had a habit of seeing the best in everyone and an instance of this arose when he signed a Pakistani leg-spinner named Nasir Zaidi, in the early 1980s. Jack thought he could be the next great thing; I felt he was a poor signing, not only because we already had sufficient slow bowling but also because he was not good enough. As a senior player – though not as captain – I went to tell Jack my views, to question the signing and suggest that what we really needed was another batter. Jack retorted that it was nothing to do with me and, in essence, told me to clear off.

I can understand it now, as Jack by then had identified me as a frustrated agitator and he wanted to clip my wings. He might have been right to do so, but I will never accept that he was right on two other occasions that showed up his a surprising lack of management subtlety for one who had captained the side so adroitly. One Sunday, when we gathered at midday before lunch and our warm-ups, he announced to the dressing-room that if a certain player was not fit, I would be captaining the side but that if he passed his fitness test, I wouldn't even be playing. Intentionally or not, this came across as a slap in the face. Another day, it fell to Jack to break it to me that I was losing the vice-captaincy to the up and coming man of the team, John Abrahams. Broached properly, in his office perhaps, I don't think I would have taken offence but Jack chose to tell me in the toilet at Old Trafford, which I considered tacky.

These were isolated contradictions to the man I knew for many years as a friend, advisor and wise tactician. He was never a flamboyant captain, first because he sensed we were not ready as a team and then, when we were strong, because he was naturally a cautious man. He liked to strangle games, to ensure that the opposition could not win and then grind them down, taking the wins where and when we could. One might question his methods at times but it was impossible to question his results.

There were some strong characters in the dressing-room, which was part of my inheritance, and I feel I profited from watching Jack's handling of those who had a lot to say – such as Peter Lever and Ken Shuttleworth. Despite my later reservations about his judgement in a case or two, I also had nothing but admiration for Jack's eye for a player who could do a job for us. The best example of this was Peter Lee.

'Leapy', as he was known, had hardly taken a wicket for Northants, who were happy to let him go, but Jack had spotted something in him and he was unerringly right. He was not even deterred when Lee came to Old Trafford for a full-scale trial on the back field and Frank Hayes and I clattered him to all corners of Manchester. Jack signed him regardless of this and regardless of the fact that Lee had a dreadful run-up, colourfully likened by the Middlesex opener, Mike Smith, to 'a Federation of London Boys' Club bowler'. What he had in his favour was a barrel chest that would not have looked out of place next to Mike Tyson, a classic, side-on action and an ability to surprise people with his pace. Essentially, Peter was no more than medium-fast but he just kept hitting batsmen on their heads and hands until it could no longer be dismissed as a coincidence. And he took wickets – eventually by the bucketload. I was lucky enough to captain him for three seasons and he was a dream bowler. It was a case of me saying 'tell me when you're finished', because if you tried to take Lee off after only ten overs or so, he would feel affronted. He took 100 wickets in a season twice in his time at Lancashire and became an indispensable member of the side. Yet when Jack Bond said we must have him, the majority in the dressing-room could not have told you why.

In handing over the side to me, Jack handed over some richly diverse personalities, none more intriguing than Frank Hayes. Frank was a mix of professor and nutcase, a mix with which he loved to confuse people. He was, and is, a very bright bloke – a

BSc from Sheffield University who, these days, teaches Physics at Worksop College. He arrived at Lancashire straight from university and it was immediately plain that he was a wonderful athlete, no matter the sport. He played rugby for a good Broughton Park side and walked straight into our team with remarkably little effort. He was a natural.

Frank had a reputation. It was said that he had a vast capacity for drink and it was said that he was always looking for trouble. I think he cultivated these images and enjoyed the notoriety, but in all our time together on the staff I never saw the reputation justified. Much the same things were said about Bryan Robson in his days with Manchester United and the parallels do not end there. Frank, too, was first to the practice ground in the mornings and often the last to leave. He never shirked anything, was easily the fastest and fittest lad in the side. He had a God-given talent to bat, which did not translate to Test cricket quite as fully as many had thought likely, but he remained a good, provocative and always interesting companion. Dull, he was not.

Frank might not have been the hell raiser he was painted but he did have a difficult, stubborn side to him and – along with Peter Lever and Barry Wood – he was at the centre of the most difficult weeks I endured as Lancashire captain, weeks when our previously bonded dressing-room was torn apart. It happened in 1975 and, unsurprisingly, it involved money – or rather, the lack of it. The entire squad was pushing for a better deal from the club but the three current England players felt they were worth more and should be able to negotiate for themselves. This, of course, flew in the face of the team ethic and caused considerable bad feeling.

Players were still regarded like factory workers then, expected to be deferential to the bosses upstairs – in our case, the committee. But although attitudes have changed unrecognisably in the succeeding quarter of a century, the central conflict is unaltered. Players everywhere will always believe they are worth more money and those who have to pay them will say they are not. A very similar 'us-and-them' situation afflicted the England team around the time of the 1999 World Cup and to say it was unhelpful to the priority of focusing minds on a single goal is an understatement.

As a player, I think I was in the minority. I never felt I was underpaid, which probably has a lot to do with the way in which I was brought up – not simply the straitened circumstances but the sheltered contentment. Money has never been a driving motivation to me; it worries me when I am short but I don't go chasing it. I have never been able to understand players having agents, because they only have to pay them, and my enduring belief is that if you are any good at what you are doing, someone will reward you for it. Naive? Simplistic? Maybe, but it is a code that has not done me much harm.

This philosophy was strikingly absent in the Lancashire dispute of 1975 and, as captain, I found myself caught in the crossfire between frustrated players and a protective committee. A no-win situation, in other words. It had all been building up for some time, a noticeable undercurrent of tension developing in the dressing-room. We were happy enough socially but this rising discontent was never far from the surface. We were the best one-day side in the country, drawing big crowds and, as we saw it, making the club good money. At long last, we were also making a concerted challenge for the county championship. The general view was that we, the players, were entitled to a larger share of the rewards.

Lever, Wood and Hayes led the revolt by their natures as much as their status. Being England cricketers, they doubtless felt they could take a public stand and challenge the committee without the fear of losing their jobs that cowed most of the others. But all three were naturally confrontational types, anyway. Lever was a barrack-room lawyer, a clever schoolmaster capable of challenging authority eloquently and loving every minute of the debate. Wood was an instinctively militant character who might have been a clone of Arthur Scargill. A Yorkshireman by birth, he came from a massive family and started with nothing, working hard and ruthlessly to achieve what he wanted from the game. I often used to room with him and found him great fun to be with but his popularity in the dressing-room waned in latter years, when he took on arrogant airs that might be compared to Geoffrey Boycott, who I suspect was a role model. Jack Bond always reckoned that Wood was one of the best players he'd seen in county cricket and, certainly, he was tough. In fact, he was like one of those things you put in a budgie's cage that keeps bouncing back no matter how often you peck it.

The three of them had been part of the England squad in the first World Cup, early that summer, and our troubles climaxed as soon as they returned to us. Essentially, they refused to play, went on strike. It happened on the morning of 21 June, the day Australia and West Indies were meeting in the final of the World Cup at Lord's. We were playing Derbyshire at Old Trafford and, having stayed unbeaten through our first seven championship games, I was keen to maintain the pressure at the top of the table. The last thing I expected was for our three England stars to turn up and down tools. To say the least, it was a bit naughty – also a bit sneaky, as they were well aware that the man at the focus of their discontent, the chairman Cedric Rhoades, was at that moment in his seat at Lord's.

There were words said in the dressing-room. I told the trio: 'You're letting us down by pulling out at such short notice.' In turn, they responded: 'You should be supporting us.' But the majority did not feel strongly enough or, more critically, in a sufficiently secure position to take such drastic action. They feared the sack. The upshot of a frenetic morning was that the trio refused to be talked round, eventually claiming they were unfit. Although both Harry Pilling and Jack Simmons agreed to play with minor injuries, we were left to start the match with only ten players – and we were in the field. An emergency call was sent out for Bob Ratcliffe, who was found doing his Saturday morning shopping in Accrington and arrived in time to take three Derbyshire wickets and score useful runs. Remarkably, we won the game by ten wickets and I was then intent on making a point by putting out the same side in our next match.

Peter Lever took such offence at this that he grabbed me by the throat in the dressing-room and accused me of betraying their cause. I stood my ground. 'We won without you,' I said. 'I'm not leaving out the blokes who turned out for me.' My view was that they had let down the rest of the team and abused their position. It was a stand that cost us dear in the short-term, because Kent easily ended our unbeaten run, but I still have no doubt it was the right thing to have done.

This conflict blew over as swiftly as it had arisen, the club acting to formalise players' salaries and the dressing-room getting back to something near normal. We finished fourth in the championship, which sounds all right until you learn we began the final round of games with a decent chance of winning it. But the saga had left its mark, not least where the relationship between players and chairman was concerned.

Cedric Rhoades had come into the post as a shining light following the en bloc resignation of the committee in the late 1960s. He portrayed himself as a champion of the members and, at first, he did an excellent job. As the years passed, however, I think he began to see Lancashire ever more as *his* club. It got to the point where he was known, to the players, as 'Cedric Power'.

He lived well, did Cedric, and had clearly done well in business, though you'd never know it from a cursory look at his dingy offices in the centre of Manchester. He was one of those commodity dealers who bought and sold such things as tea and linen without ever setting eyes on them, and plainly he did it all very shrewdly. He kept his business cards close to his chest but occasionally I would hear figures that would make my hair stand on end. He was a very wealthy man and he had a very big ego.

Not content with his authority at one county, Cedric wanted to change the cricket world. I see something of him in Don Robson, the dynamic chairman of Durham through their early years in the championship. Gradually, Cedric was ushered onto committees at Lord's, who doubtless felt he was more easily handled as one of them rather than as a militant outsider, and as these commitments expanded, he showed his first signs of neglecting affairs at Lancashire.

In his early days, nobody could have accused him of this. He was at virtually every game we played, vocally supportive by day and usually around socially in the evenings. He drank Tio Pepe, as I recall, and unlike many county chairmen, he made it his business to get to know everything that was going on within the team. He would say to the captain of the day: 'Whatever you want from the committee, I'll back you to the hilt – but I'll ask questions afterwards.' And he did. Cedric was a master at manoeuvering the committee, so that he always had sufficient yes-men to guarantee him a majority but, equally and inevitably, there were always a couple on the committee who were vehemently against him. As the years passed and his influence lost its sheen, this number increased until he was forced out by a coup.

My own relationship with Cedric changed over the years and, latterly, I really didn't like him – I just thought his priorities were wrong, too personally inclined. But this was simply a case of overstaying his welcome, the classic mistake of so many powerful men. For most of his time as chairman, I counted myself a fan and believed his influence to be good. Some of the players lived in fear of him and it is true that he always wanted his own way, no matter the degree of confrontation. I always felt I could deal with him, though, and when I became captain I followed the sage advice of Jack Bond, who told me that the way to get a good idea through a reluctant committee was to put it to Cedric in the sure knowledge that he would dismiss it out of hand, then simply leave it with him for a week. Unfailingly, he would then come back to us declaring the scheme his own brainchild and singing its praises. Basic human psychology, I suppose, but it always made me chuckle to see how it worked.

That turbulent summer of 1975 did end with me lifting my first and only trophy as Lancashire captain, in my third year in the job. It also involved me, though only peripherally, in a semi-final repeat of the match that many still recall as the greatest domestic one-dayer ever played – our Gillette semi-final against Gloucestershire in 1971, won by three wickets in virtual darkness after some wonderful tail-end hitting from David Hughes.

The reprise followed a remarkably similar course and had an identical result but managed to end rather earlier than the 8.55 pm of four years earlier, when umpire Arthur Jepson's legendary retort to concern about the light was: 'I can see the moon – how much farther do you want to see?' In 1975, there were 25,000 spectators inside Old Trafford and I was one of them. I had broken a bone in my right hand during a championship game against Hampshire and had to miss virtually a month at a critical time of the season – a time when the double of championship and Cup was still very much in our sights. I did get myself fit for the final, though. It was our fifth final in six years and we made up for the disappointment of losing to Kent, the previous September, with a comfortable seven-wicket win over Middlesex.

It was a wonderful feeling showing off a cup to the massed ranks of our supporters and it will always count among the high points of my playing career. The irony, for me, was that the presentations that year were made by Tony Greig, the new golden boy of England cricket. Tony had been made England captain earlier that summer in place of Mike Denness, one of the casualties of a bruising, losing tour to Australia. There were others who suffered for that defeat, who knew their Test careers had come and gone, and I was one of them.

CHAPTER SIX

Boycs and My Test Debut

The way things were to turn out, there was a certain irony about the circumstances of my Test debut. There had been several false dawns, including a one-day international against West Indies the previous summer in which I was run out cheaply, but when I finally got my chance in the Test side it was as a straight replacement for Geoff Boycott. He was not exactly dropped – his form was poor and the Indian left-armer, Eknath Solkar, was causing him unusual problems, but there was more to it than that. Nevertheless, I took his place as the England opening batsman. Years later, he was to tell anyone prepared to listen that he should be taking my place as the England coach.

I've always thought I got along pretty well with Geoffrey and I'd like to believe he would say the same about me. There are fundamental similarities between us – we are both from the north, of modest stock, and we tend to say what we mean – and I have never been taken in by his hectoring approach. He likes to maintain the upper hand, and he is not very selective about who he tries it on with, which can and does lead to some pretty entrenched opinions being formed about him. I believe he would have been a disaster in any coaching position with England because man-management, in its more subtle and sensitive forms, seems to be beyond him. He would clearly not be accepted by the players and in recent years he has alienated a succession of them through his stinging criticisms behind a TV microphone or in the columns of the *Sun*. Nobody minds constructive criticism, but there has been a general view that Boycott was destructive.

Once or twice, he has got through to me, and I even confronted him about it outside the BBC commentary box at The Oval during the 1998 Test match against Sri Lanka. It was one of those situations where I had just had enough of him and, rightly or wrongly, thought the only way was to sort it out face-to-face. I went up as they came off air during the tea interval. We had a five-minute set-to in what I considered a private place. It involved some raised voices and plain talking and gave the rest of the press something to enjoy, but it ended up with a handshake and an exchange of new telephone numbers, a cheery outcome that was conveniently ignored by those who wanted to make a big deal out of it. That's me, and that's him – neither of us is ever going to back off from saying what we think.

We'll probably fall out again some day, because we're two of a kind. And because he has such a facility for upsetting people, there have probably been times when he has not had the sympathy he deserved. Perhaps 1974 was such an occasion, because whatever other people were saying and thinking about his demise – and plenty would have taken a silent pleasure from it – Boycott was unquestionably going through a torrid time. It was not just his form that had been mislaid but his spirits.

I'm sure it irritated him hugely that Solkar kept getting him out cheaply, because the latter was an apparently innocuous little bowler with a bit of late inswing that consistently caught Boycott on his crease. But on top of that, I'm told, he had problems with the organisation of his benefit year, he was embroiled in the usual political infighting at Yorkshire and he had fallen out with the England captain, Mike Denness. I specifically say 'I'm told', because at the time all such matters would have passed clean over my head. I was never one to pick up on personality clashes during these early years and whatever had gone on between Denness and Boycott was a complete mystery to me. Clearly, though, it wasn't good. Boycott's subsequent autobiography was revealing when it came to the first Test of that summer, in which he was out for six and ten despite a huge England win. 'I did not score many runs, I hadn't expected to, and it was glaringly obvious that Denness wanted about as much to do with me as the Black Death,' he wrote. Wow.

The upshot is that Boycott spoke on the phone with Alec Bedser, who was chairman of selectors, and there was a mutual agreement that the wisest course was for him to take a break until he rediscovered some form and, I guess, mental resolve. Cynics might say he was jumping before he was pushed and I do know there was an alternative view that Boycott was just behaving weakly in making so much of his troubles. A piece was written in the *Daily Mail* by Alex Bannister putting this opinion strongly: 'I am certain Alec Bedser and his co-selectors, having, in my opinion, been let down, will now bide their time with Boycott, who has surrendered to the alleged pressures of two failures to medium-pace bowlers in the first Test and the anxiety of his benefit, by which he will be the richer by £150,000.'

The debate raged for days in the newspapers – some of which were unmoved from the emotive line that Boycott had been 'axed' – and on the radio but it meant little to me. All that mattered was the bald fact that I had been picked, news given to the posher end of the nation with due solemnity by the venerable E W Swanton in the *Daily Telegraph* of 15 June. 'The England team for Lord's in next Thursday's Test against India is announced today without the name of Geoffrey Boycott,' wrote Swanton. 'In his place Lancashire's captain, David Lloyd, wins his first cap as a no 1 batsman.' Swanton added of the Boycott sensation: 'This is an exclusion rather than a dropping,' a turn of phrase that will have left plenty scratching their heads.

From my viewpoint, it could not come any better than this – making my debut going in first at Lord's. It was a lot to take in and I'm sure I came out with the usual banalities during the stream of Sunday telephone interviews with pressmen. But the fact is it had come out of the blue, not only because I had not been fully abreast of the Boycott situation but because I had enough problems of my own.

To tell the whole story, it is necessary to go back a couple of years, because it was during 1972 that I seriously began to believe I would play for England. Late that summer, I scored a number of hundreds, one after the other, raising my hopes that I would get on the winter tour to India. Cyril Washbrook was an England selector that year and he told me, as sensitively as he could, that I'd made my runs too late, that the tour party had already been chosen. It upset me, because I had really started to think I would go, and although Barry Wood was a dressing-room colleague and pal, I could not understand why he was included when his self-confessed weakness was against spin bowling. Send him to the West Indies or Australia, fine, but don't make him go to India, where his results would be all too predictable. But the die was cast and I had to make do with the consolation of being told I was on standby in case of injuries. This qualified me for a fee, too – all of £50.

The call to India never came but I began the 1973 season in the same rich form that I'd finished the previous one and, in May, I was chosen for the Test trial. This eliminator for the England side, played over three days with two teams of candidates including even the automatic inclusions, was the first played for 20 years and its revival as a selectorial aid would only last a few summers. I, for one, was not sorry to see its end.

I went into that 1973 trial at Hove in very positive mood, feeling I had a great deal to gain and little to lose, but it did not work out that way. I played like a fool and managed to get out lbw for nought in the first innings and I was run out without receiving a ball in the second. My partner, commonly held to blame for this and many another run out, was none other than

G Boycott. It was a mortifying experience, one of those occasions when even the dressing-room is not sufficient sanctuary for your bleaker feelings, and I was grateful when John Snow, who was never the greatest conversationalist, took the trouble to come across. 'Think about tomorrow,' he said. 'That's another day.'

But when the next day came, or rather the next Test trial a year later, I messed up again. There was some encouragement for me in being chosen for the England XI against the Rest this time, suggesting I was at least towards the head of the queue, and I went in at no 3 after Boycott and Dennis Amiss. It was at Worcester, I remember, and Boycott made a big, unbeaten century. I made nought again, bowled by the off-spin of Jack Birkenshaw. I did fare better in the second innings, reaching 50 as Boycott proved his form was not that bad by making yet another hundred, but the game still kicked me in the teeth as I injured a finger in the field, trying to catch John Edrich in the deep.

Although I had made two centuries already that summer, including one for Lancashire against the Indians, the first Test was only a week away and that injury put paid to whatever slim chance I might have had of playing, although in truth I think John Edrich already had a stronger claim to be the top-order left-hander. What it did not do, though, was put me out of the game for the period being suggested in the press. If it had, indeed, I might never have madee my Test debut at all.

I know how the press work now, how in some areas of the newspaper business a sniff of a story can sometimes be built into a whole lot more out of expediency or simple laziness. I was wet behind the ears back then, so I couldn't understand how so many papers – whose correspondents may or may not have got their heads together – came out with a tale headlined 'LLOYD OUT FOR A MONTH' and substantiating it by revealing that I had been to see my own doctor in Accrington. Well, I had – but only to take my son, Graham for a check-up. I never even showed the overworked GP my own swollen finger, so he didn't have the opportunity to provide the mythical opinion that I should rest it for a month.

I missed the next championship match, which coincided with the first Test, but came back in time to make another 'duck' on the Worcester ground in a Benson & Hedges Cup win. We had moved on to Buxton for a championship game with Derbyshire when the news of the Test changes came through and, in the fashion that applied at that time, I recall hearing of my selection on the radio. There was no insult attached to this – indeed the omitted players tended to find out in the same way. Standards of care and communication are very different now but it is only in the past few years, specifically under David Graveney, that the chairman of selectors has made it his business to inform the incoming and outgoing players before they hear about it through the media.

This is far from being the only aspect of Test preparation that has been transformed. In 1974, and for two decades afterwards, the players did not gather at the venue until 2 pm on the eve of the game. There was no coach, no manager and practice together was confined to a couple of hours in the nets that afternoon before checking in at the team hotel and, quite possibly, having a team meal. It seemed fine at the time, because nobody knew any better, but it was a throwback to amateurism, ripe for change and modernisation.

The first thing that struck me on the morning of the game at Lord's was the eerie quietness of the dressing-room. I had been used to the buzz and banter of the Lancashire side, full of fun and characters and opinions; by comparison, this was like walking into a public library and expecting a disapproving glare if you dared to speak. To an extent, this is brought about by the circumstances of Test cricket, the throwing together of players from diverse backgrounds, but it is also true to say that we had some naturally reserved characters in that side. Men like John

Edrich, Keith Fletcher, Dennis Amiss, Derek Underwood and even the captain, Mike Denness, were never ones for provocative conversation in the dressing-room. At 27, I was the youngest of the batsmen but there were one or two inexperienced bowlers in Mikie Hendrick and Bob Willis and I found myself moving in the same circles as them. Gradually, we livened the place up a bit and Willis, especially, became a central character of the dressing-room for the next decade.

It was not that the team of 1974 had anything to be solemn about. Far from it, in fact, as India were showing once again that they were poor travellers and England were overwhelming them with something to spare. We made 629, England's highest-ever score at Lord's, with centuries from Amiss, Denness and Tony Greig, before shooting the Indians out twice to win by an innings and plenty. England haven't won too many in that fashion in recent years.

There were piles of good-luck telegrams waiting for me on the first morning, several of them from friends and family back in Accrington, and every one of them was welcome in helping to settle the nerves. So too was the toss, which Denness won. Get to it straight away and there is no time to fret. At lunchtime, we were 100 for no wicket and I was 39 not out. Solkar and Abid Ali was not the most intimidating new-ball attack I had ever faced, but the mental stresses of playing for England were all there, just the same, and I came in feeling pretty pleased with myself.

I was out soon afterwards, caught in the leg-trap off Prasanna, but 46 was a solid start and the one regret was that neither Susan nor my parents had been able to come south to watch. I later discovered that Dad had 'scored' every ball of my innings in one of his scrapbooks, and I am pretty sure he would have been a sight more nervous than I was.

There was a sense, still, that I was in the side as a temporary measure, holding the fort for the inevitable return of Boycott.

This would have rankled if I had allowed it to get to me, but I knew well enough that the one sure way of establishing myself, and securing the dream of a winter in Australia, was to make so many runs that the selectors could not leave me out. And that is precisely what I proceeded to do in my second Test.

My England career was destined to be a short one but that game at Edgbaston in July 1974 ensured there would be something tangible to remember it by. I set out my stall to make a hundred and I did so; then I turned it into a double-hundred. Rain had washed out the first day but it made no difference to us; Geoff Arnold and Hendrick swept the Indians away before tea on the Friday and I batted through the rest of that day and all of the Saturday. I have no memory of feeling tired, just immensely proud, and because these were the times when Test matches adjourned on Saturday night, I was able to drive home that evening and spend Sunday with my equally proud folks. I was disappointed to turn up on the Monday morning and discover Denness had declared, because I felt I could go on and on. It really was one of the flattest pitches I ever played on and I recall Farokh Engineer – India's wicket-keeper but my teammate for Lancashire – continually muttering to me: 'Keep going, Bumble, you'll get a lot here.'

It was apparently the first 200 by an England player at Edgbaston and, as we again needed to bat only once, I became just the fourth man ever to be on the field for an entire Test match. Such records were so much trivia to me, though, compared to the thrill of the achievement and the warm knowledge that, barring something horribly unforeseen, I could begin to think with confidence of making my first overseas tour.

During three drawn Tests against Pakistan that made up the second half of the international summer, I did nothing further to grab headlines but I did make a century in the one-day internationals that followed. By then, the news I craved had been confirmed. It came through during a championship game against

Notts, in which I hardly made a run but took four wickets – including bowling the great Garry Sobers – in an increasingly rare spell of bowling. To no great surprise, but to my own profound relief, I was included in a squad of 16 for the tour of Australia and New Zealand.

We left England in late October and, for me, the journey itself was a massive adventure. Australia was just a mystical, far-off land to me. I'd been as far as Wales and that was about it, so a 30-hour air trip was just mind-boggling. Until then, the only time I'd set foot on an aircraft was for a holiday flight round Blackpool tower as an 11-year-old. This was just a little different.

We travelled in optimism, as you always do, but in this case it was more than mere patriotic cheer. Hindsight shows we were sadly misguided but the pre-tour expectation, believe it or not, was that Australia would be short of firepower in their bowling. Dennis Lillee had sustained a career-threatening back injury in the Caribbean more than a year earlier and we were smugly anticipating that he would play little, if any, part in the series. As for Jeff Thomson, we'd never even heard of him. He'd played one Test, a couple of years earlier, and taken nought for a hundred and plenty. Why should we waste time worrying about him? There were some nasty shocks in store and I was destined to be on the sharp end of them.

This should not be taken to mean the trip was a misery. The general retrospective has typecast this tour in a poor light and it is true to say that it was a chastening experience for everyone involved. It also brought a number of England careers to an abrupt end, my own included. That's the downside. But I have any number of indelible memories of what was to be my solitary tour as a player, and the good times do not exclude some of the cricket.

Of course, I was looking at it all in wide-eyed innocence. It was all so new to me and I was determined to make the very best of it in case I never had the chance to visit Australia again. We stayed in modest places, Travellodge style rather than the five-star luxury often afforded today, but I was always among the first to rise, eager to know what was planned for the day. At times, this was not a right lot, because even without Boycott, who was brooding in his self-exile, we did have a high proportion of gnarled old pros on that tour. The likes of Edrich, Titmus, Arnold and Luckhurst would do their own thing and I recall seeing very little of them away from the grounds. As with all such situations, though, the more sociable souls gravitated into each other's company. Tony Greig was the life and soul but the group I found myself joining contained Bob Taylor and Chris Old, along with Willis, Hendrick and the assistant manager, A C Smith, whose sober-suited image as a subsequent chief executive of the Test and County Cricket Board was very different from the companionable man of that tour.

The weather was the most striking thing about the country. I'd never been anywhere hot before and my first postcard home to Mum and Dad summed up my feelings: 'It is absolutely stifling here from morning to night,' I wrote – and I can imagine them trying to picture the scene as they stared out at winter in Water Street, half a world away. Once the acclimatisation was over, I was agog at the sights and sounds of the place. I didn't always find the natives friendly but I thought our trips upcountry were full of excitement and I treated the whole thing as the adventure of a lifetime.

The cricket had its intense disappointments but the impression that we were bullied into submission by a team intent on all forms of verbal and physical aggression is just not accurate. The Australians were hard and you always knew you'd been in a match. They were not shy of using the bouncer, and they had the bowlers to do it, but as far as 'sledging' is concerned, it just didn't happen. I never heard them say a word on the field.

I knew both Lillee and Ian Chappell from the Lancashire Leagues but I'm certain that made no difference to their attitude to me – I was an opponent to be beaten but never, in my experience, abused. It became fashionable to portray Chappell as a crude and impossible Australian but he was just a brilliant captain as far as I was concerned – through his personal example, his toughness and his tactics, he had it all.

The focus of the tour, of course, was the bowling of Lillee and Thomson, and at times, certainly, it was better to be watching rather than batting. When they got it right and the pitches gave them some help, as most did, they were an awesome pairing. Get through an over from one of them and there was not a moment of respite with the other one pawing the ground. We were still playing by the old Australian regulation of eight-ball overs and there were times when five of the eight were flying past nose or chest. As has happened to England far too often in more recent years, they hit us hard with big pace and, with the exception of Bob Willis, whose dodgy knees limited him to one flat-out spell each day, we had no answer.

In such an arena, injuries were inevitable and they came at us thick and fast. I missed the first Test myself, though frustratingly that was through breaking a finger during catching practice, and when both Edrich and Amiss were crocked in Brisbane, the call went out for Colin Cowdrey to join us. Almost 42 years old, and 20 years on from the first of his five previous Ashes tours, Colin had doubtless been enjoying winter at home in Kent but he answered the SOS and arrived to spread his usual benign goodwill. I was slated to room with him straight away and I plucked up courage to relate the story of how we first encountered each other, almost ten years earlier.

Colin was captaining Kent in a championship match at Southport when a couple of injuries meant they needed to borrow a substitute fielder from Lancashire. As our 12th man, I was deputed to the duties and in three overs on the field, I managed to throw down two comfortable chances at mid-off. Colin was never one to give much away on the field and as his fielder returned to action and I began to slink away, he made a point of saying in his most courteous voice: 'Thank you very much indeed.' There wasn't even a trace of irony, for which I was truly grateful, but I subsequently heard that he raised the subject with Brian Statham at close of play, asking him: 'What role does that young man have in the game?'

Colin remained the archetypal Englishman despite the various indignities to which the Australian fast bowlers subjected us. He arrived in time to play in the second Test at Perth, on the quickest and bounciest pitch in Australia, and class and experience overcame age and rustiness. Colin was restored to his traditional position at no 3 and the room-mates were soon together when Luckhurst was out. He bade a cheerful 'good morning' to Thomson, who looked at him as if he was mad, calmly avoided the inevitable first-ball bouncer, then took another short one on his backside without the hint of a flinch. Between overs, he strolled down the pitch, greeted me as if we were neighbours out for a Sunday walk by the river and chuckled: 'This is good fun, isn't it?' I muttered that I'd been in funnier situations but his apparent lack of tension certainly had its effect and, together, we put on 55 for the second wicket despite a constant peppering of what Colin quaintly referred to as 'bumpers'.

From 99 for one, though, we were skittled out for 208 and the Australians built up such a huge lead that we struggled to make them bat again. With Luckhurst the latest to be injured, Cowdrey and I went in first in the second innings and put on another fifty-odd. Colin was by now a hero with the locals and a record Perth crowd cheered his every move, but it was the applause of those who knew their team had won. The best we could manage was a delaying exercise and I felt we managed that pretty well. In all, I batted for six hours in the game but it was not without pain and certainly not without a little luck. My second innings should have been over in the first over from Thomson when I tried to leave a short one and it ran straight along the face of my bat on its way to Rod Marsh. I had gone so far as to put my bat under my arm and take the first stride towards the pavilion when I realised that the Australians had no idea I'd hit it. Chappell, from slip, called 'well bowled', Thommo was halfway back to his mark and the game was carrying on. I gave a self-conscious cough and joined in but I'd only got to 17 when retribution was served. Thomson hit me in the box, doubling me up and forcing me to retire hurt temporarily. It was not an experience I would recommend.

The Christmas Test in Melbourne was much the best game of the series. We might easily have won it, but so might they. We led by one run on first innings and, chasing 244 to win in the last innings, they finished on 238 for eight. Amiss and I put on 100 for the first wicket in our second innings and the partnership was kept together for the fourth Test at Sydney. We entered that game with improved confidence but came away with another roasting and the Ashes were gone.

Maybe I was too naive to notice but I really don't think our spirit vanished at that stage. This was not the most compatible of tour parties and it was not the strongest of teams but we had some very gritty characters – Greig and Alan Knott prominent among them – and we kept battling away. We just weren't good enough to stem the onrushing tide from Lillee and Thomson.

In Adelaide, the Test traditionally scheduled to coincide with Australia Day, we obliged their script by losing again, this time by 163 runs. Until then, I was averaging above 30 for the series and felt I had coped as manfully as anyone with the situation – and certainly batted longer than most. But scores of four and five in that game were not only my lowest of the series but my last in Test cricket.

My neck had given me periodical problems for some years and these had recurred in a game against New South Wales. I was fielding at short-leg to Bob Willis when Alan Turner played a pull shot. I adopted the usual evasive position and felt a searing pain through the vertebrae. I thought it was just a trapped nerve, painful enough but something that would wear off. Only this time it didn't. I had damaged two vertebrae and although I got through the Adelaide Test that followed, I was in constant discomfort and by the time we reached Melbourne for the sixth and final Test, it was pretty clear I needed to give it a rest. I flew home as the game began and missed out on a feast. Thomson was ruled out by injury and Lillee bowled only six overs before breaking down. England won easily and Denness saved his job as captain – albeit briefly – by making 188.

For me, it was already too late. Nice things had been written and said about my courage in the line of duty but nobody pretended I was the next great thing anymore and I knew in my heart I was not. I was realistic enough to appreciate that I was never going to be a household name as a player because only my very best was good enough to register at Test level. Perhaps I was one of the scapegoats that must always accompany a bad defeat for England on tour, but I couldn't complain. It had only lasted nine games, and a little under eight months, but I had relished every minute of my England career.

CHAPTER SEVEN

Disenchanted, Resentful and a Bloody Nuisance

The uphill journey from Lancashire debutant to Test cricketer had taken me nine years, and after no more than a swift visit to the summit I was now on the downward slope. Or so, after a while, it seemed. You can spend a long time in this game being a promising youngster with England potential and just as long being a 'veteran former Test cricketer'. Wisdom and experience are all very well but give me the aspirant side of the business any time. Every cricketer, every sportsman, needs the ultimate goals to inspire him; once those are taken away, like the toys at Christmas, a degree of sourness and lethargy can creep into the most committed soul.

It would be quite wrong of me to dismiss the second half of my career. Some of it was contented and much of it contained sufficient attainable ambition to sustain its purpose. But I think I knew pretty quickly after the tour of Australia that, rightly or wrongly, I had retreated a long way down the wish lists of the England selectors and that it would require a series of compelling county performances to shift the name of Lloyd back to the head of the queue. I was not the first or last player to be so summarily demoted and there was no slackening of my desire to succeed. But apart from one cameo reappearance in the summer of 1980, when the England side was in a transitional chaos under Ian Botham and I was chosen for a single and distinctly unsuccessful one-day international against West Indies, I was now more of a has-been than a wannabe.

It is when this syndrome breaches the player's mind-set, pervades his daily routine, that he can become disenchanted, resentful and just a bloody nuisance to have around the place. I've seen it happen to countless other players and I know it happened to me in the final laps of my career. I got out with my cricketing enthusiasm unscathed and most of my friendships still in shape but, looking back now, I can see I was a difficult beggar for a year or two, agitating and questioning in a pretty negative way.

All of that still seemed impossibly remote in the spring of 1975. Apart from continued discomfort from my neck, which was destined to plague me for the rest of my playing life, and the nagging suspicion that I had missed out on the one chance I would get in Australia, there seemed a whole lot to anticipate.

My optimism was fuelled by selection for MCC against the Australians, when they started a Test tour after the first World Cup, and by Lancashire generating a run of form that had us all believing we were about to win the championship for the first time in a quarter-of-a-century. Both events turned out to be false dawns, though. I made runs for MCC, putting on 100 with a young and uncapped Graham Gooch as I recall, but that was as close to the England side as I was to come. Gooch was picked instead and made his famous 'pair' in the first Test at Edgbaston – but it didn't do him much harm in the longer term.

Lancashire's prospects were harmed in unquantifiable fashion by the background of the wage dispute that summer. We did win the Gillette Cup again, this time against a Middlesex side led by a studious young man called Mike Brearley, but the members were a bit blasé about that, and they felt fourth place in the championship to be a failure. With our support and resources, perhaps it was.

My own form had been patchy. I scraped past 1,000 runs, for an average in the mid-30s, but managed only one hundred all

Above: An early family holiday at Morecambe.

Left: Mum would insist on dressing me in a girl's coat and growing my hair long.

Above: Water Street was as good an outdoor net as any for the short-trousered Lloyd.

Left: Ideas above my station on a family speed machine.

Above: It's 1956 at Peel Park Junior School and the nine-year-old Lloyd, second from right front row, clutches his first bat.

Above: Early teens – the quiff in place, tie neatly obscured.

Left: Football was always more Dad's game and he got me playing at an early age.

Above: Lancashire team picture, at The Oval in 1968, with a young Lloyd second from right, back row.

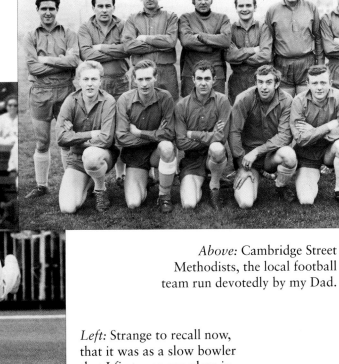

Above: Cambridge Street Methodists, the local football team run devotedly by my Dad.

Left: Strange to recall now, that it was as a slow bowler that I first won my place in the county side.

Above: Diving forward to gully to catch Mike Edwards of Surrey, with Farokh Engineer observing.

Below: They called him Cedric Power, and not without good reason — the autocratic chairman of Lancashire for most of my playing career, Cedric Rhoades.

Above: A natural ballplayer and more dedicated than he cared to pretend – Frank Hayes knocks up at Old Trafford.

Above: Peter Lever and Jack Simmons, two of the characters of the Lancashire dressing-room in my playing days.

Left: Jack Bond, never the greatest of players but a captain who commanded respect and loyalty.

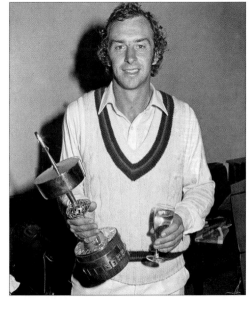

Right: A proud moment – lifting my first trophy as Lancashire captain, with the Gillette Cup in 1975.

Right: Note the 1970s sideburns and the lack of helmet. Not a bad shot, though...

Below: Richard Hadlee looks on as I play the sweep shot at Trent Bridge, during a Benson & Hedges Cup tie in 1982.

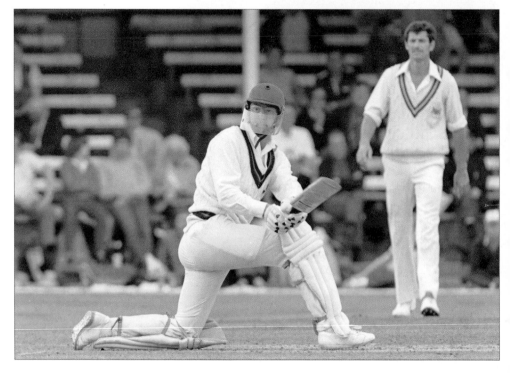

More easy runs on my way to a Test double-century at Edgbaston. My mate Farokh, behind the stumps, kept muttering 'Keep going, Bumble.'

This one flew safely past my chin – they were not all so painless against Thommo, fired up on the fastest pitch in the world at Perth.

Above: Get them young, keep them keen. This is the indoor school facility at Lord's during the launch of the Rover National Coaching programme. The one on the right forgot his boots.

Above: Technically, there is no-one better equipped than Geoffrey Boycott to coach young batsmen. A pity his personality never suited the team environment.

Left: Early April in the Parks at Oxford – sweater weather for all and Lloyd a new man in a white coat.

season. It was not a fast and fluent one, either, but it certainly had its funny side. We were playing at Stanley Park in Blackpool against Leicestershire, who were on a winning roll and heading for the first county title of their history under the canny captaincy of Raymond Illingworth. This was the season when each first innings in the championship was restricted to 100 overs and it had been such a battle for me all day that I was just about keeping pace at one run an over. I must have batted awfully and I didn't need the mutterings going on around me to know that, but when Peter Booth began the 100th over, I still only had 98 to my name. Determined not to suffer the ignominy of falling short, I swung the second ball to leg, aiming to at least complete the hundred in style with a boundary over mid-wicket. Instead, it went straight up in the air and there was Raymond calling for the catch at square-leg. He had to retreat a few yards, then pirouetted under the ball, grabbed at it and dropped it. While all this was going on, I'd scampered through for the two runs I needed, but I had no illusions about the way I'd played and nor did Raymond allow any to be broadcast. Grumpy about the catch and the way the game was proceeding, he told the press that it was the worst hundred he'd ever seen . . .

Despite all this, we entered the final round of games with the title still there to be won and, as I've said, we went back to Lord's to win the Gillette again. It was hardly a disastrous summer's work, at least by the standards of most counties, yet in the immediate aftermath of the final, certain national papers were speculating that my time as captain was up. 'David to step down?' asked the *Daily Express*. 'Lloyd set to quit' stated the *Daily Mail* in its usual, categorical way.

Apparently, I was 'feeling the strain', my 'form had been affected' and both the club and I felt it might be time for a change. Such speculation was premature. It would be another two years before the time was right for me to go, and then I would do so with some relief, but I saw no reason to be getting out in 1975. I knew what I was about as captain, knew the strengths and failings of the characters around me. I was not one for big team talks and meetings – there was no vogue for it at the time – but I felt fortunate to be able to draw on my experiences under Statham and Bond and to build into the mixture some of the distinct, dressing-room humour of David Green, whose nicknames and caustic one-liners could be used to good effect. I knew that a fine team was entering its last rites but I felt neither wish nor need to stand down and the manufactured pressure rankled. It would have been a sight worse if the club had allowed it to fester for months but, thankfully, it was no more than a fortnight before the committee met to confirm my reappointment.

After the excitement and adventure of Australia, it was a different kind of winter. I went back to Burnley FC, invited by my old manager Harry Potts, though this time I didn't even put boots on, simply walked round the ground showing off the Gillette Cup. I played a little football for Dad's Cambridge Street Methodists side and I went into business, opening the David Lloyd Sports Shop in the middle of Accrington. In January, I captained the Derrick Robins' XI on a five-week tour to South Africa, something of a regular institution at that time but already encountering the harsher realities of apartheid. Back home, I progressed a little into areas that would benefit me later by making a few after-dinner speeches and learning that my humour could indeed make an audience laugh. Then it was back to Old Trafford for a new season.

At this time, I still had realistic ambitions of playing more Test cricket. There had been no MCC tour that winter and a summer series against West Indies was now to be followed by a long winter tour to India and Sri Lanka, culminating in the Centenary Test match in Melbourne. Tony Greig was captaining England, having taken over from Mike Denness, and I knew both he and the other selectors would be seeking skilled players

of spin bowling to take with them to the dustbowls of India. I
could envisage there being a job for me there and set out to
advertise my claim. Circumstances at Lancashire helped, because
the emergence of Andrew Kennedy as a specialist opener allowed
me to drop into the middle-order for the first time in years. In
case anyone thought I was stepping delicately out of the firing
line, however, the opening championship game of the season put
them right.

Helmets were still a few years off at that time and although I
had publicly expressed a view that short-leg fielders should wear
facial protection – and had even experimented with a homespun
mask – no batsman had even considered the idea. So when I
went in to face Bob Cottam of Northants, who was then among
the quickest bowlers about, all I had on my head was my
Lancashire cap. Bob, a mate of mine then and later to become a
close professional colleague as bowling coach to England, had
already taken a couple of early wickets and was working up a
decent pace. I was seldom shy of the hook shot, though, and
when he dug one in I duly went for it. Whether it came off the
Old Trafford pitch quicker or slower than expected, I'm not
sure, but it took me full in the face and I crumpled to the
ground. I was unconscious for five minutes, apparently, before
being wheeled off to hospital. Just too add insult to injury, I'd
also fallen on my stumps.

It might nowadays seem surprising that this kind of accident
did not happen more frequently but fast bowlers had always
been around and batsmen had just learned the arts of self-
defence. Crude and primitive this will appear, in the modern
climate of protective equipment, but the risks were accepted as
part of the game. The inevitable, tasteless press beat-ups about a
bumper war that followed my injury were way wide of the mark.
Bob was just doing his job and meant no malice whatever – in
fact he was the most mortified at what had occurred.

I missed a couple of games while the effects of concussion

wore off but there was no lasting damage, physically or mentally, and the newspaper story that claimed I had spoken to my family about giving up the game was simply laughable. There was a lot for me to do yet and I had a chance to show it when we played the West Indies in mid-June. I shelved my pre-season plans and went in first in the second innings, playing as freely as I had done for more than a year in making 82. Sadly, I left the West Indies to make 192 in two hours, which I thought might be stretching it even for them, but they knocked the runs off easily.

Throughout my time in cricket, I have never shied away from confrontation. As a player, I simply loved a battle. I savoured the days when the odds were against us and we came through, and I think that attitude showed in my batting. I remember one innings that summer on a shocking pitch at Weston-super-Mare. Neither side had mustered many more than 100 in the first innings and it was a game that looked as if it might barely last until the second evening. But I batted through four hours of that day and played my shots, mainly in the company of an injured Barry Wood, who just kept his wicket intact batting virtually one-handed while I blazed away at the other end. The sight of Brian Close, Somerset's captain, simmering vividly, was always one of the most satisfying for an opponent and we went on to win the game comfortably.

The bad days outweighed the good that season, though, and I knew there would be ructions to come. We were even beaten at Lord's, in our sixth Gillette final in seven years, and although the circumstances were harsh – we'd lost an important toss and then played virtually with ten men when Wood broke a finger for the umpteenth time – it was enough to open the usual floodgates of rumour. After all, we'd finished second bottom in the championship and in the Sunday League, which had started its life almost as a Lancashire benefit tournament, we were now losing more games than we won.

The fact was that the young, vibrant bunch of blokes who had come together under Jack Bond almost a decade earlier were now getting long in the tooth. Most of us were pushing 30 or had already passed it, while Lever and Engineer were nearer 40. The athletic fielding that first made us such a force in the one-day game no longer came so easily to us and nor was it our exclusive domain any more. Belatedly but inevitably, other counties had caught up. But it was the championship form that most concerned the members and committee. Rightly so. Everyone had enjoyed the cup finals and the glamour of big crowds and big wins on Sunday afternoons but as the novelty of it all wore off, along with its annual expectation, far more attention was being given to the classic form of the game that we seemed unable to conquer. We'd had our chances to nail the elusive title and not been quite good enough; now, we were down among the dead-beats. I received a vote of confidence from the committee after we finished 16th in 1976 but when we could do no better the following year, I knew in my heart that the club needed a new captain.

The summer of 1977 was miserable in a number of ways. The weather was dire, for one thing. Down at Water Street, where the scrapbooks were still being faithfully maintained, Dad calculated that we lost 125 hours of championship cricket – that's the equivalent of 20 days out of the programme, or almost seven three-day games. And when we did get on the field, we just weren't very good, as a record of two wins indicates. We'd signed Colin Croft, hoping he would provide the leverage we needed to fire sides out, but he was a big disappointment. On top of that, the players just weren't gelling as a unit any longer. I knew changes were needed and that they should start at the top. The team needed a new direction and I needed a new challenge, so at the usual October committee meeting to review the season, I offered my resignation and, when asked, recommended Frank Hayes as my successor.

This was not exactly a youth policy, as Frank is three months older than me, but I had come to the job relatively young. It had not gone as well as I might have hoped and many might have expected but the years under Jack Bond had left the supporters feeling spoiled; it was always going to be a very hard act to follow. I was in charge for five years and that is sufficient time for almost anybody, especially when the team concerned is in decline. Frank had a good brain and I felt he should be allowed the chance to use it in authority, but in truth the alternatives were slim. Harry Pilling and Jack Simmons were the senior professionals but neither was keen to take it on, while Clive Lloyd had just signed up for Kerry Packer's World Series Cricket.

They say you only know how much you enjoy something when you haven't got it anymore and I can assure you the opposite is equally true. The extent to which the captaincy had worn me down, doubtless affecting my moods and spirits, was not apparent while I was in the midst of it but as soon as I came out of the job, I was a different person. I had said to all who asked that I was very happy to play under anyone else and they probably put it down to diplomacy, the need to say the right thing. Perhaps it was, at the time, but it also turned out to be true. A burden had been lifted from me and I enjoyed the liberation of being simply a player again.

I'm not sure how long this feeling lasted. Probably only as long as my next bad trot, when people would inevitably start looking at me as a dispensable over-30. But I recall having a few solid summers of enjoyment, free of responsibility, and I can't have been playing too badly if England thought it worth going back to me, more than five years after my last international appearance.

I had only played six one-day internationals before and I was relishing the chance to show what I could do against the West Indies' pace attack. They were out in force – Holding, Marshall, Roberts and Garner – and to say I did myself little justice would be an understatement.

I batted low, at number seven, but there were plenty of overs left when my chance came. Botham had just got out for 30, Chris Tavare was digging in determinedly and we were 81 for five in pursuit of an apparently modest target of 199. I marched out purposefully, complete with helmet, arm guard and sundry other protectors, all of them to prove useless.

Marshall's first ball to me was short, I misjudged the bounce and took it painfully on the upper arm, indeed on the very bruise I was still nursing after a blow in the Roses match a week earlier. Things could only get better, I thought, but I got that wrong, too. I'd made only one when Clive Lloyd brought Gordon Greenidge on to bowl. This seemed a case of playing the joker, as Greenidge had not bowled a single over for Hampshire the previous year, but any thought that Clive, my pal and Lancashire colleague, was doing me a favour was banished when Greenidge bowled me with his second ball.

At 33, I could not realistically hope for another chance. That one game was more of a bonus than most people realised because I had been very close to packing up at the end of the previous season. The Lancashire side of my generation was fading into memory and I just felt inclined to move on and do something different. The club wanted me to stop on, though, and the fact that Barry Wood was causing a stink by leaving at the end of his benefit year helped persuade me to sign a new two-year contract.

It might not have been the greatest decision of my life, because I can see now that I became more cynical with each season I stopped on. Jack Bond was back as manager, trying to recreate the glory years, and in retrospect I'm sure I wasn't much help to him. I got left out a couple of times and began to lose that sense of worth and pride that is essential to every cricketer.

On the full-time county circuit that is peculiar to English cricket, it is also necessary for those involved to enjoy the lifestyle and it no longer held any appeal for me. The constant round of motorway travel and late-night check-ins at soulless town centre hotels, the repetitive social life and the sense of isolation from the outside world – all of this had lost its charm. Even the club itself, a place and community I had loved dearly – and would come to love again – began to annoy me. For the first time since I started out, going to Old Trafford was purely a matter of turning up to work. It wasn't fun anymore, and I didn't like that.

Like so many sportsmen in their thirties, I was also finding that I could no longer count upon my eyes to trigger the correct reaction. This is a natural deterioration but it is much more important in cricket than most walks of life. If your eyesight is not as sharp as it should be, batting and fielding become much more difficult. I became so convinced I wasn't seeing the ball well enough that I went to an optician. He gave me a prescription and the eyes did improve for a time – sufficient, certainly, for me to score almost 2,000 runs in all competitions during the summer of 1982.

By now, however, I was simply delaying the inevitable and, to make matters worse, I was spending a lot of time unfit. The principal problem was the neck condition that had detracted from my England tour to Australia. It had nagged away at me periodically down the years, persuading me at one point to alter my stance to a more square-on position so that I could stand more comfortably. I'd had manipulative surgery on it more than once, without noticeable benefit, and early in 1983 it let me down so badly that I could no longer stand up straight without a dreadful, debilitating pain down my right side. Nobody could diagnose it properly and nobody was able to grasp how significant a problem it was to me, but it ended up with me missing half of that season.

When I reported fit and reclaimed my place, it was as if I was playing for a new club. There were new players everywhere and I just didn't know them. I batted one day in what I thought were pretty trying conditions against a West Indian named Winston Davis, bowling at the speed of light. I was joined at the wicket by a youngster to whom I'd barely been introduced and he proceeded to smack the bowling to all corners of the ground. His name was Neil Fairbrother and I think it was on that day that I realised Lancashire no longer had the need of a left-hander in the middle-order.

I woke up one morning and knew I'd had enough. It wasn't difficult, wasn't remotely painful, just a load off the shoulders. I'd probably been complaining a good bit and I'm pretty sure the club and the dressing-room were ready for me to go – certainly, when I told the club that I intended to retire at the end of the season, they announced it pretty damned quick.

Somewhat perversely, though, they kept picking me and I played like a dream. I called it a day at the end of August, after a championship game at Northampton. I had opened the batting with Graeme Fowler, an Accrington lad of the next generation, and we had both made hundreds. There could be no better moment.

CHAPTER EIGHT

Umpiring and Coaching

It is often said that you are a long time retired and I was weighed down by that feeling for fully a year. Knowing that the time was right is one thing; coping with the void is quite another. The routines that had seemed stiflingly predictable through my last season or two were now being keenly missed, because nothing a cricketer does in retirement can ever replace the special camaraderie of a county dressing-room. I missed the adrenalin of the big games, too, and that precious sense of authority which comes with playing big shots and long innings. In short, I felt lost without it.

I was not out of work. Never have been. During my twenties, I had done some menial winter work in a brewery and, some years later, I progressed to an upmarket wine shop. I suppose I felt this had given me a grounding in the drinks industry and that I might take to it full-time. But when I took a job with Wilson's Brewery, as one of their representatives in the field, I hated it. It was impersonal, even lonely, and I could not accept the change from the life that had consumed me for 20 years.

Worse still, I tried to perpetuate that life by going back to Old Trafford during the summer of 1984. I would wander up to the dressing-room and sit out on the balcony with the lads, distinguishable by my suit and my sense of loss. This was not only self-defeating from my own viewpoint but dreadful for the team.

I shouldn't have done it and it should not have been allowed, but I suspect most people there felt a bit sorry for me.

For all that, the change of circumstances gave me more time at home, and welcome opportunity to take in the advances of a brood that had now swelled to four children with the arrival of Ben to join Graham, Sarah and Steven, I was restless and unfulfilled. The one thing I did right that summer was to accept an offer to play Minor Counties cricket for Cumberland. It was not the same, not remotely so, but it was great fun.

Bernard Reidy, a team-mate from Old Trafford, had already made the same move and he encouraged me to join. It was good for me, recreating a little of the spirit of a team environment but offering a more social outlet, too. We played nine two-day games and we were always brilliant on the first day and dreadful on the second, which tells its own story.

Our home games were played around the Lake District, which enhanced a love for the area I had already begun to develop. They were lovely grounds, especially Netherfield, though you would not want to be out without a sweater when the wind got up. Home advantage meant exactly that in our case, but we did not often make the best of it. We were decidedly mid-table, capable of some big days and some absolute shockers. But we certainly enjoyed ourselves.

My first captain there was Alan Wilson, a building society manager from Kendal, a very solid character who was later to become manager of the England amateur team. When he gave it up, we were led by a schoolmaster from Cockerham called John Moyes, a decent batsman and a committed socialist. John drove a little CV6 and one night, during a game at Kendal that had developed into a drink or several, a group of us sneaked out of the bar, lifted up the captain's car and hoisted it over a stile into a cowfield.

Jokes, practical and verbal, were never far away with this team and the butt of many was David Halliwell. 'Hally' was a fast bowler with an attitude. Older than me, but possessed of a formidable head of hair, he would charge in ferociously, mane flowing, and produce genuine pace with a slingy, excitable action. He was the scourge of the league clubs in Lancashire, not only because he frightened a few but also because his temper often ran just a bit too free.

More than once, he was banned for threatening behaviour towards the opposition or even umpires. We had a problem with him during a Minor Counties game at Bedford, when he accused an umpire of being 'bent' after he had turned down a string of increasingly desperate lbw appeals. The incident brought an inevitable phone call from Donald Carr at the Test and County Cricket Board, informing us that they had received what he called 'a little complaint'. We assured Donald, with due solemnity, that David had been suspended for the remainder of the season and, suitably disarmed by such pre-emptive action, he rang off. What we had omitted to tell him, and he did not appear to realise, was that the fixture against Bedfordshire was our last of the season.

There was no malice in 'Hally' but when the red mists descended he would shout and argue on the field with anyone in his compass. He could not survive in the game as it is monitored today but he was an unforgettable character, as gently gullible off the field as he was pantomime-fierce in the heat of battle. Late one night, with the team sat round over a final drink, I was acceding to some prompting from the others and indulging in one of those fantasy selections – a World XI to play the moon. I had worked my way through the batsmen, the all-rounder, a spinner and a wicket-keeper, and then I said I needed three quicks to complete the side. Lillee was a certainty and I needed someone to frighten them with pace, which had to be Holding. Then, milking a moment that one or two others were already anticipating, I reflected that every team needed one fast bowler who would give it everything into the wind, someone who could always be relied upon and would never complain. 'It's got to be Hally,' I said, straight-faced. I expected an explosion of laughter from the chair containing D Halliwell but it didn't come. He took it all seriously and got really emotional, until I no longer had the heart to tell him it was a wind-up.

While I was playing for Cumberland, where I even revived my spin bowling to some effect, I also went back to Accrington. I played as an amateur first, then for a few seasons as professional and captain. I enjoyed devoting time and energy to the club, trying to improve its facilities and its outlook. I found that rewarding.

At 36, I had the chance to become second XI coach at Essex. This was a successful, well-organised county and the job doubt-less had scope for promotion but I turned it down on several grounds. I felt it was a bit soon after retirement, and that I needed more time away from county cricket to get the playing days out of my system. Just as important was the geography of it; Essex is a long way from Lancashire and I just did not feel this was a good enough job to justify uprooting the family.

I actually went on playing until I was 42, six years out of the Lancashire staff. Then, one day, I snapped an Achilles tendon batting against Rishton. It was a bad injury but it was also a signal. That was it. I was too old and I had no inclination to play again.

The Cumberland experience had lasted three seasons and for the last two I was combining playing with umpiring. This is not a job that appeals to every past player and there are aspects of it, within the modern media world, that are pretty thankless, but I had no immediate thoughts of aspiring to such heights. I consid-ered it was one way I could solve the dilemma of wanting to retain a contact with the county game without being consumed by it. I also thought I probably had the natural attributes to do it reasonably well.

I telephoned Lord's to discuss my prospects before the 1985

season started and they made encouraging noises. The list was full but they offered me a place among the standby umpires, which meant I could expect some games between the universities and the counties and needed to be available to fill in where vacancies occurred. My duties expanded quicker than I could have expected, though sadly through an illness to David Evans, and by the middle of the 1985 season I was standing regularly in county games, and loving every minute of it.

Some people might be surprised that it is possible to become a first-class umpire without formal training or qualifications but, for someone such as me, the apprenticeship has been served by playing the game. It is an incalculable advantage, because an ex-player knows how games are conducted and, unless he is an especially difficult customer, will relate far more comfortably to the ways of the players he is supervising. This should not mean he is soft on them, simply that he has the best chance of getting on the same wavelength, which is so very important. If an umpire is confrontational, the instinct of players is to lead him a dance. Commonsense is a pre-requisite, even more crucial than a detailed knowledge of all the Laws. A sense of humour also comes in handy and you will not find many good umpires without one.

The first game I stood in was at Fenners in April and the visitors were Essex. This, remember, was the Essex side of the early 1980s who carried all before them and yet existed on an exhausting diet of pranks and parties. Characters like Ray East and Keith Pont remain the subject of many stories doing the rounds of dressing-rooms even now, and John Lever, a superb left-arm bowler who just enjoyed life to the full, is not far behind.

'JK' opened the bowling from my end when Essex took the field and his first ball was a slow half-volley. Something not quite right, I thought, but exactly what did not register until the 'ball' struck the bat and disintegrated. Lever had bowled an orange. Only the most pedantic and humourless of umpires would not see the funny side of that and I had no problem.

Different players needed treating in different ways. With Ian Botham, the sensible umpire would cajole and indulge, without quite letting him run the game. I was standing in a Sunday League match at Taunton when Ian was batting against Wayne Daniel, Middlesex's West Indian fast bowler. It was a televised game and 'Both' – perhaps with his future career behind a microphone in mind – was milking the drama of a good finish.

We were midway through the last over and Somerset still required 12 to win. It seemed a long shot but Botham relished those and, as Daniel turned at the end of his run up, he stood up from his stance and strolled halfway down the pitch, giving it a prod and calling out to me: 'Who are you backing?' Only Botham could do this but I needed to keep the game moving. 'Three to come and 12 to win is a good contest,' I replied. 'Now, is there any chance of getting on with it because *Songs of Praise* is next on and we're running late.' Predictably, two huge sixes decided it.

I had very few problems with players. Most of them knew me well enough, and vice-versa. A working knowledge of the laws and regulations is necessary, of course, but knowing how and when to impose them is even more important. Just occasionally, though, every umpire will arrive at a moment when he has to assert himself. One of mine came at Lord's on the first morning of a championship game between the metropolitan neighbours, Middlesex and Surrey. I was umpiring at the pavilion end and, although my back was turned, I could sense the binoculars of 'Gubby' Allen, one of the great guardians of the game, focused on me from behind the committee room window. I could even picture him in his usual seat as Tony Gray, Surrey's West Indian fast bowler, let out a wailing lbw appeal after hitting John Carr, the Middlesex opener, on the pads.

It was not a bad shout but it failed to convince me. 'He's not out,' I said, at which point this huge man from Trinidad dropped theatrically to his knees and started thumping the pitch with his fists. Quite what 'Gubby' was making of this I hardly dared imagine, but I knew I could not let it continue. I walked smartly round the stumps and down to the point where Gray was still taking it out on the turf. Jerking him out of this performance by tapping him on the shoulder, I reminded him that the game was due to last three days and that there would be occasions in that time when I would be saying the words 'not out'. 'If you go on doing this every time you hear those words, we won't have a pitch to play on,' I added. He grinned a bit sheepishly at this and got on with the game. By lunchtime, he might have wished he hadn't bothered as Middlesex were making the most of a pitch on the bottom side of the square and had peppered the Tavern boundary relentlessly on their way to 199 for no wicket.

Peter Roebuck gave me a different kind of problem one day at The Oval, where he was captaining Somerset. The umpire is supposed to be kept informed when players leave the field, and why, but Roebuck ran off to the pavilion without a word. The Somerset substitute trotted down the steps to replace him and I went to intercept him. 'Hallo, who are you?' I asked innocently. He said he was on instead of the skipper and I told him he'd have to go straight off again because I had not been told of his movements. As he retreated, Roebuck peevishly leaned over the balcony and shouted down that he had hurt his hand. He should have thought to tell me earlier but I'm told he got his own back by giving me a mark of one out of ten.

Somerset were never short of characters, even when Botham, Richards and Garner were no longer around. They had a fast bowler called Adrian Jones, who used to thunder in off a very long run and turn increasingly red in the face as his spell progressed. We used to call him 'Puffing Billy'. Jones would chunter to himself all day, especially if his bellowed lbw shouts were drawing no response, and on this particular morning I had turned down plenty. After lunch, he came out holding his inhaler and asked me to look after it for him. I was well aware what it was – even used one myself – but thought I'd have a bit of fun with him, so I told him I'd got quite enough clutter to carry anyway. He set off towards square-leg, where Roy Palmer was standing, but I beat him to it. 'Mr Palmer,' I called, 'do you want to hold this for Puffing Billy'. Roy, a Somerset player in his time, caught my drift and said sternly: 'I don't want that, I'm loaded down.' Jones, turning scarlet, indignantly said that he would use it to mark the end of his run-up. 'That's fine,' I said, 'but it's five runs if the ball hits it.' He stalked off, now an impossible shade of red, and proceeded to charge in ever more furiously for the afternoon session.

I was happy as an umpire, in some ways happier than I'd ever been. The nature of the job, its hours and routines and variety, suited me fine, even if the pay was unbelievably poor. I honestly do not know how some of the umpires of that time got by. I do know that Ray Julian used to paint the fences on the county ground at Leicester to earn a few pounds in the winters, and that he, among others, would think nothing of sleeping in the dressing-rooms during games to save on the puny expenses allowances. It sounds desperate but I prefer to think of it as dedicated. Ray, like me and many others, loved the job and was prepared to make sacrifices to go on doing it. Others cut corners in different ways – David Constant and Alan Whitehead travelled the country in caravans to save on hotel bills, while Roy Palmer went one better by converting a single-decker bus into a mobile home. For him, though, it was a tortuous way to get around the circuit, as his 'home' had a governor device on it, restricting him to a maximum speed of 50mph.

My good fortune was that my umpiring earnings were regularly topped up, at first by playing for Cumberland and Accrington and later, when the boots were finally hung up, by speaking at dinners. I am told I have a natural talent for this, which is flattering to hear, but the idea that I can just turn up, stand up and perform is a long way from the truth. Of course, I have a formula, certain lines I always use and stories I will routinely tell, but it is the unavoidable lot of the after-dinner speaker to sit around, smiling soberly and fretting over an unwanted meal, while his potential audience has a ball. I have never enjoyed that aspect of it, because, believe it or not, I do get very nervous before a speech.

To me, it is a lot more difficult and a lot less rewarding than sitting behind a microphone commentating for radio or television, which was another direction my life was beginning to take me in the late 1980s. Sky had started to televise cricket, and to use me in their team, and I was then approached by Peter Baxter to work on *Test Match Special*. This was a wonderful outlet for me, surrounded by very special people and with the licence to do what I do best – talk passionately, occasionally humorously, about cricket.

All things considered, then, life was becoming quite hectic, and yet I still loved the umpiring and had no wish to give it up. There was a feeling among us, soon to be justified, that an international panel of umpires was on the way, innovation that was to make the job at top level far more lucrative and glamorous. My ambition, at the time, was to become a part of that panel, but I did not stay around long enough to find out if I might be chosen.

The next stage of my life in and around cricket, the move into full-time coaching, had in some ways been coming for years. I had done all the coaching exams while I was still playing, taking off-season courses at Lilleshall and working my way through the grades up to Advanced, a truly testing course which was run, in my year, by Les Lenham and Keith Andrew from the National Cricket Association.

Keith had dual roles as the national director of coaching and chief executive of the NCA, the body responsible for administering all non first-class cricket before it was absorbed into the new creation of the England and Wales Cricket Board a few years ago. The phone call from him, asking me if I would consider coaching at some of their junior sessions, offered a fresh diversion from the course I had been happily taking. I could not then imagine it would have its ultimate extension in the invitation to coach England, but then I guess that thought was also farthest from the complex mind of K Andrew.

Keith is a generation older than me but I had played against him at the backend of his career, when he was captaining Northamptonshire. A very fine wicket-keeper, good enough to have played two Tests for England nine years apart, he would have suffered in the modern game from being a particularly poor batsman. He might also have attracted more attention than he did in his own era for being a true eccentric, not above a spot of gamesmanship. Keith would think aloud when keeping wicket, muttering something like this: 'It's a green-top, bit of dampness in it . . . I'll put the spinners on . . . that'll fox them.' Once he had put this thought in the mind of the batsman, and duly summoned his spinner, he would engage the batter in conversation. 'You don't want to play this fellow from the crease,' he'd say, with a pretence of concern. 'You need to get down the wicket.' The unwary would be sucked in and stumped almost immediately.

Keith's origins were in Oldham and he was actually on the Lancashire committee during my time as captain, so I came to know him pretty well. In that sense, his approach did not surprise me and, as I had always wanted to do some coaching, I willingly took it on. Keith, who by then had moved south again to fulfil his duties at Lord's full-time, would sometimes turn up on the coaching days, or at games I was attending, and habitually carried a rolled-up newspaper, which he used as a mock telescope, honing in on the batsman's hands or the wicket-keeper's stance.

It was not long before coaching began to take me over. Keith used me as a locum for the four national coaches, so that I would travel to wherever an extra man was wanted. I became more involved in the junior representative teams and helped with efforts to break down the barriers between the NCA and the English Schools association. In this, I discovered a precious ally in Derek Day, who had been manager of the Under-15 schools side when I played and is not only doing the same job today but looking virtually no different 35 years later. Derek lived in Great Harwood, three miles from Accrington, and as we took a softly, softly approach to the problem, he, at least, could see the benefits of the different administrations working together for the benefit of all young cricketers. It took a long time to convince certain others that such change was desirable.

Kwik Cricket was the innovation that really launched me on the coaching ladder. The problem in our country, as Keith and I agreed, was that we had no flagship system of junior cricket, no hook to lure the kids into the game. Mini tennis and short hockey were doing their bit for sports that could not, traditionally, call upon such a captive audience, but every sport was vying for attention and it was time for cricket to get competitive. We knew the Australians were developing an introductory form of the game called Kanga Cricket and that New Zealand had Kiwi Cricket, so we logged onto a similarly snappy title and, with backing from Lord's, took the show on the road.

Keith put me in charge of the Kwik Cricket roadshows, along with a decent club cricketer named Mike Gear who also had a brief spell as a county chief executive. Our target was to get every primary school in the country affiliated to the scheme and supplied with kits, which may sound simple enough until you realise there are 26,000 of them. We started from scratch, very much the pioneers and evangelists for this scheme, and aimed to get around 500 schools a year. As you can imagine, this was no longer a part-time commitment and I was now effectively employed by the TCCB.

Gradually, I was also becoming ever more involved with the national age-group teams, and thoroughly enjoying it even if the experience was sometimes deeply frustrating. The Under-15s became my pigeon and my ambitions for them to progress were consistently stalled by reminders that many of them were still treated as little boys by their doting parents. Some would even come in the dressing-room during games, giving their lads sandwiches and calling them their 'popsy'. I ask you.

We had some highly talented kids in that age group and some of them are now coming through at the top levels. Marcus Trescothick was always captaincy material in my eyes and had enviable ability both as a batsman and a slip fielder, but he was a big lad and he was into bad eating habits. He would eat nothing but sausages and crisps, along with litres of lemonade. I talked to his parents but without any noticeable result. I was trying to get more steel into him, to tell him he would need to get his flannels dirty if he wanted to succeed in this game. He was worrying about his tea. Marcus went to Somerset, where great things were expected, but it took him a good many years to fulfil his undoubted promise. He is 24 now, nine years on from when I first had anything to do with him, and he has just made it onto his first England 'A' tour.

He was not alone in his pampered approach to the game. I thought Robin Weston was one of the most talented 15-year-olds I had ever seen. Nobody could get him out and he would have been an absolute banker to play Test cricket by the age of 21 if one did not know the English record in this regard. Robin was just too soft to grab his opportunities and it took a move away from the home comforts of Durham and into the rough and tumble of Derby to begin bringing out the best in him.

Even at Under-19 level, the English inclination lacks hunger and determination. I went as coach on two winter tours and saw some very fine young players but the same frustrations were around every corner. Once, in Zimbabwe during a junior Test match, Paul Hutchison, the Yorkshire left-arm bowler, was swinging the ball round corners, so favourable were the conditions. Overnight, he had taken three wickets for very few and it was pretty clear that his bowling would win us the game and make something of a name for him. Did this bring a sense of resolve and determination? Did it hell. The next morning, he turned up at breakfast croaking pitifully. 'I can't make it today, coach, I've got a sore throat. I think I've got tonsillitis,' he said. Quite apart from the fact that he was awarding himself unsuspected medical prognosis skills, I found it depressing that he was not bursting to get back on the ground. I thought it worth investigating further.

'So you were in your room all last night, were you Paul?' I asked. 'No, I went out,' he replied, as if this was the most natural thing in the world. That made up my mind. 'Look,' I said, 'you've won the last Test, you've already got three wickets here and you are the talk of the town. If you're not feeling well, tough, just try and get out there. You might knock one over early, then have a rest. You'll easily knock over ten and eleven with that swing and then you'll have six-for. You'll be headline news.'

There was a pale-faced, rather unexcited compliance. 'I'll give it a go, then,' he offered. But he did get six wickets and we did win the game, so I took him aside later and asked how he felt now. 'Still not well at all, coach,' he said. Yet at nine o'clock that night he had his hair gelled up, beads round his neck and he was off on the town. That's what we are up against in trying to instil a different, harder attitude into our young players. They have grown up in a culture of comfort and complacency, in which success at sport is a nice bonus but no more.

Responsibilities at this level brought me into contact with Graham Saville, a former Essex batsman who had gone into coaching administration and found his niche. When I was asked to coach the England Under-19s on these tours, Graham was the manager, and excellent at the job. In some ways, he is very similar to another Essex man, Brian 'Tonker' Taylor, a barking, sergeant-major type but unfailingly well-intentioned. 'Sav' would crack the whip and there would inevitably be a love-hate relationship between him and the lads, but at the essentials of organising their lives on tour he was invaluable.

At Under-19 level, there is a need for the managers to understand that the players are just like your teenage sons. They will be absent-minded and slovenly and the job of those in charge is to take this into account while running a team in the most professional manner possible. Ben Hollioake was a classic example of this syndrome. There was always a perception of him as capital city cool but it was hopelessly wrong – at heart, Ben was just an average, forgetful teenager and if you tore him off a strip for some silly misdemeanour, he would drop his head, lift his eyebrows and mumble modest apologies.

'Sav' had spent years around talented kids like this and I found his experience invaluable on tour. He was not a tranquil man to have about the place, though. In fact, he was on blood pressure pills as he tended to get over-excited rather easily and there were times when I had to calm him down pretty quickly for his own good.

Early in 1996, the Under-19s were staying at the Holiday Inn at Bulawayo. It was a free day between games, the weather was gorgeous and the lads were having great fun around the hotel swimming pool, hurling a ball from one side to the other and diving in to execute the catches. There was an element of cricket practice to it all but it was essentially rest and recreation. Harmless, too, especially as there were no other guests in the pool and none within sight apart from an elderly lady with a small West Highland terrier who sat alone at the rear of a large lawn. She can hardly have been within earshot but she took it on herself to summon the manager and complain about the noise levels. When the manager came to me, I told him I did not accept the boys had done a thing wrong and that they were causing no offence to anyone. The manager was placated but the lady with the terrier was not and she shouted across at us before going back to her chair and turning it to face away from the pool. The dog did not follow. Instead, perhaps beguiled by the sight of a ball, it toddled across towards the lads and suddenly, it was in the pool. I am still not entirely sure if a cricketer's foot helped his dive but I was not inclined to make anything of it and, after a few moments of righteous pandemonium, he was restored to dry land as good as new.

'Sav' was unaware of all this but at 6 am the following day, when we were loading up the bus for a drive back to Harare, the hotel manager made another appearance. Any fear that he might be about to raise the subject of the lady and her dog was replaced by news of a different complaint. There were some unpaid bills, which is unacceptable on any tour. 'What names are on them?' demanded 'Sav' with a warning flush of anger? 'Mick Jagger, Cliff Richard and Prince Monolulu,' replied the manager with no hint of a smile. 'Right,' bawled 'Sav', 'that's it, everyone off the bus. I want the culprits to report to me immediately.' As often happens in such cases, one lad took the rap. We told him he could be sent home, a threat designed only to shock the entire team into avoiding a repeat. My main concern was the tour manager's blood pressure.

CHAPTER NINE

England Calls

You do not plan to be England coach. Unlike playing for your country, it is not an obvious ambition. Certainly, on the late January morning in 1996 when I went to collect Michael Atherton from the airport after he had captained an unsuccessful tour of South Africa, I felt miles away from the job. It simply had not occurred to me that a vacancy may soon exist, let alone that I might be in the running for it, and I was genuinely taken aback when Athers told me: 'You've got to get involved.'

It was not as if I was looking for work. Indeed, it could be thought I had more than was good for me. Since 1993, I had been back with Lancashire as first-team coach, a role I had combined with various coaching posts with England age-group sides, some radio commentary on *Test Match Special* and a fair scattering of after-dinner speeches. It was a varied life, doubtless an enviable one to many, but it had taken its toll on my personal life. While working my socks off, here, there and everywhere, my marriage to Susan had fallen apart.

There is no point in pretending this was anything but awful, for all involved, and I blame myself. For all of us, and notably our four children, it was a really bad time. The situation is common enough, sadly, but that does not make it any easier to deal with when it is happening to you. Time, thankfully, has been a terrific healer; we got through it, all of us, and are back on good terms, but the months when discord turned into distance were tough and upsetting.

Being back 'home' at Old Trafford was in many ways a comfort. I had returned after the 1992 season ended in complete disharmony, failure on the field prompting some difficult decisions by the committee. Paul Allott and Graeme Fowler, who were thought to be behind some agitating in the dressing-room, were released before the end of that season (though in Allott's case the separation was short-lived and he is back now as an active member of the committee). Alan Ormrod, who had been in complete charge of team affairs since 1987, left the club acrimoniously and his duties were divided between David Hughes and myself.

David, not long retired after a successful stint as captain, became team manager, with my title being coach, but this arrangement was destined to last only a year before Hughes went the way of Ormrod. Looking back, this was a shame and a loss for the game. David is a good man and, if coaching was not his best suit, he was certainly a terrific organiser. He is firm, fair and great company and in this age of England managers and administrators he could have been a box-office appointment if he had stayed involved. Instead, though, I was given an enhanced role and it went pretty well. After three deflating years in the lower reaches of the championship, we finished fourth in 1995, and also won the Benson & Hedges Cup. I felt sure we could have done even better but for losing six players to England – a problem I was soon to be observing from the opposite camp.

That still seemed a remote prospect to me. I was enjoying my involvement with Lancashire, relishing being back where it all began. Despite the fractured spirit I sustained at the end of my playing days, Old Trafford has always felt like home to me; I have a deep, abiding affection for the place and a native's desire to see the team succeed and the environment improve. There is still much to be done, even now, for I look around Old Trafford and see not the smart, modern stadium the club deserves but something vaguely scruffy and unclean. It should be like a new pin and it pains me that it is not.

For all that, it is a brilliant place in my biased eyes and, in those mid-1990s, we had an improving team, re-establishing itself as a major force in one-day cricket while proving that the championship need not always pass us by. With a pace attack led by Wasim Akram, and batting headed off by the likes of Atherton, John Crawley and Neil Fairbrother, why should it? In common with many other counties, our weak area was spin bowling, yet even here we provided a Test player. Mike Watkinson, newly encouraged to bowl off-breaks in addition to his seamers, delighted us all by winning his first caps in the summer series against West Indies.

My input at England level, thus far, had been confined to the teenagers and to a few unofficial scouting missions, mostly during the time of Micky Stewart as England manager. Kwik Cricket, an all-consuming project for a year or two, was up and running efficiently by the early 1990s and in addition to an involvement at England Schools level, where I saw the developing talent of Michael Vaughan and Aftab Habib to name but two, I was occasionally enlisted by Micky to have a look at a player or, more likely, a pitch England were soon to confront. There is a sensitivity, for some strange reason, about the England coach or manager being seen taking too close an interest in the pitch that his team is about to play on. Micky felt this, and so did I in later years, but it did not stop him asking me to go along and assess conditions, a small duty I was happy to perform.

I always got along famously with Micky and I think we are similar in a number of ways – the football background is shared, for one thing, and we both have a real passion and enthusiasm for cricket that, I like to think, transmits itself to players. Micky had me along to help with some England get-togethers and coaching sessions in his final years in the job and it was instructive for me to see that, for all his experience, there were players he plainly found difficult. Well, one in particular, actually. Micky just could not get along with David Gower, couldn't come to terms with David's frivolous ways and reluctance to embrace the tight team ethic that was Micky's aim. They had not been a natural combination as captain and manager and the fact that they were operating on different wavelengths was well known within the game. The irony is that the public fuss over Gower's omission by England – leading to a special general meeting of MCC members to debate a motion of no confidence in the England selectors – came immediately after Micky had handed over to Keith Fletcher.

There is a general impression, promoted by the nudge-and-wink type of journalism, that Fletcher's number was up as soon as the Test and County Cricket Board elected Raymond Illingworth as their new chairman of selectors. This happened early in 1994, when Fletch was managing the side in West Indies, and Raymond's reputation went before him to the extent of an expectation that he would soon want overall power. I know little of what went on between the two of them in the year that followed, but I do understand that communication, and the chain of command, were damagingly confused during the 1994-95 tour of Australia. Few were totally surprised when Fletch, a decent man and a quite brilliant county coach, lost his job after that tour and returned to his beloved Essex. Illingworth, for the time being, was to be team manager as well as chairman – all things to all men.

There were flashpoints, as will always be the case with straightforward Yorkshiremen like Illy, but a 2-2 draw with West Indies, and the emergence of Dominic Cork as star material, gave the arrangement an encouraging start. In South Africa the following winter, with Raymond running the cricket and John Barclay in charge of administration, England hung on at

0-0 until the final Test in Cape Town, then capsized in the one-day series that followed. All was far from contentment, though I did not know that until the morning when I set off to do my duty both as friend and Lancashire coach by collecting the captain off the plane.

Mike Atherton had been leading the side for almost three years by this point. He had dealt with two managers and two chairmen and he knew his mind about what he felt was right for the team. In his view, Raymond should not continue to do both jobs – it just wasn't working. He knew nothing could be done before the World Cup, which was due to start in India and Pakistan in a matter of weeks, and I think he feared the worst about England's prospects – rightly so, as it turned out. But he was adamant that I should make myself available for a coaching role with the team. Clearly, he intended to lobby for me. I sat back and listened for a change. I can't pretend I was dismissive or uninterested but I did feel this was something out of my control. You cannot apply for a job that does not exist. I just had to wait and watch – in the event, not for very long.

The World Cup campaign was by all accounts a disaster. England progressed through an uncompetitive first stage without beating another Test-playing country and were then trounced by Sri Lanka in an embarrassing quarter-final. The fact that Sri Lanka went on to surprise the cricketing world by winning the Cup was small consolation; inquests were in the air. When the team returned home in mid-March, things began to move quickly and it was only a matter of days before Illingworth relinquished the coaching and management side of his job, though he wished to remain as chairman of selectors. Now, suddenly, there was a vacancy to interest me and Athers made certain I retained that interest. By now, I did not need any further encouragement. The TCCB made it plain that the post of team manager was to be discontinued and that they were seeking a coach. That suited me fine.

Lancashire were in the habit of visiting some far-flung spots on pre-season trips and, that spring, it was Jamaica. Although my name was now officially in front of the TCCB, along with a couple of other serious candidates, my place was with my county and I duly flew across to Montego Bay, the holidaymakers' part of Jamaica on the tranquil north coast of the island. I was enjoying some April sunshine when I received a call from Lord's that hastened my return. They were proposing a trial period but the job was mine for six months if I wanted it. I flew home to sort out the fine print.

My initial dealings were with A C Smith, who was seeing out his final months as chief executive of the Board. This was no hardship to me, as I knew and liked AC of long acquaintance as a player, and then as assistant manager on my one tour with England. His image was as a fusspot, inclined to obstruct and prevaricate, but I had always found him accessible and amenable and it was no different now. The money was quickly agreed – £25,000 for the six months – but, plainly, this was a short-term offer lacking any sense of security and I needed to feel I had a fallback position. Lancashire, characteristically, were supportive. Bob Bennett and his committee pledged to keep my position open and sent me off to the national side with their blessing.

I have said before that the politics of cricket life have never greatly interested me but I had to pay close attention to the saga that was unfolding around me now, as it impacted directly on the England team. Illingworth was being challenged for the chairmanship of the selection panel by David Graveney, a challenge that came to nothing when Grav's employers at the Professional Cricketers' Association deemed that it would constitute a conflict of interests. The business must have ruffled Raymond's feathers, though, and strained relations between him and David. At the same time, the election process for the two remaining positions on the selection panel turned into an unprecedented auction with nine people involved. Brian Bolus and Fred Titmus, the two allies Raymond had positioned alongside him, both fell by the wayside – Titmus eventually making his own statement about the inflated number of runners by withdrawing his candidature – and the vacancies were taken by Graveney and Graham Gooch.

Given all this upheaval, and his own greatly reduced power, Illingworth might have been expected to be difficult when we got together for the first time, but he was fine. I gathered the impression immediately that he was happy to work with me, which was an encouraging start. I also pretty quickly concluded that he was not the autocrat he was so often painted.

Of course, I knew him reasonably well from playing days. We were years apart in age and experience but I came up against him with both Yorkshire and Leicestershire and he never altered a jot. Within the Yorkshire side of the late 1960s, he was just one of several immense figures who, to be frank, frightened us to death just by striding into the lunch-room in their blazers and looking down on us. They had the stature of winners, which always goes a long way. It said a good bit for Raymond, however, that he could translate his shrewd and effective leadership to another, more alien county and make them winners, too. Leicestershire won the championship under his captaincy; they also adopted some Yorkshire ways. Raymond, meanwhile, was just Raymond – a dour, thinking cricketer, short on smiles but never on moans and famously inclined to blame the pitch, the umpire, the setting sun or some slight movement in the sponsor's tent whenever he had the misfortune to get out. He was the caricature Yorkshireman on the field, sometimes even in the bar, but he would always socialise at the end of a day's play and I found him one of the most interesting of cricketers to have a chat with of an evening. Later, when both of us had hung our boots up, I spent some time with him on the commentary circuit and found there was a bit more fun and mischief in his soul than he often let on as a player. I enjoyed his company, so I had no great qualms about entering a working liaison with him now, even if others feared for me.

If he is honest, I think he will admit that it simply had not worked when he put the tracksuit on to try and combine his roles. The game had moved on since his days, largely in methods of preparation; Raymond was reluctant to move with it. He had also taken on Peter Lever and John Edrich to help on the coaching side, men who may have been thought redolent of another generation by the players. Peter, who I knew so well from Lancashire, was nothing if not diligent, but I know there was a feeling in the dressing-room that John and Raymond spent plenty of time on the golf course.

I cannot fault Raymond in his dealings with me, though. I had heard plenty about some of his conflicts, not least with Athers himself and, infamously, with Devon Malcolm in South Africa, but then I knew life would never be dull with him. Like any Yorkshireman, he likes a good row but he was always straightforward and I had no reason to doubt his sincerity or his support. I also found out quickly that he is a good bit more sensitive than he likes to let on. He gets hurt as easily as anyone, and in a position that equates to being manager of the England football team for scapegoatism, there was plenty of opportunity for pain.

When I joined the selection panel for the first meetings of summer, I was surprised on a number of counts, not least by the atmosphere in which the process took place. There was something sociable, almost Corinthian, about getting together over a nice dinner, with some bottles of decent wine, to perform the task of picking the national team. I'm told it has always been this way and I have no reason to feel the ambience clouded anyone's judgement, but at the time I still felt it was an inappropriate way to conduct the business of picking a team that the nation would be arguing over by the middle of the following morning.

Raymond's approach surprised me, too. There was plenty of talk about him banging the table to get his way but, in my time, this simply didn't happen. It was nothing like that at all, in fact, and the usual procedure would see Raymond having his say on a position in the side, then sitting back quietly to hear what the others had to offer. As often as not, he would allow himself to be swayed to a general view. On one occasion, when we wanted to pick a load of youngsters for an England 'A' tour, he even did something quite out of character by admitting his own vulnerability. 'I don't know many of them,' he confessed, 'but if that's what you all believe we should do, fine.'

Illy did like to have his fun during selection, and hardly a meeting went by without him setting out, tongue in cheek, to provoke either Gooch or Atherton. I remember one evening when he stated firmly that Martyn Moxon was the best opening batsman in the country. He went on to name three or four more who might run him close but Goochie, who was still playing at the time, was not among them. Graham kept bringing this up at subsequent meetings and asking the chairman in that plaintive voice: 'Have I moved up the rankings yet?'

Later in my time with England, I took the decision to come off the selection panel. This was not a fit of pique over any individual episode but my private acknowledgement that it was pointless being one voice in five. More pertinent still was the feeling that, as coach, I was the one who was closest to the players and therefore obliged to justify the decisions of the selectors in the dressing-room. If it was a matter on which I had been outvoted – and there were several – this became a sensitive area, because I would have to be supportive of a decision I felt was wrong.

Players are always wondering which of the selectors supported them, and which did not, and to have the coach involved in this area is counterproductive. I felt this acutely in the Caribbean, early in 1998, when I wanted Mark Ramprakash in the side for the first Test but the other tour selectors did not. 'Ramps', who has periodically been let down by his inability to handle such setbacks, went bananas and it was my job to calm him down and look him squarely in the eye without letting on that I had fought his corner and the others had not wanted him.

The longer I was in the job, the more convinced I became that one man should pick the team, creating a clear accountability. The number on the panel was reduced from five to three but subsequently increased once more to four. There are still observers to be consulted and others – even the chairman of the Board – who can have a say if they so desire. It is still selection by committee, which must by definition lead to compromises and trade-offs, let alone intrigue. Even when Raymond did everything, which was the closest we have come to the system I believe in, he still had a selection panel and he did not have a proper coaching staff.

I firmly believe that modern sporting teams cannot be effectively chosen by committee and I see no reason why cricket should now be regarded as any different to football in this regard. My solution is to institute a role for the England team equating to that of Sir Alex Ferguson at Manchester United. Alex is in total charge of football matters; he picks the team and will take the credit for getting things right and the flak if he is wrong. He does, though, have a coaching staff beneath him to run the team on a day-by-day basis.

It is time someone was put in similar authority in our game. In fact, it should have happened already. Yes, I would like to have been that man but I would have been equally at home with someone else in that position and me working the team as coach.

Water under the bridge now, as far as I am concerned. When I set out on my 38 months in the job, the priorities were of a lower order. We had to stop the rot, stem the tide of public scorn and indifference towards the team. It was a big job, but then it had been a long time since England were a genuine power in Test cricket and I had no illusions about the size of the task ahead. Nor did I kid myself that it could all be done in six months.

There were adjustments to be made in my life, some of them quite difficult. I had been comfortable at Lancashire and had neither sought nor expected the upheaval from county to country. It was very different. I have never been one to linger in bed when the sun is up and my daily routine had been to arrive at Old Trafford early, sometimes at 7.30 am. I would meet up with the head groundsman, Peter Marron, and we would chat over a mug of coffee before addressing ourselves to the day ahead. I knew everybody who was employed in the place and, it sometimes seemed, most of those who came to watch. To me, moving away was like a teenager leaving home with only his rucksack and his grand plans for company. Just as exciting, too.

On the face of it, England offered me little but headaches. The team was not very good, there was no established base to work from, no proper staff and no set routine. Looked at in another way, the optimistic way I always prefer, this offered me fantastic scope. I was like a painter sitting down at his easel with a blank canvas in front of him and a head full of ideas. My problem, as ever, was that I was keen to implement them all at once. I wanted to run before I could walk.

Nobody helped me more, in those early weeks, than Medha Laud. Many people reading this will not even have heard of Medha, but I do not flatter her falsely if I say that the entire England operation would many times have ground to an embarrassing halt without her tireless efforts. Medha was, and is, based at Lord's and however her job title has altered in recent years she has remained the principal point of contact for all of us – players, coaches and staff – involved with the England team.

She was put in place by Micky Stewart, for whom she previously worked at Surrey, and she has been one of the finest appointments ever made at Board level. You would not think so, however, from the shameful way in which the Board officers distanced themselves from her when she dared to make a passing comment about a controversial employee, or from the high-

handed way in which her influence was diluted by the appointment of Simon Pack in the obscure role of International Teams
Director. I have no doubt that Medha felt slighted by all this; I
know for a fact that the players were so united in support for her
that any further diminishing of her position would have brought
strong words and actions.

All this was ahead. In the spring of 1996, Medha was simply
invaluable as my guide through the people and procedures of
Lord's. If I had questions – and I had dozens, every day – it was
always Medha I would turn to for answers and she would invariably have them waiting. If I had ideas – and there were plenty of
these, too – I would run them past her, first. Pretty soon, she
realised she was dealing with someone who had big plans and
she told me that I was unlucky not to have become involved at
the time when Patrick Whittingdale, the city financier, was spon-
soring the England team. There were funds available for all good
schemes during that period but I quickly discovered the purse
strings of the counties, who effectively call the shots at Lord's,
were not to be loosened so easily.

They, in turn, would find that I was not easily deflected. It did
not take me many weeks to form a view that the England team
had fallen behind the times in many ways. The human side of
things I could deal with without cost – it was down to me to
make the players feel better about themselves, to create a more
congenial and positive atmosphere, a workplace likely to bring
the best out of them. But we also needed to catch up with our
opponents in staffing and technology.

I identified two things, in particular, that would make the
coaching of the players more effective. One was a video system
first introduced in Australian rugby, from which a coach could
pick off exactly what he wanted from the filming of a match or a
series. If he wished to know how many times his number eight
had tackled, for instance, he could programme the system, press
some buttons and produce the evidence on a tape. After seeing a

demonstration of this, I was excited about its use within cricket and put it to the Board. Around the same time, I proposed that we should have some digital cameras for use in and around the nets, so that players could have instant access to their own practice performances in a way that should make it easier for them to identify and acknowledge faults.

I got what I wanted. Most of it at least. The counties jibbed at my idea of spending £23,000 per club so that each ground around the country could have a video system, building up a library of knowledge. I still maintain that this was short-sightedly and miserly of them, especially as I note that every state and provincial team in both Australia and South Africa now has the system installed. At least the first priorities of technology for England affairs were met. At that time, I got a good and enthusiastic response, a sense that the administrators were behind England and fully supportive of what I was trying to do. It would not always be like this.

CHAPTER TEN

Utterly Unaffected Athers

Michael Atherton and I were good for each other, I'm sure of that. It was not merely our friendship and our shared roots that smoothed my path into the England job but the fact that we worked well together, complementing each other with a mutual understanding of our often misunderstood personalities. I have always liked Athers but I also happened to think he was bloody good at being captain of England, something for which he may never get the credit he deserves. It is not much fun captaining a struggling team and that was Athers' fate for most of his five years in the job, yet he carried it off in a way that gained him the respect and admiration of the players under him. If I was not greatly mistaken, most of them idolised him.

He and I go back a long way, though initially I knew his parents a good bit better than I knew him. He was playing for Lancashire boys at 16 and I remember chatting to his mum and dad under the bell at Old Trafford, asking about his plans when he left Manchester Grammar School. It did not surprise me to hear that he was aiming for university – Cambridge, as it turned out – but I told Alan, his schoolmaster father, that if it was down to me, I would play him in the Lancashire first team straight away. It never happened, though.

For years afterwards, he was the butt of dressing-room jokes about his batting as a boy, when – not to put too fine a point on it – he could hardly hit the ball off the square. You couldn't get him out, because even then he had this focused, blinkered approach to an innings, but time and again he would chug along to an unspectacular not out while the middle order players had to come in and slog. He also had what I would call the Manchester Grammar approach, later to be emulated by John Crawley and Mark Chilton. They could all bat precociously well at a young age, but none of them could field.

For as long as I have known him, which is through some high times and some desperate lows, Atherton has never changed his personality. I find it hard to think of anyone who has achieved so much in his chosen area yet remained so utterly unaffected. Through it all, he has remained stubborn and scruffy and I imagine he always will. Through it all, he has been a loyal and trusted mate.

This, however, does not mean we are a mutual admiration society. Far from it. Athers delights in telling me what he thinks – the more unflattering the remark, the more he enjoys it. These days, he can let loose on my media work and he does so with relish. Midway through the 1999 summer, when I had moved out of the coaching job and into a commentary seat with Sky TV, we went out to dinner together. I thought I was doing okay on Sky but Athers soon disabused me of such complacency. 'Absolute crap,' was his judgement. 'I had to turn you off, it was so bad.' Then he turned his attention to my articles for the *Daily Telegraph*. 'Read your column on Monday,' he said. 'Thought it was rubbish, didn't agree at all.' And we would have a lively debate about this player or that game, lively enough for anyone listening in to wonder if we were really quite so friendly at all. With Athers, though, it is immediately forgotten. We have fallen out plenty of times, because we both say what we think, but neither of us has ever borne a grudge for a moment.

If I come across to the public as a buzzy, animated, ever cheerful type, Athers is the opposite. He knows this, but chooses to do nothing about it. Indeed, during his years as captain, he actively cultivated the grumpy image as a perverse reaction to what he considered the excesses of the tabloid press. He simply didn't care what people thought about him, so the perception the public formed of him became steadily less flattering. He damaged himself and it frustrated me to see him do it, but he would never once admit that he got it wrong. To me, like it or not, there have to be concessions made to the huge media presence around the England cricket team, but Athers would have none of that and he suffered for it.

Most people, who have little option but to believe the popular portrayal of the man, would be amazed to see Athers in the dressing-room, or on a night out or a day's fishing or horse-racing. He is terrific company and he has a robust sense of humour but he likes to keep that to his own circle. Often, he is at his funniest when having a moan. Get him on the subject of car parking at Old Trafford, for instance, and he is hilarious. Athers will insist – as he has done to me scores of times – that he parked his car there one day and a high-ranking official of the club let his tyres down because he was in his space. Whether it is true or not, I couldn't say but Athers brings it up all the time.

I would love to have seen him captaining a team of good players, because I think he would have brought the best out of them. With England, he had the rare ability to be one of the boys when it was appropriate but to back off and be aloof when more authority was required. He will be judged poorly and unfairly as captain of England, partly through the inadequacies of the teams at his disposal but also because he did not encourage the media – and through them, the public – to like him. But I observed him at close quarters for two years and I can vouch for his qualities.

Athers was never shy of expressing a view to a player, telling him he'd messed up. Generally, he would do this privately rather than in earshot of the entire team, but he would do it firmly, too – and then, so far as he was concerned, the matter would be finished. When he gets serious, he is really earnest, because he is a winner by nature and he cannot abide anyone showing a lack of commitment. He expects every player to know his business, because it is his job.

Another misconception about him as captain is that he was remote, even self-absorbed. This doubtless stemmed from his totally undemonstrative manner and his unwillingness to make passionate public utterances, but it was completely wrong. He was nothing of the kind. On tour, no matter how well or badly he might be playing himself, he retained a broad and compassionate view of the players around him. He would identify and seek out those who were low, either from lack of form or opportunity or through more personal worries. Many times, I saw him turn down the chance to spend an evening with the gregarious group on a tour and instead go and knock on the door of someone feeling down, drag him out for a meal and cheer him up. The team knew this but nobody else would appreciate such a side to the Atherton character.

Of course, he was not perfect. His body language on the field could be poor and there were days when I longed for him to look more sprightly. At the same time, I recognised the physical restrictions imposed by his back problem, which was severe enough to justify a hangdog look in anyone. His contrary behaviour with the press also grated on me at times. He would regularly reserve his most morose expressions for the press conferences, almost deliberately antagonising the newspaper writers with his demeanour and the brevity of his answers. He considered the press as incidental and such formal conferences as an unnecessary way of writing their stories for them − so he set out to be as little help as possible.

The fact that he held a section of the press in such open contempt sat uncomfortably alongside his open friendships with a few journalists. The rejected majority simply took greater offence and became still more reluctant to acknowledge any of his good points. The problem was not solved by the appointment, in 1997, of a full-time media relations officer to travel with the team. Brian Murgatroyd, a former journalist himself, had a fundamental difference of opinion with Athers, who believed there was no need for anyone to be telling him what to say and who to say it to. It became a running sore.

Michael was always content to be judged on his batting, however, and in this respect it would be a very harsh or prejudiced man who assessed him as anything below the very highest class. I rate him as one of the finest openers of modern times but it is frustratingly impossible to know how much better he might have been but for the constant discomfort of his back problem. Certainly, I am convinced he would be averaging a good bit more than 39. He would always mask the effects of the injury until or unless it got too bad to contemplate playing. The fact that he missed so few games says everything about his dedication to the cause, because a great many other players would have found it impossible to cope.

Two bowlers have caused him regular problems down the years and they are significantly similar in style. Glenn McGrath and Shaun Pollock both jump into the stumps in their delivery stride and bowl a tight, wicket-to-wicket line with late movement. Athers has never been commanding against either of them and in Australia in 1998-99, he had particular problems when his back condition would not allow him to duck under McGrath's short ball. Instead, he had to play at it and it cost him his wicket more than once.

Throughout his England career, he has been stimulated by playing against the very best. The downside of this has been evident in periods of mediocre county form. Michael has never sought to hide his scepticism over the role of county cricket and he expressed it again in a radio interview in January 2000, immediately after his return from the Test tour of South Africa. It met a predictable reaction from the counties themselves and

Tim Lamb gave his usual speech, taking 'a dim view' of comments 'that could bring the game into disrepute'. This was a nonsensical response for two reasons – nobody in their right mind could argue with Athers' assertion that county cricket, in its present form, fails to prepare players for Test cricket; and he was saying nothing that Lord MacLaurin, the chairman of the Board, had not said in his own way during press conferences in South Africa. Like Michael, I bow to no-one in my love of county cricket and my anxiety to see it prosper, but it is just so obvious that it needs re-styling.

Michael also sometimes betrayed a lack of enthusiasm for minor games on tour. I remember a match in Hobart during the last Australian tour, in 1998-99, when he made 200 for the first time in his life, yet dismissed its significance because the opposition – an Australian 'A' team – 'had got no bowlers'. He even refused to talk to the press about it at first. Athers was captaining that game, because both Alec Stewart and Nasser Hussain were resting – a mistake, in my view – and he declared our second innings to make a game of it, when the ruthless thing to do was to grind the opposition into the dust. It was something he would never have contemplated in a Test match and I was anxious we should replicate the mood in each game. He couldn't see it. We lost the game, too, which caused an overnight frost between us, but it was an example of Athers being utterly uninspired by what he saw as a meaningless contest. He is just the same in certain county games and there are days when a little dibbler of a bowler, scarcely good enough to tie his boots, can get him out cheaply.

Set this against his batting when the best bowlers in the world are ranged against him, there is tension in the air and a prize worth fighting for. In such circumstances, there is nobody I would rather have on my side. Athers thrives on confrontation and there are times when he helps create one, just to boost his reserves of concentration and motivation. It is not a tactic you would ever wish to teach, because it would be self-defeating for the majority of mortals, but to produce Atherton at his best you want the atmosphere of a bullring.

He had been badly disappointed by the decline of the tour to South Africa, and particularly by the ineptitude of the team in the World Cup, but when we came together in the early weeks of the 1996 season I was struck by his belief that we could turn things around. We made a good start, too, getting things moving in a variety of directions off the field and creating a vibrant mood in the dressing-room.

One of the most notable features of England's cricket, early that summer, was the quality of the fielding. It was remarked upon whenever we played. There was such a visible energy in the side and it was as much a cause of encouragement to me as it was consternation to unwary opponents. With versatile, predatory fielders around such as Nick Knight, Chris Lewis and Nasser Hussain, we were spectacular. One of my great regrets in later years was that the energy faded away. It got to the point where we were static in the field, nothing happening at all, and, back in the pavilion, I would tear my hair out watching it happen. It was not for the want of work – we would put in more and more fielding drills but just seemed to get nowhere – and I came to the conclusion that it could easily be down to the players simply being too familiar with my methods. They knew me too well. Here, perhaps, was evidence for the theory that a cricket coach has only a limited time to impact upon a team, though my hope that it was not entirely down to this was endorsed when things got even worse after I stood down in 1999.

During those first few months out of the job, I crossed the floor into journalism and caused something of a stir by writing in my newspaper column that two players new to the England team – Aftab Habib and Chris Read – had been 'traumatised' by the atmosphere in the dressing-room. Athers and I fell out over it. 'Strong word, that,' he admonished me one evening, having greeted me without much amusement as 'Controversial Dave'. I could only repeat to him that it was a sincerely held concern of mine and that I knew how those youngsters felt as they spent time amongst senior players who had grown to regard the dressing-room as their own domain and, in some cases, the game as a job. When I first came into the England side from the buzz and clamour and democracy of the Lancashire dressing-room, I found it all intimidatingly quiet. I carried on being myself, broke down the reserve and had fun but I could sympathise with youngsters who felt unable to do that.

It was for this reason that I consciously set out to make the England dressing-room a noisy, animated place. One of my first briefs, according to those in charge of the game, was to restore some pride and passion. I told them they would get plenty of that. I tried any number of things to create the right mood of uplifted patriotism, from sticking big, motivational signs on the dressing-room wall to playing stirring anthems on the ghetto-blaster. We started off with 'Jerusalem' and 'Land of Hope and Glory', which always made Jack Russell stand earnestly to attention; later, to appease the Welshman in our midst, I recorded a version of 'Land of my Fathers', and it duly brought a tear to Robert Croft's eyes.

I would do card tricks, make stirring speeches, quote Churchill – anything to get through to the players that they were not in that room just to represent themselves, that they were there to represent their country. Of course, I knew there was the risk of not being taken seriously and I had to balance that, but I always felt safe in the knowledge that the players could not take me for a fool, and in the conviction that every one of them would prefer to play in a happy, united atmosphere.

It took me some time to generate an understanding with all the players around me. Longer with some than others. With Hussain and Ramprakash, I reckon it was 18 months before I fully appreciated what made them tick, and consequently the best way to handle them. As a coach, I believe it is utterly misguided to feel everyone must be treated identically, because this assumes that everyone is the same, which is demonstrably untrue. Nasser probably caused me as many anxieties as David Gower caused Micky Stewart – not because they are remotely similar but because neither fits easily into the doctrines of team togetherness. I know now that the coach needs to offer space and scope to such players but that the trick is to persuade them to observe the team ethic for long enough to present a united front.

Hussain was the prime example of this in my time, because he always wanted to prepare for a Test match in his own, private way, which was inclined to leave the unit thoroughly disjointed. In the nets, he would want to bat first, last and then bat again and he would try to nominate who should bowl to him, when actually the bowlers were there to work on their own game rather than servicing the batters. Nasser would invariably want to continue fine-tuning his batting, maybe with some throw-downs, when the net session broke up and while this was admirable in itself, it was also disruptive to any team planning. I wanted everyone involved in the fielding drills and I had to explain to him more than once that there was a given time when we would all be together – if he wanted to do his own thing, he must come early or stay late.

During the time we were together with England, I felt Nasser became a better team man and a far better person. There was a time when I could not envisage him captaining the side and com-manding the essential respect of his peers but he has come to realise that an awareness of the needs of others is part of being a cricketer, no matter the level. This 'New Man' tended to take leave of absence on the morning of a match, however, and then it was always wise to leave Nasser alone, because he worked himself up to a crescendo like a kettle about to boil.

Darren Gough is different again. When we gathered on a

Tuesday afternoon, Goughie would puff out his chest and bellow, in that timid Yorkshire way of his, that he had just bowled 60 overs in a championship game and he was exhausted. I had a lot of sympathy with this, having believed for years that our Test cricketers are obliged to play far too much county cricket, but Gough just needed a bit of bluff and a bit of bluster. 'Take a rest,' I would say. 'Don't bowl until Wednesday morning.' He would perk up at this, in time to hear me add: 'But you must stay around for the fielding session – no golf.' Briefly, that expressive face would fall again. 'Just a walk round nine holes,' he might venture, before conceding defeat with a mock scowl. He would soon be himself again, because Darren has that rubber-ball mentality, never down for long.

If only Chris Lewis had been so straightforward to manage, I honestly feel we would have had an outstanding all-round cricketer. With Lewis, though, the great problem was that you never quite knew what you were going to get – or even who you were going to get. That first summer, I swear I had to handle two Chris Lewis's. The first was brilliant against India, both in performance and attitude, but when the opposition switched to Pakistan later in the season it was as if a different person turned up under Lewis's name.

There is always a lot of hearsay about Lewis. He is that type of bloke, thoroughly individual and distinctive enough to provoke comment. So I had heard plenty about him when I started the job, but scarcely knew him at all. I could not help wondering what he would be like but, such is the chameleon within him, I am still not sure to this day. He earned his selection for the three Texaco Trophy games against India in May and performed so well he won the man of the series award. Nothing could have pleased me more, because I had set out to make things simple for everyone, sitting them down in the dressing-room and spelling out how things were to be conducted from here on; Chris had seemed to respond eagerly to this directness and his performances said as much. Misguidedly, I felt I might be succeeding in an area that had left others frustrated.

He remained outstanding through the three Tests against India, bowling with genuine pace and aggression. I especially remember him dismissing Sachin Tendulkar twice in a superb over at Lord's, the first of them with a no ball. He was on a hot streak, looked a complete athlete and, just as important in the general scheme of things, was not a scrap of trouble. He was one of the first names inked on the team sheet when the Pakistan series began but it seemed he had come back in disguise – literally so, as he had taken it into his head to turn up dressed in denim dungarees, which just didn't seem right for an England cricketer. The rest of the lads, inevitably, would rib him about it, demanding to know what he'd come as this time, and even those who were his own age considered it strange. Chris, though, seemed to like being the centre of attention and began to regard the dressing-room as more of a catwalk than a team area.

Worse still, his performances dropped off alarmingly. We could no longer rely on him on the field and we certainly could not rely on his attitude. He turned up 40 minutes late on a practice day, which strained the patience and credulity of many, but I dealt with it by telling him he must buy four bottles of champagne for the rest of the lads. He agreed and apologised, but no more than a couple of weeks later he was late again – this time on a match morning during the Test at The Oval. As he lived just down the road from the ground, and had opted to stay at home rather than in the team hotel, there was absolute no sympathy for him and his excuse of a burst tyre on his car was deemed totally unacceptable.

Athers and Raymond were both furious; Illy, indignant and sceptical, said: 'Let's go and look at his car, then, and see if he's changed that tyre.' When I talked to Lewis in the dressing-room my own disappointment in him was magnified by a complete lack of contrition. It just seemed beyond him to say sorry, a gesture which might have meant enough to keep his punishment to a fine. Instead, with the mood as it was, the faith in this enigma utterly exhausted, there was no alternative but to make an example of him. He was excluded from the one-day series scheduled to follow that Test and not even considered for the winter tour. It might seem harsh, and he was later to complain in a newspaper that he had been hard done-by, but he had brought such problems upon himself with a complete disregard for the others in his team.

If Lewis provoked resentment and bewilderment, Graeme Hick brought out only sympathy and support. He was already five years into his Test career when I became coach, and had already heard more than enough barbs about his background, his character and his flawed technique. I doubt if any cricketer has ever come into the international game burdened by such impossible expectations and Hick, being a shy and slightly negative personality, had not coped well with early failure. Through it all, though, he had retained the backing of the players around him, not only because they all knew how he could bat but because they liked him as a genuine guy. In his own way, though, he could be as frustrating as Lewis. In the first one-day international of that summer he made a lordly 91. Then he scarcely made another run until, reluctantly, we left him out one match into the Pakistan Test series.

This had been the way of it for Hick since he came into the side against West Indies in 1991. Always flattering to deceive, never quite delivering the goods. From afar, I had found this impossible to fathom, for I knew only the commanding figure in a Worcestershire sweater, racing out from the pavilion, announcing himself as soon as that first wicket fell. Time after time, he would slap us everywhere. We never bothered discussing what we might do if we got down to the likes of Damian D'Oliveira or Steve Rhodes against Worcestershire, because more often than not we couldn't get Hick out.

I did see the hint of a chink in his armour when we played Worcestershire in the Benson & Hedges Cup final of 1991. Wasim Akram was properly fired up for Lord's and he hit Hick twice with short balls of extreme pace. Suddenly, Hick's feet looked leaden and his mind seemed to have gone into neutral. It was only a fleeting vision – Hick recovered to make 88 and Worcestershire won the game – but it did make me wonder, especially as by then the West Indies bowlers were starting to expose him, too.

My memory of Hick in 1996 also relates to Lord's and a duel with a Pakistani, but this time one he was not destined to win. Hick had managed only 35 runs in four Test innings against India and his place was plainly under threat. In this first Test against Pakistan he had already been cleaned up once by Waqar Younis's yorker and on the final afternoon, as we scrapped to try and save the game, he had to go in and face him again at a critical moment. As he left a tense dressing-room I was struck by the unanimous desire to see him succeed. 'Come on, Arnie,' the players shouted at him, a reference to the Schwarzenneger muscles under his shirt. They were to do him no favours now. The ability to dominate with bat and head had deserted him; he was limp and hesitant compared to the Hick we knew from county cricket and Waqar scattered his stumps with his second ball.

Graeme is a naturally reserved lad who could not be expected to be gung-ho all the time but I felt he suffered for being unable to cross that line into ruthlessness when on cricketing business. You come across many mild-mannered individuals who change character completely once on the field – Allan Donald is one who springs to mind immediately – but Hick took his meekness with him to the middle, and at Test level that will not remain a secret for long. He is a lovely, caring bloke, the type I could never see kicking a dog, and we did everything possible to try and make him feel secure within the team. There is a limit, though, to what you can do for a man whose mind is full of negative thoughts.

I did feel he improved within himself, that eventually he felt more comfortable contributing to team meetings and having his say on policy, but he would countermand this by talking himself into poor form. In Australia in 1998-99, he fretted more and more, demanding an ever greater number of throw downs to correct some perceived blip in his game. It was no surprise that when he went out to the middle, his head was full of failure.

Hick has been in and out of the side more than almost anyone in the past decade and, of course, it is not an ideal situation. It is not a normal situation, either, for here is a man still capable of making such a vast volume of runs in county cricket, often look-ing on a different plane to everyone else, that the selectors will always be under pressure to pick him – then under equal pres-sure to leave him out as soon as he shows the vulnerabilities at the highest level with which we are now all so familiar.

On tours, I noted other players rallying round him protec-tively whenever he was down, and in Alec Stewart he had a man who would champion his cause endlessly. Red herrings were fre-quently thrown into the Hick debate, however, none more so than his potential contribution as an off-spin bowler. To me, this was never a factor worth discussing because he hardly ever bowled in county cricket, let alone for England. Still, whenever his place in the side was in doubt, someone would raise this in his favour.

That sequence of low scores in 1996 was the first of several such crises we were to go through with Hick, yet no matter how poor his Test match form he remained an automatic pick in the one-day team and I strongly fancied him to have a serious influ-ence on the World Cup in 1999. Until, that is, I called the play-ers together during the build-up and raised the subject of a flexible batting order. This was something I wanted every mem-ber of the side to buy into as we approached the tournament, because I was convinced we needed it to compete with the starts being achieved by the likes of Sri Lanka. At a team meeting, though, Hick simply refused to countenance it, insisting that he should be assured of going in at his preferred number three. His argument was that he needed time to get going but that if he got set, he would get the big hundred we needed. My response was that if he took up that time and failed to get in, we would be missing our chance to capitalise on the 15-overs fielding restrictions.

It was a frosty team meeting, with everyone except Hick in agreement as to what we should do. He remained blinkered about it when I tackled him alone later, and although we eventually talked him into the concept for the good of the team, I know he was uneasy about it. As it turned out, he was to have a disappointing World Cup, though he was not alone in that.

CHAPTER 11

The England Set-up

If there was a time and a place for me to make an entrance as England coach, the fates were kind to me. The publicity could hardly have been more upbeat during my first weeks in the job and I kept hearing flattering phrases like 'breath of fresh air', 'eternal optimist' and 'witty and inventive'. I think the country, and most certainly the cricket media, had decided that the expressions around the England team had become too solemn and their cricket too po-faced. I am sure they identified me as someone who would brighten things up, make life more interesting. The comments were pleasant enough to hear, of course, and the most confident of men benefits from such an eager welcome, but I had been around the game quite long enough to know that the honeymoon would not last. Or, to be accurate, it would last only as long as the first bad defeat.

There were some hard decisions to be taken and some tough matches to come. There would be times when I made myself unpopular and times when the press and public, flailing around for someone to blame after a disappointing defeat, selected me for the brickbats. I knew all this, prepared myself for it thoroughly, and accepted all the nice words with a polite smile and a pinch of salt.

In the few, hectic weeks open to me between taking the job and sending the team onto the field for the first international of the summer, I worked like a dervish to get things in place. Poor Medha Laud did not know what had hit her but she responded to every call for help, every impossible request. A C Smith, who was seeing out his final year at Lord's, was always a willing listener, too, but most of my hours were spent with the men who were to be my closest allies – none more so than our physiotherapist, Wayne Morton.

Wayne was an Illingworth appointment, prior to the tour of South Africa the previous winter, so I was not a great deal newer to the job than him. An outgoing Yorkshireman with a mop of dark hair and an intense enthusiasm for bowling in the nets, I knew nothing about him when we first met up, but Athers told me he was all right, so that was a good start. We hit it off straight away and became very close in the three years we worked together – so close that I grieved with him when my departure from the scene was so closely followed by his own. Wayne did not go voluntarily; he was dismissed to satisfy the craving for a new broom. It was shabby treatment of someone who had done a great deal to help create a better, more caring environment for the players.

What I found in him immediately was someone capable of doing much more than his primary job. Wayne has never been lacking in self-confidence, which has been known to set him against those who persist in the old-fashioned view that the likes of physiotherapists should be seldom seen and never heard. This disapproval did not concern him at all – he just went on conducting himself in the way he thought worked best – and the players, though they might weary of him, also gave him a great deal of respect.

His priority, of course, was the prevention and treatment of injuries, and he can produce a dossier of evidence to prove that great strides were made in this direction during his time. He never shirked the opportunity to take on other roles around the team, however, and in time he would become nursemaid, psychologist, social companion and sergeant-major. The last-named duties did not guarantee his popularity – that he achieved in other ways – but it meant he and I could complement each other effectively. Wayne bawled them out, while I used the cajoling calming tactics. Naturally, there were times when I, as the man in charge, had to administer a rollicking and if it involved the whole team I would do it there and then. If it came down to one errant individual, though, I would instinctively leave it until later. Confront it on the spot and you have a stand-up row sure to disrupt the camp more than the original bit of insubordination. Go to the player later to talk and invariably, I found, he would be defensive if not openly contrite.

I had only the vaguest idea, when I started, about which players might make my life difficult and I did not intend my own suspicions, or the whispered warnings of others, to cloud my judgement. Find out for yourself and take people as you find them were two good mottos to be going along with. Even so, I was pleasantly surprised that when the selection panel sat down for its first dinner of the season to pick the party for the Texaco Trophy games against India, I pretty much got everything I required. Whether this had anything to do with Raymond being embattled on another front, his recently published book causing some serious ructions at Lord's, or whether it was a conscious effort to give the new man his head, I took the opportunity gladly.

There was a surprise or two in the squad, at least to most observers. I introduced Ali Brown to open the innings on the strength of his explosive striking for Surrey, and I brought back Lewis as the all-rounder. I knew very well that he had disappointed people and that there were those who thought he should be given no further chances, but I was adamant that he fitted into our best one-day team. If he was to be a problem, I wanted to discover how and why for myself, and see if there was a better way of dealing with him.

India were beaten 2-0 in these games and it would have been a whitewash but for rain intervening in the first of them, at The Oval, when the touring side was 96 for five in hopeless pursuit of almost 300. Brown made runs in that game, albeit sketchily, and Lewis took four wickets, so the new coach was spared an immediate fall from grace. Indeed, it was to some while before the sunny disposition of the nation towards me showed any sign of developing clouds, and by the end of that Texaco series the sour memories of the World Cup had been shoved just a few yards further out of sight.

Of course, there were extenuating circumstances for India. We are good at finding them when a team comes to England and gets beaten. If England lose, there is something wrong with our game, but if the opposition get stuffed it must be down to the pitch/the weather/the injuries/the toss. As a patriotic Englishman, this has always rankled with me. In this instance it was the weather that was to blame. Sure it was chilly and damp in late May – it usually is, in England – but they could not go on offering that one for long.

Any fears that may have entered my head about the essential working relationship with Illingworth so far seemed quite misplaced. He was encouraging when we spoke, and I think he enjoyed my sense of fun around the team even if it was something he would never have attempted himself. Most of all, I think he was happy to let me get on with running the side because he was now seriously sidetracked by the issue of his book and a fine imposed by the board for 'bringing the game into disrepute'. He was later to get the decision overturned but the whole affair cast a blight over his last summer as chairman and it was sometimes hard to get him to speak of anything else.

Devon Malcolm, the central figure in the book controversy, did not feature in our discussions when we picked the team for the first Test at Edgbaston. He didn't deserve to, purely on form. We did make some interesting alterations, though. Hussain was brought back to bat at number three – and for the benefit of all those who are now scratching their heads, I do mean brought back. Now that he is captain of England, and seems to have been a resident in the batting order for ever, it is hard to recall that this was to be his first Test appearance in three years. It had been a long time out in the cold, a time when even he had begun to doubt if there would be a way back. But Nasser found the way and he was also to mark it with a century.

That apart, we gave out three new caps, to Ronnie Irani, Min Patel and Alan Mullally. Two of these are easily explained. Patel was thought worthy of a go because he had been taking stacks of wickets for Kent and our slow bowling resources were as thin as ever. He did not prove up to it, however. Mullally had also forced his way in on county form for Leicestershire and, as a left-arm seamer, he offered us something different. He was no overnight sensation, either, but there was clearly enough to work on to suggest he would improve.

Irani was a different case. He had done reasonably well in county cricket and he had his vocal supporters. Ian Botham had been going on about him on television, which is always a help to a young all-rounder, but Ronnie's greatest ally in selection was Graham Gooch. Graham had seen a lot of him since he moved from Lancashire to Essex and thought he was ready. I did not share Graham's enthusiasm and nothing I saw in the next nine months would alter my view, but these are the trade-offs imposed when a national team is chosen by committee. I repeat again, sport has come too far for such a system to remain sustainable. Put somebody in charge and let them get on with it.

There was one other issue in my first Test selection that needs recalling for its rarity value. Alec Stewart did not play. He was fit and available but just not picked. Alec had been in poor form during the winter and it was no secret that he had not seen eye to eye with Raymond on everything, but to be omitted on form was a rare indignity for him and it has not happened again. He came back in the next Test at Lord's after an injury to Nick Knight and has never left the team since. Nor, to my great and lasting regret, has his most effective role in the side ever been satisfactorily resolved. The saga of what to do with Stewart has been a running sore at selection meetings for much of the past decade, under four different coaches. Those who watch the game, or comment upon it, are polarised by whether Alec should always play as a specialist batsman or should always keep wicket. Everybody agrees that it is unsatisfactory for the team and unfair to the individuals involved to keep chopping and changing, yet year after year we have gone on doing so.

I had known Alec as a young player, partly through his Dad, Micky, and partly through encountering him while umpiring. I knew he had played winter club cricket in Perth and the benefit of the quick, true pitches in that part of Australia was obvious in the fluent way he played. I actually stood in one of the first games in which he kept wicket, a championship match against Somerset at The Oval, when he did the job tidily and got 97 with the bat. That night I phoned Micky, who was England manager at the time, and told him I had seen a wicket-keeper-batsman he should have a look at.

The fact was he coped with the dual job expertly and there was always going to come a time when he would be asked to do it in Test cricket, usually when the state of a series dictated that we should strengthen either our batting or bowling at the expense of the specialist 'keeper. The problems here were twofold; whenever Alec kept wicket in Tests, his batting appeared to suffer, while the man who had to be the fall guy when this plan was activated just didn't deserve the suffering.

Jack Russell is everything a coach could want from a team member, and rather more besides. When I think back over my time with England and the players who epitomised the spirit I required, I think first of Atherton and Angus Fraser and Jack. He's dotty, of course, but endearingly so, and rising above the patriotic fervour that drives him on is a wicket-keeping ability rivalled by very few in the modern game. Jack made runs at Test level, too. Not as many as he would have liked, nor with a method that had any place in a coaching manual, but when the chips were down he would scrap and scrape and come up with a score. He did it in this first series of 1996, at Lord's, with a first-innings century and some vital, fighting runs when we needed them on the last day. Everyone was really made up for him, not least because he had just been awarded an MBE. But then everyone loves Jack, which always made it much tougher to leave him out when the fault was so seldom his own. And by the end of the summer, in a typical win-at-all costs situation at The Oval, Jack was to be left out again so that Alec could keep wicket.

Russell was always the model tourist, diligent and uncomplaining, even when he was not playing and to me he embodied the essence of playing for your country and respecting everything that meant. His eccentric ways are well chronicled, from his faddish diet to his intensely private family life – so private that nobody at his county even knows where he lives, let alone his telephone number. I don't mind any of that; I enjoy Jack's company and still love going down to his art gallery in Chipping Sodbury, where he is making such a success of his second career. But I know there were a series of disappointments in his international cricket career and I wish it could have been different.

He did annoy me at times. Not with his eating habits or his reclusive nature or even the individual way in which he worked on his 'keeping; these were things that made him feel good and affected no-one else. The way he batted was a different matter. His batting could drive a coach to distraction and sometimes seemed designed to make the opposition think they could get him out on any ball. While I was prepared to indulge his whims, there came a day in the West Indies when I decided he had gone too far. I went to him and suggested he cut a few of the contortions out of his batting, because the poor bloke at the other end can be chugging along, thinking the pitch is decent and he's playing all right, and suddenly he looks at Jack and feels he's batting in a minefield. He took it in good part and asked for some extra practice, which, in typically improvised Caribbean style, involved asking a groundsman if he could cut out a pitch on what resembled a cow field. There was no net, so I found a local lad to throw the ball back, and Jack in full regalia proceeded to bat like a novice. 'How's my shape?' he shouted down to me. I gave up the struggle for a straight face and laughed. 'You look dreadful,' I told him. 'The best thing you can do is buy a proper bat to replace that old thing.' He pretended to be upset and told the lads I'd put him down, but he loved the banter and involvement of a tour.

Great man though he is, there were times during my years in charge when I felt we were a stronger, better balanced side without him. In Test cricket, I always wanted our batting to be as long as possible and the easiest way of accomplishing this was for Alec to keep wicket. The trouble was, we never came to a definitive agreement as to whether he should bat when he was 'keeping, so one series he would be at three, then at five or six, before someone would inevitably pipe up that the best opening pairing was Atherton and Stewart and could he possibly go in first as well as 'keeping?

Alec never said no, which in one way did not help the issue. Whenever I went to him to discuss the permutations, he was the model professional, ready and waiting for whatever job or jobs we put his way. I always knew that his preference was to concentrate on opening the batting but it was only when he took on the captaincy that he came out and said so. By then, he had occupied too many roles to be remotely fair to him and, by changing our policy so consistently, we had kept putting ourselves in perceived 'must win' situations and leaving ourselves open to the inevitable criticism if it did not work out. I like to think quite a lot of advances were made while I was coach but we never did get to the bottom of this conundrum and the massive, ongoing confusion was undoubtedly damaging to the stability and outlook of the team.

Oddly enough, the one Test match we won on 1996 was the one Stewart missed. No reflection on him, we just outplayed India in a game that barely hobbled into its fourth day on another Edgbaston pitch that bounced unevenly and aroused widespread criticism. People will say the conditions suited our bowlers, and all I had been hearing in the build-up to the game was that Srinath and Prasad, the Indian seamers, were the danger men. I pointed out quietly that Srinath had yet to take five wickets in a Test innings; Lewis did so here and I thought he was the best bowler on view.

We had done plenty of homework on the Indians and I had enlisted John Emburey for some detailed reports on those players we did not know. 'Embers' had seen something of them while coaching the England 'A' tour, and again when they met his new county Northamptonshire in May, and he came to the fore now as they introduced two debutant batsmen, Ganguly and Dravid, for the Lord's Test. Sometimes, though, the dossiers of knowledge get you nowhere – Ganguly made 131, Dravid 95, and two stars of India were born. When we lunched on the last day at 170 for six in our second innings, only 85 ahead, an equalising win for India was on but Russell and Irani batted well and we drew the game comfortably enough.

Trent Bridge was never going to be anything other than a draw – 500 apiece and much public muttering about featherbed pitches – but we had won the series and that, to me, was the outcome that mattered. Still, people were saying the Indians were cold – it was July by now, remember – and that the opposition had been poor and that things would be different against Pakistan. Well, we had done our first job competently. I knew without being told that the next one would be tougher, because we were now facing a crackerjack team. Bring them on . . .

I was well aware that there was a residue of bad feeling between the countries, if not the current players, dating back to the business between Mike Gatting and Shakoor Rana in 1987. There had even been some flashpoints when Pakistan toured here in 1992 but as we now had two captains, in Atherton and Wasim Akram, who were good mates, I thought we had a good opportunity to put things right. The first Test was scheduled for Lord's and a night or so beforehand four of us went to dinner in St John's Wood High Street – myself and Athers representing England, Wasim Akram and Aamir Sohail for Pakistan. I made a little speech, saying they could take it as read that we would respect them as people and players and I was confident we could expect the same by return. Wasim got the message back to his players and, since then, I honestly believe we have got along better with the Pakistanis than most other teams.

They can be a rag, tag and bobtail outfit at times, the next bit of political turbulence or change of captain never far away, but most of them are good lads and I think the series that summer was enjoyed by everybody. This, however, did not remotely make up for the fact that we lost it, pretty comprehensively, with defeats at Lord's and The Oval surrounding a drawn game at Headingley that I still feel we ought to have won.

With the possible exception of Edgbaston, where the present generation of players have habitually done well and so feel comfortable, Headingley suits us better than any ground in the country. When conditions are right there, we should win, and conditions were perfect that year. It was overcast, damp and there was water on the covers – water for which I had a good use.

The Pakistan bowling strength came from the reverse-swing achieved by Wasim and Waqar with an old ball. I had no problem with that. From the deep early suspicion, it is now accepted as a skill-enhancement in the game, a throwback to the fundamentals of trying to hit the stumps. Nothing illegal about it, just an adept use of a ball that has been roughed up over a dry outfield. The solution here was obvious and the groundsman obediently disposed of all the water from the covers in the third-man and fine-leg fielding areas, where it would quickly drain away but leave the surface lush and damp – precisely what the Pakistanis did not want. Wasim went berserk, waving his arms and demanding to know what was going on. He knew the answer perfectly well. He also knew that it was a legitimate practice and no more was said.

The force remained with us, Atherton won the toss and Mullally got rid of Saeed Anwar straight away. Now let's get into them, I thought, exploit the conditions. But it never happened. Everything was in our favour, everything pointed to a big performance from Andy Caddick – and, not for the first or last time, Caddick chose such circumstances to shrink in stature. He even shortened his run-up and loped in as if it was a Sunday league game, which had Ian Botham bounding down from his seat in the commentary box demanding to know what was going on. We sent a message out to Caddick, urging him to crank it up, but at lunchtime he said simply that he felt his control was better off the reduced run. I ask you. With so much in their favour and an early wicket down, would Dennis Lillee or Curtly Ambrose have throttled back to concentrate on control?

Caddick, I am afraid, has been like that for much of his career, which helps explain why he took so long to become an established member of the side. Plainly, he is a Test match bowler, with a wicket-taking pedigree, but time after time, he failed when he just had to succeed. A frustration, then, but not to my mind a difficult lad to deal with, although he was definitely not one of the boys. He was always seen by the cool customers in the dressing-room as a nerd, and it is easy to see why. He doesn't talk their language or move in their circles, doesn't really fit into the dressing-room culture, but I still think he is a genuine, misunderstood guy.

He will have a view on everything, which also grates on plenty of nerve-ends, but he can never do enough for you. Andy will fetch it, mend it and lend it – he's your old pal Andy-Man, like a Harry Enfield character come to life. He was, however, very insecure about his cricket, especially in high pressure situations, and responsibility appears to intimidate him, both in the sense of being able to grab the initiative and of owning up when he has got things wrong. It is as if he gets fazed by an atmosphere of expectation, then applies a selective memory to is own inadequacies. Bob Cottam has tried very hard with him since coming on board as England bowling coach, and I think decent progress has been made, but in his time with Somerset I know Bob found Caddick very difficult because he would not accept criticism. He is much better now, though.

Back then he was inclined to say silly things. 'I've got a ball for Brian Lara' just about took the biscuit as Lara, naturally enough, read this boast and made it his business to take him to the cleaners. Caddick bowled poorly for most of that tour in the Caribbean in 1998 and it cost him his place for a while, but what riled me just as much was that he would never put his hand up in the sanctuary of the dressing-room and admit that he had bowled like a drain. In Trinidad, after his wastefulness with the ball had been influential in West Indies sneaking a win, he piped up at a team meeting and claimed he had only bowled four bad balls all day. Ranged around him were 14 or 15 professionals who knew this was utter nonsense, yet not one of them would say as much. This disappointed me hugely, because I knew full well that some of them would leave the meeting and mutter about Caddick behind his back. The situation that developed, in which he became ever more isolated, could have been avoided if he had shown the courage to admit he had bowled rubbish or if others had made certain he knew it. Instead, silence bred resentment, which was a shame. Andy Craddick is a high quality bowler, a five-wicket man in Test cricket, but his inability to accept his own failings has held him back badly.

Back to 1996 and the upshot of our failure to capitalise at Headingley was that we went to The Oval in just the situation that Jack Russell came to know and dread. We probably reached a stage when the phone call to Jack was unnecessary – he would already have looked up Gloucestershire's programme and packed his bags accordingly. Sure enough, we left him out to go into this critical game with a properly balanced attack and as much batting as we could muster. This meant retaining Lewis, who had bowled poorly at Headingley and was now to spurn his reprieve in the most foolish way, asking Stewart to keep wicket and go in first, and creating an intriguing spin pairing of Robert Croft and Ian Salisbury. It was Croft's first Test and he did well – only two wickets but bowling with a loop and control that made him a ready-made inclusion for the winter tour. It was Salisbury's ninth Test, spread across almost five years of frustration, and I am afraid the romantic idea that a leg-spinner would weave the necessary magic held no water.

England's cricket has had a variety of shortcomings over the years but the recurring Achilles heel has been the absence of a big-spinning leg-break bowler. Other countries have stolen a march and we have been obliged to admire Shane Warne, Mushtaq Ahmed and Anil Kumble, to name but three, while our stocks have remained depressingly bare. Well, not quite. Salisbury has been around for years now, taking his share of wickets at county level and frequently looking something close to the complete article. Even recently, when the leg-spin initiatives I put in place began to bear fruit around the counties, and bowlers like Chris Schofield made their advance, I still harboured the hope that Salisbury would solve the problem. I was happy to play him in that Oval Test and felt that with another spinner alongside him, the pressure might be eased. But he just couldn't cope.

It's a big arena. A lot of people, a lot of cameras, a heap of anticipation. And Salisbury could scarcely land the ball, let alone spin it. He took one for 116, going for four runs an over without hinting at the penetration that would compensate for the bad balls. He was mortified about it all and I really felt for him, because this was an example of a gifted cricketer, desperate to please, who simply did not have the steel in his temperament essential for this level. His anxiety seeped into his action, which became jerky and unnatural during that game, but when I later asked Richie Benaud to pass a view on him, he viewed some videos and told me his basic action was fine. Here, then, was a bowler who was comfortable only at the lower levels – and to make his remorse the sharper, Mushtaq won the game for Pakistan by taking six wickets in our second innings.

The result was a disappointment but this game did have one indelible session of play, the reaction to which illustrated a lack of appreciation of the essence of modern Test cricket. Atherton and Stewart went in on the third evening to open our second innings, facing a deficit of almost 200 and a mountain to climb to save the game. They were also facing Wasim and Waqar at their fast and furious best. Sure, there was plenty of short stuff, ample opportunity to check the resolution and pulse-rate of the two batsmen, but it was wonderful entertainment, a true Test match battle involving four of the fittest players of their generation. Those who chose to write it up as 'over the top' and suggest that the umpires should have taken a more authoritative line with the short balls might care to reflect that there were four men left in the corner of the dressing-room when I left that night – Atherton and his Lancashire team-mate Wasim, Stewart and his Surrey side-kick Waqar. They'd had a ball and were ready for more of the same the next morning. The kick, the buzz, the stimulation of such duels is one very good reason why such men, the best around, want to play at this level.

The summer was not quite over and we had the opportunity to take a small slice of consolation by beating Pakistan in a Texaco Trophy series. We did so in some style, actually, winning the initial two games by wide margins, but there was to be a sting in the tail of Pakistan's two-wicket win in an exciting final game at Trent Bridge. Rashid Latif, the wicket-keeper, won it for them with a dashing 31 not out just when it seemed we would wrap up a third victory. The fact that there was no overt celebrating from the Pakistanis did not register at the time and it was a while later before the stories began to filter through that Rashid, far from being acclaimed as a hero in his own dressing room, was allegedly something of an outcast. The rumour that reached our ears – our astonished ears, I might add – was that Pakistan's intention had been to let us win but Rashid, unaware or uninterested in such goings-on, had foiled the scheme.

My instant reaction to all this was one of scorn and I am still not sure if that was the right response to maintain. At that stage, we had never heard of matches being thrown to order and, for England cricketers, it was impossible to comprehend. Subsequent events, including a long-running judicial enquiry in Pakistan, have thrown a somewhat different, if still shaded light on the matter and I think if you asked anyone in cricket now for an opinion on whether international games have been thrown they would say there's no smoke without fire.

Being an avid student of the history of cricket, I suppose this should not surprise me. Betting, after all, was responsible for much of the development of the game in this country, where vast wagers of land or baronial homes were made on the outcome of long-ago games. And if that seems a distant irrelevance to the modern debate over match-fixing, I can remember much more recent episodes in county cricket that we thought nothing of at the time but, in the present climate, make uncomfortable memories.

It was not so long ago that three-day championship matches had a Sunday League game sandwiched in the middle and, all too often, August and September would find one team more interested in the championship and the other gunning for the Sunday title. It was commonplace for captains to drink together on a Friday or Saturday night and come up with some apparently innocent 'agreement' that team one would be given a reasonable declaration to chase in the championship – even if they had to employ some 'joke' bowlers to achieve it – but that by return they might see their way to 'resting' a bowler or two on Sunday. Nobody thought twice about it and there was no feeling, so far as I recall, that this was in any sense corrupting the spirit or integrity of the game. It was a means to an end. In hindsight, it looks pretty bad and I am very pleased that four-day cricket has largely banished the nonsense of joke bowling and captains' collusions.

I still have no idea whether Pakistan wanted to lose that game at Trent Bridge and I don't suppose I shall ever have a definitive answer. Betting on your own team losing remains complete anathema to me and I am convinced that no England player of my knowledge has ever been involved. We did, of course, discuss the subject from time to time and the bigger the issue became the more difficult it was to retain puritanical beliefs. Sharjah, the Middle-Eastern venue for annual floodlit one-day tournaments, is regularly cited as being a hotbed of such corruption and, again, I have no evidence either way. I do recall feeling distinctly uneasy, though, as we watched a match there between Pakistan and West Indies in which a host of catches were dropped for no good reason. It just looked wrong, and so did the scene in the viewing area where, unless my imagination was running riot, too many mobile phone calls were being made and too many apparently furtive discussions involving players and other unknown characters were taking place. I sincerely hope I was wrong, because I would much prefer to believe that all of cricket is straight, but I am afraid that has become an increasingly difficult belief to sustain.

CHAPTER TWELVE

'We've flippin'
murdered them ...'

It did not take long. By the time 1997 was a few days old, my honeymoon period in the job was well and truly over. I was being lampooned in the newspapers and my conduct in the aftermath of a Test match had earned me some sensational headlines and an official reprimand from my bosses. On top of all this, the England team was being castigated as useless for failing to beat the newest of Test-playing nations and as graceless for failing to exhibit the true spirit of touring. It sounds a dreadful mess; it certainly requires some explaining.

I know that, to my detractors, Zimbabwe will always be a rope to hang me with. I know that we played some shocking one-day cricket on that tour and that many have concluded – wrongly, in my view – that we were also poor in the two Test matches. I know that my behaviour attracted a great deal of attention and that in one incident, on one day, I was out of order. The circumstances of the tour, however, have not properly been aired or appreciated and I have waited a long while to tell the full story.

It was to be a split tour, with two Tests and three one-day games in Zimbabwe followed by three Tests and a longer one-day series in New Zealand. We were to leave in late November 1996, not returning home until the second week of March. In planning with this itinerary in mind, we made two immediate mistakes. We scheduled nothing but fitness work between the end of the home season and the start of the tour, and we decided that wives and families would not be allowed to join the players at any stage.

The first decision was the easier to make and the quicker to cause the captain and myself regret. Our thinking was simple enough: it had already been a long year for the players, with an arduous South African tour followed by a World Cup and then two home series. Some were showing signs of fatigue and the need for practice must sometimes be balanced by the benefits of rest. After much thought, we scheduled a fitness camp for late October and the entire squad travelled to the Barringtons Health Club in Portugal, where Wayne and Dean Riddle, our fitness expert, left them in no doubt that they were not there for a holiday. In terms of getting them physically into shape, it was a great success, but our deliberate policy of avoiding bats, balls and tactics backfired when we began the tour with only two first-class games scheduled before the start of the international programme. It was not enough and it left us rusty. It was our own fault, no-one else's, and a lesson to take forward into future years.

The issue of families was obviously more contentious and several players were openly unhappy about it from the outset. We knew this would be the case but there was a strong belief, emanating from both Athers and Raymond, that the collapse of English resistance in Cape Town the previous winter was not entirely coincidental with the families being present over Christmas and New Year. Both of them felt it had been a distraction and, at the time, I went along with their opinion without real reservations. It was wrong, though, and by the mid-point of the tour I think we all knew it. My firm view now, with the virtue of experience and hindsight, is that families should be accommodated on every tour for as long as is practical, and I truly believe that if all parties work at the arrangement, it benefits the players, the atmosphere and consequently the performance.

There will always be some players on tour who are more self-sufficient than others. Equally, there will always be those who go through agonies of homesickness but never let on. Graham Thorpe was the prime example in Zimbabwe. His wife had just given birth and he had come out on tour in a surly disposition that he could not or would not shake off, at least for the duration of the stay in Zimbabwe. I had some sympathy with him, as anyone of compassion would have, but he presented this forlorn picture of the reluctant tourist which unfortunately rubbed off on several others who considered it 'cool' to be with him.

Thorpe is one of our box-office players, a rare batsman capable of scoring runs all round the wicket, and for England to be at their best he has to be in the side and firing. He has a rebellious streak, though, declining to conform in areas that he would regard as a joke but we must impose for team unity, and the danger is that he takes impressionable acolytes along with him. There were a few candidates on that tour.

I firmly believe in the principle that you must look like a team when on tour. This does not mean slavishly donning blazers and ties at all times – not very often at all, in fact – but it does mean adhering to a few basic rules of dress when travelling or attending team functions. An incident on a later tour of West Indies come to mind here, and it was all the more irritating to me because it was an evening in a lifetime. John Paul Getty was in the Caribbean, not least to watch some cricket, and he issued an invitation to bring the team onto his yacht. Now this, you understand, is no ordinary yacht, more like a luxury liner on a compact scale, and to be asked aboard for the day was a privilege. The players were told that we would dress, as a team, in what we called our 'number two's', smart chinos and a blue polo shirt supplied by Boss. Thorpe flatly refused. He turned up, albeit reluctantly, wearing jeans and a check shirt hanging loose. He stood out like a sore thumb and Mr Getty made just one comment: 'He's not part of your team, then?' It may be easy to say we should have been more insistent with Thorpe, or we should have disciplined him, but these are not kids we are dealing with here, they are grown men with families and mortgages who really ought to be capable of conducting themselves in an adult way and recognising the damaging effects of such unconformity.

There was an impression gathering momentum during the Zimbabwe tour that painted our players as slovenly. Personally, I believe this stemmed only from a few individuals and that the great majority of the players upheld standards. It is true to say, though, that dress codes were not a priority, either in my eyes or those of our manager, John Barclay, who understandably felt there were more important things to worry about. He did not waste time chastising players if they had put on the wrong shirt, or neglected to shave, and in this he offered a sharp contrast to Bob Bennett, who took over in the role the following winter. My own instincts are far closer to John than Bob, but I realise that as an international side with an avid press following it is necessary to play the game, watching your back if things are not going well. Winning, as Atherton never tired of pointing out, is the key to all perceptions and publicity. Everyone said Mark Taylor was marvellous as Australian captain. Well, he didn't shave very often, did he, but that was easily overlooked because his team was usually in the process of giving out another drubbing.

John Barclay was a very caring manager, probably more popular with the players than the press. He had his own views about some of the side, believing them too shallow for their own good, but he conducted a difficult tour with unfailing efficiency and geniality. He also made certain that the players saw one of the great sights of the world by personally sanctioning the hiring of two nine-seater planes for a day trip to Victoria Falls and it was this, I shall always believe, that cost him his position. He felt strongly that the lads should see the Falls, that it was the chance of a lifetime, an adventure, and he was undeniably right – not least when it is recalled that the team was at this stage taking some unwarranted criticism for adopting a siege mentality. So John made the arrangements and pressed ahead with them above the disapproving head of Tim Lamb, successor to A C Smith as chief executive of our Board. I believe that was always held against him. Moreover, I am convinced John was shafted on the juggernaut of misguided condemnation that followed the Zimbabwe tour.

So what was it really like, then, and why did our team come across so poorly? It was difficult and inhospitable is my answer, and the players came across as they did because that is how the Zimbabweians planned it. If this seems a fanciful claim of conspiracy theories, let the evidence bear me out. It has been said that I was suspicious of Zimbabwe after my experiences with the Under-19s there the previous winter. Well, so I was, but I was also forewarned. I knew the facilities we could expect and those we could not. At least, I thought I did. In truth, nothing could adequately have prepared me.

We were to fly into Harare and, there being only two cricketing centres in the country, we were to spend most of the tour there, too. So we were destined to get to know our hotel pretty well, which was one reason I had raised doubts about the choice of the Monomotapa. We stayed there with the Under-19s at a time when it was being refurbished, and there was not a single soul there apart from the 16 of us. I had no fond memories of the place and strongly believed we should be put up in either the Michels or the Sheraton, two hotels of better class in the city. Medha Laud went out to inspect the Monomotapa and reported that she had misgivings about it. Tim Lamb overruled her, stating that it was 'adequate', though I thought it significant that when he appeared in Harare later in the tour, he checked into the Sheraton.

The Monomotapa is in a poor area and has basic accommodation. It would have been fine for a single game stay but we were due to spend a lot of time there and I considered it inadequate. If my views need independent endorsement I can call no better witness than Lord MacLaurin of Knebworth – Ian to us – the new chairman of the England and Wales Cricket Board. Ian took the chair during the tour and quickly made it his business to fly out to Zimbabwe to make himself known. Rather than recall things he said to me in conversation, I shall quote his own book, *Tiger by the Tail*:

'When I rang the Board's offices at Lord's to say that I would like to join the tour, the first question I was asked was where I would like to stay. There was only one thing I could say: "With the team, of course"'. A shocked silence greeted my reply, which was matched only by my disbelief on being told: "But that's never happened before. The management always stay in a different hotel." It did not take me long to find out why. On arriving in Harare, Ann and I were driven to the team's hotel and were horrified by what we found. Our own room was bad enough but the team's quarters were even worse: two players apiece to each pokey room in which, at best, the air-conditioning worked to a regime of its own. And this in a climate where the daytime temperature often reached 110 degrees. Small wonder that the management preferred the luxury of either the Michels or Sheraton Hotel to the accommodation provided for our players. And small wonder, either, that it was proving to be such an unhappy tour.'

Well said, chairman. To that summary, I can add that the South Africans, visiting Zimbabwe for the first time, checked into the Monomotapa and immediately booked out again. They deemed it unacceptable; we had to get on with it. Before that, however, we were ushered into a side room as hot as a greenhouse, where a briefing was given by some officers of the Zimbabwe Cricket Union. Their message, paraphrased, was that Harare is a dangerous and tacky place, a fact we were to appreciate ever more. They warned us not to go out alone, nor to wear jewellery in public places, and to beware of prostitutes and Aids, both apparently rampant. It was probably well-meaning but after a long flight this was not quite the time or the place to make an impression.

Once this was over, we were given a schedule for practice. As is customary before every tour, faxes had been exchanged between the relevant Boards and we had set out the usual requests for local bowlers to help out in the nets. On our first morning at the Alexandra Sports Club, we arrived to find there were no nets ready, no food or drinks laid on and certainly no bowlers. I subsequently discovered from the two English county players in the city, James Kirtley and Matthew Rawnsley, that they had been told they were not to help us.

When we moved on to practice on the Harare Sports Club, their Test match centre, we were told that we could not use the main ground even for physical exercises. Instead, we were confined to the adjacent rugby ground, with goalposts placed inconveniently. Sometimes, the ground authority refused to provide stumps for practice, saying we should bring our own, and there were days when I had to put up the nets and roll the practice pitch myself just in order to get a session started at the appointed time. Usually, the nets were wet, without explanation or apology, just one more example of the obstructiveness and negativity we met at every turn.

Worse was to come when the cricket began. Each morning, I would arrive at the ground to find that our dressing-room had not been cleaned and that piles of rubbish from the home dressing-room had been swept into ours. Bottles, leftover food and general debris littered the floor and I took to cleaning it up myself before the players arrived. At the other end of hot and sweaty days, the players had little alternative but to head straight back to the hotel, because there were no shower facilities at the ground.

My first mistake was in bottling this up, keeping it all to myself. I did so because I was determined we would not show that this treatment was getting to us, but I have since realised that a wiser tactic would have been to apprise our travelling media of all these events and get them on our side. Instead, the press turned against us, feeding on the half-truths and accusations being slipped their way by opponents who wanted to portray us as aloof and superior – which, ironically, was just the impression we were drawing of them. I imagine Dave Houghton, the Zimbabwe coach but a man very familiar with the English press from his time with Worcestershire, had done his job thoroughly and captured the ears of the English press. My only view on that is 'well done', and a reflection that it was partly my own fault for not trusting our media to back us.

There was a notice pinned to the wall of the Zimbabwe dressing-room during the early international games, beating up the idea that this was their one and only chance of beating England. There were references, too, wherever we went, to the fact that our Board had not supported their application for full Test status. Well, true enough, but that had nothing to do with the players on tour and it was this group that was now being painted in an unjustly poor light.

It was said that our players spurned hospitality, that they shut themselves away and behaved unsociably. The truth of it is that there was no hospitality offered, other than one wonderful and greatly enjoyed day on the Streaks' family farm. After that initial, uncomfortable briefing, the Zimbabwe CU officials were conspicuous only by their absence. The team management did attend one dinner at the home of Don Arnott, the chief executive, and one evening in Harare four or five lads from each team got together for dinner – a journey made in the back of Andy Waller's pick-up. There were no bad relations between the sides. No relations at all would be nearer the mark. Even when Ian Botham, who was out there with the Sky commentary team, organised two golf days and issued a general invitation to the two teams, only one of their players, Craig Evans, turned up, though I subsequently learned that two England players caused equal offence by saying they would play and then failing to show, which was bad manners.

The one good facility available at the Monomotapa was a large and comfortable team room and this was our sanctuary and our salvation. There was a game some of the lads had played in South Africa, called 'Balderdash', which resumed on many an evening, and there were chess and card schools. Hardly riotous behaviour, just professional sportsmen sticking together as a team in a place that was coming across as increasingly inhospitable.

The longer this went on, and the less our own press saw of us in the evenings, the more some criticised. To me, they were on pretty thin ice, because our players would never be found in some of the joints they patronised of an evening, but it did not stop them digging and niggling. There was some public fall-out over the team decision to decline an invitation to spend part of Christmas Day with the press; we were told that it was traditional to share some drinks and to watch a pantomime put on by some of the journalists. My view was that it would have been very difficult, very artificial, to create some jollity and festivity with people who had been slagging us off in such a personal and virtiolic way. I also thought this was the unanimous opinion, although certain players have subsequently said they were uneasy with the decision, seeing it as a snub that could only make things worse. I am not sure that was possible. I fell out with Martin Johnson, who was covering the tour for the *Daily Telegraph*. Clever writer though he is, I just felt he set out on a one-track crusade to belittle the players in general and me in particular. It wasn't funny any more, it was cruel and monotonous. Other pieces we had faxed back to us were misinformed and grossly unfair, the slant being that the players were hiding themselves away from paradise, when the truth in my view is that Harare is the pits.

Outside its capital city, Zimbabwe is a beautiful country, thoroughly unspoiled and a tourist's delight. But we were not there on holiday and we had no time to goggle at the game parks. Harare was our focus and, of all cities where Test cricket is played, it was at that time among the most dingy and depressing. It was also home to a faction for whom I had nothing but contempt as they continued to represent the worst excesses of the old colonial empire. Their bar-stool conversation was frequently anti-English, harking back to UDI and the 1970s, times for which we cricket folk had little recall and no influence whatever.

Outside our changing room and away to the right, a modest temporary stand was built for the international games. Its occupants were members of the outdated and outmoded Colonial Club immediately behind. From early in the morning, and right through each day, these guys would sit in the stand drinking beer from bottles served to them by black waiters. Each time one of the members finished a bottle, he would throw it onto the grass between the stand and the boundary line, from where one of the waiters would have to collect it. This demeaning process became nauseating after tea, when the effects of the beer would be kicking in and the party piece was to throw bottles while the waiters were picking others up. It looked terrible, like some long-forgotten racist ceremony, and after observing it, quietly seething, for a day or two I made a point of walking across, picking up a bottle and looking up into the stand. I picked out one of the biggest blokes, a massive red-neck, walked towards him and offered him his bottle back. 'I think you've just dropped this,' I said. They went mad, the lot of them, and the bravado of my gesture dissipated pretty quickly. To be honest, I was a bit frightened as I walked away but that did not ease the sense of loathing for what I had seen. I thought of my black friends in cricket and wondered what on earth they would make of it. What would Viv Richards have done if he had witnessed such a scene?

This, then, was the unsettling background to the cricket we were to play on that tour. None of it constitutes an excuse for the way we performed, which was often disappointing. I had set out believing that we should win both the Test series on tour and that we certainly ought to win the one-dayers in Zimbabwe. By the new year, I had been disillusioned on both counts, though to this day I will maintain that our cricket in the Test series entitled us to win.

We were ridiculed for losing the opening first-class game to Mashonaland and, however much the rustiness contributed, it was a poor performance against aggressive opposition. By then, we had also lost a one-day game to a President's XI and played unbelievably sluggish cricket. The transfer from Harare to Bulawayo came as a relief, the place and the people being much more friendly, but after an uplifting win over the Matabeleland first-class side, we underperformed dreadfully in the opening one-day international and lost by two wickets – quite an achievement after having Zimbabwe 106 for seven chasing 153.

It was in this game that we encountered our ICC referee, Hanumant Singh, for the first time. He came into the hotel restaurant at 8 am just as I was on my way out and I thought he said: 'You all fine?' I gave a cheery response to the effect that we were all keen to get on with the cricket, whereupon he interjected: 'No, you are all fined.' The former Indian Test player was taking issue with the size of the logos on our bats, a problem we were able to deflect successfully back to the ICC chief executive, David Richards. Hanumant was a fussy man by nature but John Barclay thawed him out a little by talking to him about Colin Cowdrey, who turned out to be one of his heroes. On another morning, he came into our dressing-room with a huge dollop of bird droppings on the shoulder of his blazer. The players hooted with laughter, thinking he was unaware of it, but he solemnly told us that it had to remain there all day to bring him good luck.

Bulawayo did not bring us much luck. Three days after that initial one-day international we began the first Test, a game in which we played much the better cricket and certainly deserved to win. I shall always believe that we were deprived of that victory by our opponents being allowed to flout the spirit of the game on a dramatic final afternoon that was to leave me in a temper with considerable consequences.

Zimbabwe made 376 in their first innings and, at 306 for four in reply, we were dominating the game. The eventual lead of only 30 was disappointing but, with Philip Tufnell to the fore, we reduced them to 107 for five by the end of the fourth day. It then took us longer than ideal to wrap up the innings and we were left with the kind of target familiar to our players from Sunday League games rather than Tests – 205 from 37 overs.

To sustain a rate of almost six an over, when the opposition can drape all the fielders round the boundary if they so desire, is a taxing task and I think we surprised the Zimbabweians by going for the runs from the start. At 154 for one, midway through the mandatory last 15 overs, we are winning, but then, as so often in frantic chases, wickets begin to slip away and the essentially dormant opposition suddenly began to have half a sniff of stealing the game themselves. I never really gave this outcome a thought, though, believing that if we did not make it we would certainly not be bowled out. And it was never a danger, as the target slowly came down to 21 off two overs, then to 13 from the last, with Nick Knight still there, 86 not out and facing Heath Streak. A six and two twos left us needing three off the last ball; we managed two before the run out that ended the game with the scores level. Epic draw? Honour satisfied, everybody happy? Well, not quite.

I had watched the closing stages from close to the sightscreen. The one television in our viewing area was on the blink. I preferred to be alone and I was also keen to make a proper judgement of the line the Zimbabweians were bowling. Pretty wide was the answer to that one, and the closer we came to the climax, the more liberties they took.

I was not entirely surprised by this. At the start of the Under-19 tour a year earlier, their boys had consistently bowled very wide of the off stump with only one fielder on the leg side. We made overtures to their management, suggesting this was hardly what was required of age-group cricketers and that we had come to play proper, constructive cricket. The negativity, though, had been there for all to see and it raged again now at senior level, largely unchecked by the umpires, Steve Dunne and Ian Robinson, who called only three wides in the innings.

Towards the end it was shameful and the most blatant wide of all, the third ball of Streak's last over, went uncalled. On that alone, the result altered, but the general tenor of a session that was undoubtedly tense and dramatic to a neutral was that only one team had any intention of playing the game properly.

To say I was incensed is an understatement, and doubtless I showed it. In my view, cricket simply should not be played like that, let alone in a Test match, and I am afraid I was in a mood to give my opinions voice. I stormed into the umpires' room to tackle them on the issue of wides but got no further than the door before Steve Dunne, impressive in his authority, pushed me out again. Next, I went to see Hanumant Singh, who had been keen to stress to both teams before the match that he expected to see it played 'in the spirit of the game'. I challenged him on this. 'It is down to the umpires to interpret that,' he replied, which did not placate me one bit.

Finding no satisfaction, I stood on the peripheries of the presentation ceremony, still vividly seething. When the formalities were over, a chap with red hair and beard came across to me – a face I felt I had seen before but could not place. He observed that we had failed to beat his team and I responded hotly that if that was the way they wanted to play the game, they deserved everything coming to them. 'You were an absolute disgrace,' I added.

He came back at me with another remark and I am sorry to say I gave him a mouthful, expletives not deleted.

There were other people looking on now, one couple in particular taunting me. 'You couldn't even beat us,' they kept saying. I reacted badly. It has been said that I gave them the two-fingered sign. In fact, I stuck one finger up at them, not that this excuses it. Someone later told me that the couple were the parents of Alistair Campbell, the Zimbabwe captain; if so, they should both examine what they were saying and the part they played in a pretty regrettable scene.

Back in the dressing-room, Ian Botham spent a few minutes with me, and he was firm. 'You're not going in that press conference until you've calmed down,' he said. It was sound advice and, at the time, I felt I carried off the conference all right. I had not set out to be controversial but I had given my view that we were the better side, given it in my own way. It was only when I detected a scurrying activity among the journalists that I became aware that I had presented them with a headline that was to haunt me.

It was an English journalist, believe it or not, who asked me if I thought we were fortunate to get a draw. I replied that the opposition had thrown the ball here, there and everywhere in their desperation to survive. 'We've flippin' murdered them,' I added. 'And they know it.'

CHAPTER THIRTEEN

Yellow-carded by Tim Lamb

Christmas came and went. So, too, did Tim Lamb. Neither were much fun. The players made the best of things on Christmas Day in Harare, the tour newcomers putting on a show to make us laugh, but the wounds of the last Test were still fresh and anticipation of the next one, due to start on Boxing Day morning, was strong. It was during this game that the new chief executive of the Board came to see me in my hotel room and ripped me to shreds in a manner I could scarcely comprehend.

Of course, I knew by then that there would be some questions asked. It could hardly be avoided. The immediate aftermath of the match in Bulawayo had made more newspaper headlines than the dramatic and controversial cricket. I was disappointed by this but I understood it – I have been around journalists long enough to know that a 'row', whether genuine or fabricated, will always seem better copy than a straight report, and my position was not exactly helped by the revelation that the man with whom I had clashed after the presentation ceremony was none other than the chairman of the Mashonaland Cricket Association, one Ian Goggin. I was not especially proud of losing my temper in public but I had little sympathy with those who had provoked it, either.

There had also been some pretty fierce letters about me in the

Zimbabweian papers. One, published on Christmas Day if you please, said it was 'distasteful' that I should have made such 'loutish and unsporting remarks'. Another correspondent, having viewed my post-match interview, said he thought he must be watching the commander of the Barmy Army, which at least made me chuckle.

Well, even in cool repose, I saw nothing wrong in the 'murdered 'em' quote that was to follow me around. I still don't. It was delivered with passion but that is me – nobody who knows me should expect any different. Essentially, though, it was a sound byte, the sort of northern turn of phrase that might be used up my way if Manchester United had won 1-0. Hanumant Singh had looked into it, as he was empowered to do with anything that might constitute a controversial remark, but he had seen no cause to take action. Yet plenty of people were judging it differently, taking it literally, and one of them was knocking on the door of my hotel room.

It is worth saying here that Tim Lamb and I always got along okay, so far as greetings and superficial conversations go. We still do. He and his son follow United and we will usually chat about the club if we meet. Perhaps it is safe, neutral territory; certainly, from the time of that meeting in Zimbabwe, I had the feeling that we were working to distinctly different agendas. Tim, I came to believe, saw his responsibility as running a smooth ship for the contentment of the county chairmen who elected him, rather than offering wholehearted support to those who were out in the field doing their best for the national team. Perhaps this is being simplistic, perhaps I expected too much. But I do not think it unreasonable for an England coach or manager, doing his best for the national team, to feel entitled to some understanding in private and backing in public. With Tim, I went short on both.

I felt no such misgivings about Ian MacLaurin. Both in Zimbabwe and later, I always felt he was supportive. It has been said, even written in other books, that MacLaurin issued a reprimand to me in Zimbabwe. This is totally untrue. All he did, both verbally and in writing, was offer sympathy. The bludgeon was wielded by Lamb.

I had no problem with him coming to talk about the issue. He was simply doing his job. What I objected to, and I told him so immediately, was the source of his information and the angle of his questioning. Tim went through a whole raft of matters, many of which were one-sided complaints, and when I asked him where he had got his information from, he stunned me by saying he had consulted 'English journalists he respected' and 'members of the crowd'. So there it was: in the eyes of the man who could be thought my immediate boss, I was to be judged on the word of reporters and spectators. Would this happen to the England football manager, I wondered?

Taken aback, I decided I should commit what Tim was telling me to paper. I grabbed a hotel envelope from the desk and wrote down the points he had made to me. I still have that envelope and one side of it is covered with my alleged bad points and Tim's threats. From top to bottom, it reads:

Learn to be more diplomatic, to be more gracious;
Subject of ridicule at home and by Zimbabwe crowd;
Will not be in job long unless you change;
We do not like an interview you gave after Bulawayo;
Must accept hospitality afforded. You are a guest in a foreign country;
Do not like the way you spoke to players regarding umpires' decisions;
We take a dim view of England coach being subject of a hearing with match referee;
We do not like the way you were seen on the boundary at Bulawayo;
We do not like the feel we get from speaking to Zimbabwe officials and English press;

> The 'feeling' about you and Zimbabwe dates back to the
> Under-19 tour.

I passed the envelope across to Tim and asked him to check the words, which he agreed were an accurate summary of what he had said. After he had gone, I jotted on the other side of the envelope: 'I was not allowed to answer in detail any of these allegations . . . Thanks for your support.' Bitter, perhaps, but accurate. Tim, I believed, had made up his mind about the matter before he even set foot in my room and he had no real interest in hearing another side of the affair. He had given me what amounted to an official warning – a yellow card, if you like – and while this did not worry me as such, it mystified me that things could work this way in an organisation where we were both supposedly seeking the same ends. I knew now that no such thing could be assumed. Tim Lamb, in my estimation, was an efficient politician whose prime motivation was covering his own back.

Some fortnight later – after we had moved on to New Zealand, in fact – I received an official ECB letter from Tim, which did nothing more than put the warning in print. He reiterated his view that the 'abusive remarks' I made to Ian Goggin 'had the effect of tarnishing not only your own reputation in Zimbabwe but indeed that of the whole team.' The final paragraph was intended as a sweetener but it just came across as silly and insincere. 'This particular episode apart, let me assure you that you have the absolute support of the Board . . .'

A good deal had happened on the field in the interim, not much of it of cheer to me. The second Test was washed out when we were in a position to dictate terms, 136 ahead with seven wickets still standing. We had batted poorly in the first innings but battled back well. I thought we would have won the game but we shall never know. The one-day games, however, were a different story.

We lost both matches in Harare and Zimbabwe took the series 3-0. It sounds undignified and it was; our cricket was shocking and we had a lot of improving to do as we took our leave of Zimbabwe without, it must be said, much regret.

A new country brought a new problem. This one was called Dominic Cork and it was a subject that had rumbled ominously through the preceding weeks and was destined to stay with us for some time. It was only 18 months since Cork had made a sensational Test debut against West Indies and quickly become the talk of the country, the flavour of the month. He had graduated to Test cricket relatively late, after a sequence of 'A' tours, but now it seemed the game was at his mercy. How things can change.

His game, indeed his life, had tumbled downhill horribly fast since then and by the end of the 1996 season in England we were aware that his marriage was in trouble. Sad, and cause for sympathy but no reason to feel he was unique. We picked him for the winter tour and, at first, he seemed committed to it, attending the fitness week in Portugal and giving no hint of any doubts when, along with the other players, he was interviewed by John Barclay and myself on his hopes and aspirations for the winter ahead. Soon after we returned home, I received a phone call to say that Cork had asked for compassionate leave from the early weeks of the tour. In the circumstances, there was no argument but the difficulties were only just beginning.

The extent of this leave was to remain open-ended, no matter how hard and often we tried to set dates. Our firm preference was that Cork should join us in Zimbabwe, so that we could monitor his fitness and he was properly prepared for the second half of the tour. He refused this option and, instead, dictated that he would join us when we arrived in New Zealand. The effect was that he had Christmas and New Year at home, which naturally rankled with many of the other players – though, again, none of them would say so to his face. In hindsight, we were very slack and soft with him on this issue. In trying to do the right thing by his personal life, which was admittedly in turmoil, we were compromising our plans and inviting discord in the camp. I felt strongly enough on this point to propose that for everyone's sake he should not come at all. His presence, I feared, was likely to be counterproductive, but, rightly or wrongly, I was swayed by Atherton, who was adamant that he wanted Cork's bowling in New Zealand.

What made the situation worse, and very much more irritating from a management viewpoint, was that Cork was then unprofessional enough to miss the fitness sessions we had arranged for him before he left England. He had his excuses – bad weather, mostly – but he simply did not show, which upset Wayne Morton no end and meant that we had no idea what kind of state, physical or mental, he might be in when he joined us in New Plymouth.

If there was a certain frostiness in the air, it soon passed and the lads accepted him back into the fold. I understood keenly enough what he might be going through on the personal front and told him he could knock on my door any time he wanted to chat. But he never did. After an initial burst of enthusiasm, he regressed into a brooding, unhealthy mood and often seemed to be deliberately drawing attention to himself and his problems. He was on the phone all the time and he carried his misery with him onto the field, where it undoubtedly had an adverse effect on his cricket and his outlook.

This, though, is the man. If it is not one thing with Cork, it is another. I sometimes feel that his problem is simply cricket itself, and a basic inability to handle it. He always gives the impression that he wants to change the world, and a taste of the high life in 1995 doubtless convinced him he could, but his attitudes both on and off the field are sometimes infuriatingly misguided.

In the dressing-room, his humour can be cutting and I have known him prey unpleasantly on the more timid or sensitive members of the side. At other times, he can be lovably impish – put him in civvies, take him out for the evening and you will probably think he is jolly good company, mischievously funny and willing to own up apologetically to all the flaws in his cricket. Dress him in whites, though, and all too often he becomes the type of character who can be as unpopular with his own team-mates as he is with the opposition.

It was not so much his form that attracted concern in New Zealand but his boorish behaviour on the field, frequently involving himself unnecessarily in baiting matches with the Kiwis – Adam Parore usually to the fore. It became unseemly and Ian MacLaurin, making his second visit to the tour in Wellington, spotted it straight away. After watching a few days of the Test match in that windy city, he came to me and said he thought we should send Cork home because his conduct on the field did not fit his image of what an England cricketer should be.

I agreed with the sentiment but not the cure, and I do not think I was just taking the soft option. If we had sent him home then, the tour would have been finished. The press would have focused on that to the exclusion of all else and whatever the merit of the statement we were making, it would have been obscured by sensationalism. My view was that we should deal with the situation when we returned to England and Ian eventually agreed. Cork received some pointed remarks from coach and physiotherapist in his tour report and he was visited by the chairman of the Board back in Derby, where Ian – caring man that he is – tried to unravel the mysteries of a misfit.

It was Cork and his attitude, as much as anything else, that prompted me to put in writing, after that tour, my view that we needed to get away from players managing the managers. I had various other instances and episodes in mind, a number of players who had known no different and just thought it acceptable in a team situation to say: 'I don't do that.' My answer, unfailingly, was: 'You do now.' For any team to be united and successful, there are a lot of routines and instructions that cannot be negotiable but too many England players had grown up taking liberties, and Cork took it to the limit. Now that he is settled, England need the Dominic Cork of old. He can be world class; it is not too late.

He was not the only problem player. A clique developed on that tour and it had some unfortunate side-effects, felt most keenly by Craig White, who was summoned on standby when it became clear that Ronnie Irani was physically incapable of doing the job he had been picked for. We had seen Irani as a bowling all-rounder but the tour was in its infancy when Nasser, his friend and team-mate at Essex and now our touring vice-captain, told us that he could not be expected to bowl long spells because he had a back condition which had necessitated him modifying his action and taking things more easily. This came as a surprise, not least because Graham Gooch, with all his Essex associations, had helped select Ronnie and had not thought to tell us. This, though, was a communication problem I was to encounter regularly, with a variety of clubs, as I continued in the job.

There was no simple solution but what we did do was call upon Ian Botham, who had an informal agreement to be on hand whenever we needed his expertise. Ronnie idolised Ian and responded to the technical help he was given but we then received an irate fax from the Essex physiotherapist, James Davies, demanding to know what right we had to interfere with his action. Well, in my view, we had every right – Ronnie was an England player, earning good money to represent his country, and we had discovered something that was preventing him doing it to the best advantage. Botham hit the roof when he heard that a physio was questioning his technical input on bowling.

While Irani had some treatment and technical attention, it was quickly agreed that we needed an extra player. Craig was the natural deputy but I felt he was shunned, by some of the lads, for a time after he joined us, especially when he started well enough to pose an obvious threat to Irani's place. Ronnie was one of the clique; he moved in fashionable circles and his pals closed ranks around him, to the exclusion of the quiet and reserved character that is Craig. Later, on what was a pretty disappointing first tour for him, I thought Ronnie lost his focus, became both distracted and distracting, and was keener to listen to the advice of his mates than anything the management had to offer. He probably felt we gave him too few opportunities but he had an unfortunate way of trying to prove us wrong.

The clique numbered five at most – Graham Thorpe and Philip Tufnell joining Cork and Irani as regular members, with Nasser seldom quite sure whether he belonged with them or, now that he had a position of responsibility, elsewhere. We tried to draw him away from it, and to some extent he responded, but there was an engrained loyalty to those he considered his soulmates. The rest of the lads tried to bring it out in the open in a humorous way, snapping their fingers – the 'click' – as the cool cats climbed on the team bus, but the faction was never really broken down and there is a limit, in such circumstances, to how much a coach or manager can intervene.

To me, though, this group came across as slovenly and uncaring, precisely the image we were anxious to avoid. Ronnie, when challenged as to why he was not wearing team uniform one day, even said he had given some of it away, as if replacements could be instantly dispatched from Lord's to the other end of the world. I can well see why Ian MacLaurin showed such concern at this time and why he believed the players, as a group, needed to be knocked into shape.

Tufnell's natural habitat was the company of the clique but, perhaps unexpectedly, I found him much better to deal with than some of the others. He had come with a murky reputation, of course, and there were plenty willing to state that he should never be taken on tour again after some of the things he had got up to previously. I paid no heed to that, determined to judge as

I found, and I grew to enjoy Tufnell's company and to know, I think, how best to jolly him along in the fitness and discipline routines that, with the best will in the world, are alien to his character.

In the past, I imagine, he had simply been told what to do and a stand-off had occurred when he was half-hearted or openly rebellious. He does not respond well to having his hand forced. 'I'm not big on nets,' he said to me, pretty early on. 'Okay, will you just have a session?' I would reply. 'Well, yeah, I could do a session . . . maybe two if you want.' And so we would kid along. Gradually, I discovered that there is some enthusiasm for the game behind the front of studied moping, but that it has to be brought out in a gently cajoling way. He never threw a ball down or had a strop at any practice session in my time and he wrote in his own book that I was the first coach around the England set-up to respect him and leave him alone to get on with things. The problem with this, of course, is that it can be seen by other players as pandering to a maverick, even as giving him preferential treatment. Tufnell was habitually morose in the mornings and my tactics with him did not sit well with some of his team-mates. Their view was that I spent too long with my arm around him, to the neglect of others. My response was that he was doing more than he had ever done before and the extra attention was worthwhile, but it did not convince everyone.

I instituted various team routines on that tour. One was to stick a flag in the ground whenever we arrived at a base, a statement that we were in town and meant business. Another was that at every new venue, I wanted a committed, full-on practice session to impress everyone with our unity. It was at these moments that Philip would be backing off, making his excuses. His mindset was that he was there to bowl left-arm spin, that he was good at it and had no need to be an athlete with it. I won a few battles but, with Tufnell, you are never quite sure you have won the war.

Left: Seething silently. John Emburey and I inspect the conditions during the abandoned final day of the second Test in Harare in 1996.

Right: My bosses. Lord MacLaurin, chairman of the England and Wales Cricket Board, alongside the chief executive, Tim Lamb.

Left: Cork and Crawley take the glory but this was Atherton's match – Christchurch 1997 and the victory over New Zealand that secured the series 2-0.

Left: Big, bold signs on the dressing-room wall were just one motivational aid – I'd do anything to help the team ethic.

Right: Passions run high among Sri Lankan supporters, unwilling to accept that their hero, Murali, might have a suspect action.

Left: Maturity and responsibility were alien to him at first but Nasser Hussain, encouraged through my time as coach, is now a revelation as England captain.

Right: Often misjudged and maligned, Michael Atherton was revered within the confines of the dressing-room.

A video camera at net practice was one of the first innovations of my time as England coach.

At his best, he is absolute box-office. Graham Thorpe on the attack during a warm-up game for the 1999 World Cup.

Dominic Cork at practice, soon after his belated arrival in New Zealand in 1997. I would not have brought him out; Ian MacLaurin soon wanted him sent home.

Above: Just for a while, I thought we'd cracked it with Chris Lewis, but Raymond was never quite so confident.

Left: 'Golf this afternoon, Bumble?' 'What, in this weather, Beefy?' 'Oh, all right, what about a drink, then?'

Right: Talking to the media is a part of the coach's job. Structured press conferences, like this one with David Graveney in 1997, are a regular feature of a touring week.

Above: Atherton and I have shares in a racehorse trained in deepest Herefordshire by Venetia Williams.

Left: Escapism comes no better than this, especially if people believe you caught it yourself.

My three boys – Steven, Ben and Graham.

Left: A disaster waiting to happen... the pitch at Sabina Park, where the 1998 Test match was abandoned on the first morning.

Above: Headley and Butcher set off for the winning single at Port of Spain in 1998, levelling the series 1-1.

Above: Faces of defeat... Fraser, Stewart and Headley after defeat at Antigua in 1998. · Minutes later, they would hear that Atherton had resigned as captain.

Right: Wayne Morton and I rush to join in the team celebrations after clinching the series against South Africa at Headingley in 1998.

Left: Days like this made even the bad times bearable...celebrating with Alec Stewart, the captain, after victory over Australia in the Melbourne·Test, Christmas 1998.

Right: West Indies 1998 and the usual paraphernalia of a touring dressing-room.

Below: Colin Miller's stumps have just been scattered and Darren Gough has done the hat-trick at Sydney in January of 1999.

Right: Glenn McGrath's repetitive action is a model for all aspiring fast bowlers and Brian Lara, here dismissed in the World Cup, has found him a formidable opponent.

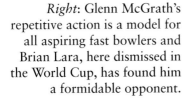

Left: Modern cricket epitomised – the coloured gear, the helmets and armguards, the sponsored stumps and the sunglasses at slip. England v India, during the 1999 World Cup.

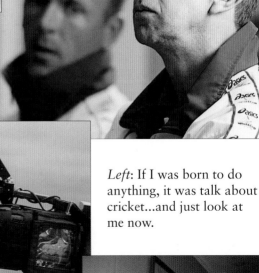

Right: So this is it, the end of the road. We're out of the World Cup and I have spent my last day as England coach. Not the best day of my life.

Left: If I was born to do anything, it was talk about cricket...and just look at me now.

Right: Singing for my supper. People still won't believe how nervous I get before speaking. It's as bad as facing Thommo at Perth.

In team meetings, by contrast, he was excellent – far more forthright than either I, or those who had toured with him before, had expected. He had some sound views on tactics and when he contributed, he wanted it heard. In one meeting, he came out with a statement about something and another player laughed. Tufnell turned on him and snapped: 'I'm f***ing serious, right.' There was not another murmur.

The public warms to Tufnell, because instinctively they enjoy maverick figures. In some ways, he is no different to Shane Warne, another cricketer who can be prone to excesses and transgressions, but the difference is that Warne gets away with it because he is so special, and Australia so patently need him. Tufnell has never quite risen to such heights, partly because he is full of insecurities, defensive both as a man and a bowler and inclined to be suspicious of most of mankind – even of me, when I was no longer his England coach. At Edgbaston, during the first Test against New Zealand in 1999, I spotted him in the hospitality area at the end of a day's play and went across, genuinely pleased to see him and looking forward to a spot of banter. I was left feeling like a stranger when he turned his shoulder and blanked me.

On that first tour, though, we rubbed along okay and I think he genuinely enjoyed the rapport. A Tufnell tour cannot pass without a whiff of scandal, I suppose, and it was in Christchurch that a local newspaper printed a story alleging he had taken drugs in a bar. We were on a free day when this happened and I had risen late and avoided the papers. I was alone and oblivious, strolling through the pedestrian areas of this very pleasant city, when I spotted Tuffers with two or three others, having lunch in one of the open-air cafés. He called me across, looking furtive and anxious, and proceeded to interrogate me about what I might or might not have heard. I didn't have a clue what he was talking about, so I sat down at the table, accepted a glass of wine and listened to his account of it all. I came away more inclined to believe his version than the one being peddled publicly, which had the strong hint of a set-up to give a certain restaurant some publicity. Tufnell is no angel but I could not see him behaving quite as stupidly as they alleged. John Barclay agreed and the story was swiftly and undramatically dismissed.

By this stage, the Test series had been won, giving the tour merit and vindication. We deserved it, too, and probably should have taken all three Tests, though it could equally be said that on the last day of the third Test we were faced with the strong possibility of coming out with only a 1-1 draw. This tense finale would have been avoided if we had wrapped up the first Test in Auckland by completing what is theoretically among the most straightforward of tasks and taken Danny Morrison's wicket cheaply.

We had a habit, at that time, of starting games poorly and then getting into our stride and we certainly did so on this occasion. The Auckland ground is primarily set up for rugby and the cricket square is on a diagonal to achieve equitable boundaries on all sides. It is a disorientating arrangement and on the first morning of the game our bowlers were so giddy they could barely hit the strip. After putting New Zealand into bat, we failed to take a single wicket in the opening session, nor even to threaten one. It was a disgraceful effort but, rather than rant at the bowlers in the dressing-room, I tried the reverse psychology of saying nothing at all. In fact, I made my point by sitting outside the dressing-room by myself through the interval.

Their bowlers fared no better when their turn came and we piled up 521 for a useful lead. At lunchtime on the last day, New Zealand were eight down and still behind. There was a 'pack your bags' feeling in the dressing-room that no warnings about complacency could entirely dispel and when the ninth wicket fell half-an-hour into the afternoon, it seemed we would only have to knock off 20-odd at most. It was then that Morrison, holder of a world record 24 Test 'ducks', made monkeys of us all by holding the fort with Nathan Astle for almost three hours as the last-wicket pair added 106 runs. It was an astonishing turnaround and I was tearing my hair out as I sat watching it helplessly.

Darren Gough, who had helped put us in such a commanding position, told me honestly that he simply 'ran out of puff', which I found revealing. The players, I concluded, were not physically fit enough, nor as mentally strong as other teams more accustomed to winning. It felt terrible, almost worse than a defeat, but we had to move on and it was my job now to lift the players for the second Test ten days hence.

At times like this, a touring team wants to get straight on to the next significant match, to purge itself. Instead, we had to play a four-day game against a New Zealand 'A' team in Wanganui and we lost it by 90 runs. The opposition, full of prospective Test players, were keen and eager; we had our minds on Wellington the following week. Their bowlers took advantage of a sporty pitch; ours did not. And all the while, I was patrolling this lovely park ground, anxious only that the next big game should be our focus. I said to the press that the match in Wanganui would have no bearing on the next Test and that was borne out by events. But my approach to the occasion still ruffled feathers and one broadsheet writer gratuitously and offensively suggested I needed a straitjacket. That was not remotely funny.

When that game ended, I strode into the press tent for the after-match conference. John Etheridge, of the *Sun*, asked what I thought of Wanganui and I knew he was hoping for some resentful response. With Tim Lamb's exhortation to 'be more gracious' in my head, I said: 'It's been really nice. The views are stunning, the ocean's only just over the boundary, the groundsman has laid on some good practice pitches and the lunches have been terrific.' I thought this might draw the sting but the headline in the *Sun* next day read: 'ENGLAND BEATEN – COACH ENJOYS HIS LUNCH'. Sometimes, you just can't win.

Jack Russell, who got a rare game in Wanganui and battled hard to try and save it on the last day, felt that the atmosphere in the team was poor. This gave me some cause for concern, because if I had given him that impression I must have done something wrong. My priority in it all was to put the team on the field at Wellington in the right frame of mind, and I think I achieved that. Victory by an innings and 68 runs was proof enough.

Robert Croft took wickets in the second innings of that game and then played a big part in Christchurch. So too, did Gough, and the two of them had struck up such a close and endearing relationship that we called them 'Pinky and Perky'. They were also so noisy and full of themselves that I labelled them 'the children', but I was delighted for them both. Robert had made a big impression and, at the time, we had justifiable hopes that he would be the wicket-taking off-spin bowler we had lacked for some years. Sadly, the great asset of drift away from the right-handers – so marked that Hussain, at first slip, felt he was in the game all the time – was to desert him the following summer. As his form suffered, so did his bubbly personality. I think his bowling might have been damaged when his batting against the short ball was so clinically exposed by the Australians but he became insecure, looking for excuses. Sometimes, he would let his disappointments out too obviously and on other days his natural exuberance was just overplayed. He thought it was good for team spirit but I told him it was being talked about in less flattering terms and suggested he calmed down. I hope he comes good again, because he is a nice lad at heart and a bowler whose best qualities would benefit any team.

The key to the Christchurch win, however, was another monumental innings by the captain. Athers had toiled all through Zimbabwe, hardly making a run but never letting his worries permeate the team. Early on the New Zealand leg, at Palmerston North, I remember him saying he wanted a net at the end of the game. The press were watching, most of the spectators were still hanging around and Atherton was absolutely dreadful. He did not let it deter him, though, and next stop, in Hamilton, he took himself away from the public gaze and practiced indoors, hour after hour, against a bowling machine. His tour was transformed in that room and the second of his two Test centuries carried us close to the winning target in Christchurch. When he was out, I sensed New Zealand still felt they would win, so highly did they rate him, but Cork and John Crawley saw us safely home. That night, the irritations and controversies of Zimbabwe seemed half a lifetime away. As Atherton often said: nothing else matters if you win.

CHAPTER FOURTEEN

A False Dawn to the Ashes

The summer of 1997 began and ended with scenes of patriotic joy and fervour. It was only the bit in between that spoiled the party. We started out giving every indication that Australia could be beaten in Ashes cricket for the first time in a decade and the country got behind us in such a big way that the enormity of the prize was clear to all. But we fell away badly in mid-series, paying an unacceptably heavy price for the demands of county cricket on key players. I began to wonder if we would ever learn, if our administrators would ever accept that the county game was no longer good preparation for Test cricket. It sometimes seemed that everybody, in our camp and even among successive oppositions, readily identified where we were going wrong but that nothing would be done to correct and reform the system so long as the counties continued to hold sway.

It is frequently said that a coach is only as good as the players at his disposal, and there is some truth in that. The real truth, however, is that he is only as good as the *state* of the players at his disposal, which is subtly different. I know now how so many England football managers have felt as they waited powerlessly before big internationals, dreading the inevitable cast-list of the wounded and washed-out when the players reported in from club commitments. At least, in football, the players are now spared any club games on the weekend prior to an international.

English cricket has blundered along for years in the fanciful belief that players can come straight off a week of hectic county cricket to give of their best in a Test match, then drive through the night to play in a knockout cup game the following day. Enlightenment, in the form of contracts which give the England management authority over the workload of the leading players, has come too late to ease my passage as coach but I am delighted, nonetheless, that something has come of one of my most persistent campaigns.

In my report to the Board at the end of the 1997 season, I laid great stress on this aspect of our game, because I genuinely felt it had cost us dearly against an Australian side so well-tuned to modern international cricket that they laughed at the muddle of our system. I told the Board that in order to prepare adequately for Test cricket, our players needed rest and quality practice time with the best available coaches, on the best possible surfaces. I added that I was so convinced this represented the way ahead that it seemed obvious to me we must have players contracted to the Board, so that we could manage them on a daily basis.

The difficulty of achieving such aims, and the apparent inaction of counties still content to live in the past, was a frustration I came to accept as part of the job. Sure, it could sometimes feel I was banging my head against a brick wall but I knew I had allies in high places, from Ian MacLaurin down, and I always believed we would get around to what was right sooner or later. I now had another eloquent spokesman alongside me in David Graveney, who had finally inherited Raymond's job as chairman of selectors, while Bob Bennett had become the first chairman of a new and rather nebulous body called the England Management Advisory Committee, or EMAC. I could work happily with Bob, who had translated his business skills to cricket and would quietly occupy his seat upstairs while knowing everything that went on at shop-floor level. We went back a long way together and our relationship had always been good but I was later to feel that the introduction of this committee was the prompt for ever more bureaucracy around an England unit that had operated pretty smoothly with Medha Laud pulling the strings at Lord's while the coaching staff got on with working the team. Too many chiefs created too much paperwork, too much justification of positions that really did not add up to much, and this became an ongoing irritant to me, rather, I imagine, as a schoolteacher must feel when the time spent with the children is outweighed by the demands of form-filling.

'Grav' had to prove to some people that he could combine his new role with his duties as chief executive of the Professional Cricketers' Association but he had to prove nothing to me. It was clear that he would become chairman from the time in late 1996 when I came out of my 'probationary' six months and took on the job full-time, and I looked forward to working with him. We had played against each other at county level and been on social tours together, and I felt confident in him as a straight, sincere and conscientious man. We lived through some difficult and demanding times together in the next two years but I never altered that view.

The new chairman enjoyed his own honeymoon period as we whitewashed the Australians in the Texaco Trophy and then emphatically won the first Test but a great deal of talking and planning had taken place before any of that. I have mentioned the Statsmaster video system and the portable digital cameras as examples of how I was trying to take the England team – or Team England as we would henceforth be known at Lord's – into the areas we needed to conquer if we were to compete with the progress of Australia and South Africa, in particular. The next step was a three-day team building camp, to be held before the domestic season began at the NatWest training centre at Heythrop, near Oxford.

We were not the first or last to use such techniques – it happens all the time in business, for one thing – but the conservatism and scepticism of English cricket is such that it was bound to produce a reaction. Interestingly, when the British Lions employed a motivational company called Impact for such a course before they toured South Africa, it was widely hailed as innovative and professional. We used a very similar company, called Insights, and received the scornful response from some areas of the media – and, through them, the public – that we were indulging in 'a love-in', or a 'bonding session'. The aim of the course was actually to help create the right environment for the team to express itself, to create a culture of awareness and togetherness. Such get-togethers will not make the difference between winning and losing but, used properly, they can be another brick in the bridge. There will always be someone who rebels against the time and trouble involved, however, and in our case it was Graham Thorpe. Back with his family after a tour he had undertaken with obvious reluctance, Graham believed his time was his own until cricket resumed. He told us he wanted a rest and would not be attending, but he had to rethink when an early-morning phone call from Tim Lamb instructed him to get there immediately. When he arrived, Ian MacLaurin took him aside and spoke to him on the subject I had been preaching – the need for the management to manage the players, rather than vice-versa. To his credit, Thorpe buckled down and gave it everything.

Two of the principal presentations made to the players, first at Heythrop and later that year in Harrogate, were by Sebastian Coe and Frank Dick and they could hardly have formed a sharper contrast in content or reaction. Coe was so poor that the players, who tend to be cynical about such things, were keen to know how much he had been paid for it.

He started badly by producing a sheet of paper with some notes he announced he had knocked out on the train, and he did little more than give his audience a resumé of his own athletics career. Dick came from a similar athletics background but he made his name as a coach and motivator, and it showed. He talked of sportsmen being either mountains or valleys – the mountains representing the doers, changers and achievers, those who wanted to knock down barriers, while the valleys were shallow, complacent, the do-it-tomorrow types. He said that at the highest level all players were coaches, too, because they should be willing and able to help each other out, and he added that the ethic of any team is trust and the word that identifies great teams is attitude. To a man, the lads were impressed. Indeed, I think Frank Dick left them all feeling ten feet tall and when they left Heythrop at the end of the three days, even the most dubious among them would have struggled to say the venture had failed.

The mistake we made was trying to repeat it in mid-season. Possibly, it was an anti-climax after the success of the initial project but I would also cite inappropriate activities, poorly handled. One part of it even involved playing with guns and we were spoken down to as if we should automatically know the mechanics of the weapon, when most of us had never held one before in our lives. The discovery of a press photographer in the bushes killed another activity stone dead and I think the players left for home resenting a costly, meaningless exercise that had deprived them of three days off. We changed companies after that and employed Impact but as the players' enthusiasm for such sessions waned, so Simon Pack, recently appointed as International Teams Director, seemed intent on organising more and more. Eventually, a good idea just got out of hand and far too much time and attention was squandered on motivational courses that nobody wanted. Wayne Morton, never one to shy away from a spiky comment, asked Simon if he had shares in the motivational company, which did not go down particularly well.

I did attend the first Impact course with real interest, however. It was staged at their centre in the Lake District and laid on specifically for ECB management and coaching staff. The top brass all took part and, especially after the events of Zimbabwe,

I thought it was a commendable show of togetherness. The various activities involved us splitting into teams, listening to expert instructions and then, one by one, performing a discipline that involved depending on the rest of your team for safety. One involved climbing up a telegraph pole, as an engineer would do, reaching the top in a stiff breeze, then jumping onto a trapeze and swinging back to solid ground. Everyone was to wear a harness with ropes stretching down to team-mates, who needed to react by pulling the ropes tightly in the event of a slip.

This was a daunting exercise for some of us and there was a good deal of shifting in seats as it was explained to us. I told my team I would go first but warned them that I wanted no nonsense because I was so frightened of heights that when I took my kids up Blackpool Tower I shrank straight to the back of the viewing area and had to go back down immediately. I strapped myself into the harness and set off up the pole, which was hard work with my old knee and ankle problems. At the top, heart pumping unpleasantly fast, I jumped for the trapeze and missed. My colleagues tightened the ropes and lowered me without alarms. End of story? Well, not quite, because I was to reflect a little sourly on that episode a year later, when the treatment I received from the Board over my comments about the legitimacy of Muttiah Muralitharan's action made me wonder what on earth happened to this avowed intention to 'support each other at all times'. The management course in the Lake District cost the Board a cool £35,000 and if I had known then what I know now, nothing would have persuaded me to set foot on that telegraph pole.

Motivational aids have their place within any progressive team and, during my time, I introduced short videos of individual England players doing well, set to music the player enjoyed, and others of prominent opponents messing up, to prove that even the best do it. It added up to no more than 0.5 per cent of our cricket preparation but it made the players feel good and was working well enough that many of them would seek out their latest tapes unbidden and play them in the team room. The videos needed professional preparation, however, and the cost to the Board was something between £8,000 and £10,000 per series. Eventually, Simon Pack, possibly at the behest of the counties, decreed that it was too high a price.

Back in 1997, I felt we prepared well for the visit of Australia and, eternal optimist that I am, I shared the belief that seemed to be sweeping the country following our striking performances in the one-day internationals. We were busy, mobile and dynamic in those games, our fielding right back to its highest standards of a year earlier. We were all over them and it was magnificent to watch.

Prior to the Texaco series, I had spoken at length to Bob Woolmer, whose South Africa team had just concluded a home series against the Australians. Bob was extremely helpful and revealing. He told me that Australia were mentally stronger than his side, which had surprised him, that they were better in the field and fitter. He went thoroughly into the strengths and weaknesses of their bowlers, whose fitness and flexibility was honed by regular swimming and warm-down sessions at the end of a day's play, when the average cricketer is thinking more about a bath and a beer. He told me that they did not waste their time in the dressing-room when batting, but worked repetitively with small weights. Having given a resumé of what was obviously a highly impressive unit, he then said that he was convinced they could be beaten, and the way we started the summer endorsed his thoughts.

The first morning of the Test series was dream-like. Edgbaston offered its usual, tricky conditions first thing and we bowled in the right areas, with purpose and pace. Before lunch, Australia were 54 for eight. Gough and Caddick had taken wickets and so had Devon Malcolm, who was playing his first Test in 18 months. Mark Butcher was making his debut and we made a show of presenting him with his cap, the sort of public ceremony that does a player good and sends out the right signals. All in all, it was a morning I could not have improved upon if I had sat up through the previous night writing the script.

The Australians made a better fist of their second innings, as they could hardly fail to do, but we won the game inside four days – a wonderful partnership of almost 300 between Hussain and Thorpe the abiding highlight but a charge to the target of 118 on the fourth evening a clarion call to the public. And did they ever respond? They poured onto the ground at the end as if the Ashes were already won and some of the newspaper headlines the following morning gave the same impression. The public chat from me was that the Australians would come back hard and that we must be ready for them.

Their two key bowlers, McGrath and Warne, were both poor at Edgbaston and while the leggie still had something to prove, I felt sure that McGrath would improve quickly because his action is so simple and repetitive. During my years as coach, England's batsmen were more wary and respectful of McGrath than any other bowler. He is so accurate, so durable, never seeming to break sweat, much less break down. He also fulfils a common trait of Australian cricketers by being a lovely chap off the field but thoroughly nasty when he has the ball in his hands. He boils over regularly, becomes abusive, loses the plot. Plainly, this cannot always be condoned but I have noted with interest that he consistently gets full backing from his own authorities when he is disciplined by a match referee, their view being that there is a mechanism in place now to deal with conduct violations and that once action has been taken it should be forgotten. Rightly or wrongly, our players have come to feel that any disciplinary action, or even interest, they attract from a match referee will bring further retribution from the ECB. In other words, they feel they should be better supported.

It is history now that Australia did indeed hit us hard. They might have won at Lord's but for the weather, yet they made up for it with emphatic winning margins at Old Trafford, Headingley and Trent Bridge, consecutive wins that were sufficient to guarantee they retained the Ashes. The disappointment in our camp was all the more intense for the deflated optimism and I am not sure I can recall the mood of a summer being turned on its head quite so swiftly. It was the second defeat, at Leeds, that really crushed us and as we were beaten by an innings it is implausible to suggest things might have turned out differently. The fact remains, however, that Australia were 50 for four in reply to our inadequate 172 when the debutant, Mike Smith, had Matthew Elliott dropped at slip by the usually safe-handed Thorpe. Elliott had 29 at the time; he went on to make 199.

Smith's selection caused a good deal of debate and there were those who tried to suggest it came down to David Graveney's Gloucestershire bias, which was nonsense. Smith was a heavy wicket-taker in county cricket and had only recently picked up 12 wickets in a game on the same ground, against Yorkshire. All reports told us that he swung the ball late throughout that game and I happily went along with the notion that he would give us a different attacking dimension – the doubter was Athers, who reckoned Smith was too small and that if the ball did not swing for him he became very hittable. We even let him select the ball for us, from the proffered box of 12, and he was utterly convinced it would swing for him, but for some quirky reason it didn't.

Throughout that series, we rarely had much problem knocking over the first three or four Australian wickets but their lower order was far more resilient and productive than ours. It was not that our tail-enders did not practice their batting – I made damn sure they did, day after day – but it seemed to bring no improvement and this was a key difference. In McGrath and Warne, the best leg-spinner I have ever seen, they also had the two outstanding bowlers, and in Steve Waugh they had a competitor I admire more than any in the world game.

Waugh is like Atherton in that he thrives on confrontation to the point where he will pick a fight on the field to aid his adrenalin. Our response in this series was to avoid talking to him at all costs. He sussed it after a while. 'Oh, it's not talk to Steve is it?' he would sneer. 'Well, he'll talk to himself then.' And he did, jabbering away nonstop just to nourish his concentration. Waugh is nasty on the field, ruthless in all senses. When South Africa's Herschelle Gibbs dropped a simple catch at a crucial stage of the World Cup semi-final, Waugh may or may not have said, as cricket legend has it: 'You've just dropped the World Cup mate', but it certainly would be in his character to say so. For all that, however, he is the first to come up to share a beer and a chat afterwards, a metamorphosis that Australians carry off far more comfortably than we English. It counts for a lot.

I admire and applaud their team ethic, bred out of adversity by Allan Border and sustained and improved by Mark Taylor, a confident, tactically sound skipper. They have factions, just like any other group, but when they take the field they are visibly, demonstrably and audibly together. I recall observing Warne, standing at second slip, clapping his hands and going round the team, calling out their surnames and goading them into greater effort. As they closed in on victory to level the series at Old Trafford, he sensed the mood was too subdued, so he shouted so all of Stretford could hear: 'Come on, Australia. This is what it's all about.'

Australia have a win-at-all-costs culture that I have not detected in any England side. Our culture, even at the dawn of the new millennium, remains a little too close to 'play up and play the game'. I am not of that ilk. I want to win, even if it does get a bit messy, and I never go along with that awful hogwash about the game being the winner. I am a terrible loser and proud of it but I will always go into the other dressing-room to say well done. The Australians could see me coming by the time we got to Trent Bridge that year.

There was still one match to come, though, and if we were determined to win it, I am convinced the Australians were equally determined not to lose. Geoff Marsh, their coach, told me that they had got a bad press once or twice before for being unprofessional at the end of a series, stepping off the gas and losing the last game. They wanted no repeat of that and despite the usual denigrating remarks after an England win, I know we beat them on merit and ended the series, at 2-3, with heads high.

By an accident of the county fixtures, we were able to prepare better for The Oval than for any game since the series began, and it made a difference. What a game it was, though, a fortnight of drama packed into three days of cricket. Australia led by 40 on first innings and then bowled us out a second time for 163, at which point there cannot have been many in a packed Saturday crowd who gave us a prayer. But we were well aware they had been proved vulnerable when chasing small targets and our strategy was to press on the psychology of that, hitting them hard and fast. Devon was roared in by the crowd and he took Elliott out with his fourth ball. Instantly, the Aussies were wobbling and we never took our foot off that pedal.

Interestingly, the match-winners were Caddick and Tufnell, two of the supposedly fragile characters. There was nothing soft about them that day. Caddick came in as we know he can and that performance should be his yardstick – he won't always end up with five wickets but, as with McGrath, the standard should be consistent. Tufnell bowled wonderfully well for his four wickets – impishly confident and getting masses of revs on the ball in the way that he does all too seldom. When he knows he is on top, as he did here, Tufnell can be irresistible; too often, when things are not going his way, it is evident in a crab-like action that seems simply to go through the motions.

My enduring memory of the dressing-room, boisterous and

barely believing that we had triumphed by 19 runs, is of Tufnell, this complex character, sitting on a locker alone and remote, his knees drawn up to his chest and a towel completely covering his head. I left him a while, thinking he might just be composing himself after the emotion of the finale, then went over to ask if he was all right. There was no response. An hour later, as we trailed noisily back into our dressing-room after a drink or two with the opposition, he was still there, silent and swathed.

CHAPTER FIFTEEN

Windies and a Shock Resignation

Michael Atherton tried to resign the captaincy twice during the summer of 1997, and twice he was talked out of it – first by Ian MacLaurin and then by me. Stubborn he may be but selfish he is not and the persuasive factor was that the team would suffer for his going. Whatever he was going through himself, he cared about the players and cared deeply for English cricket. He was to lead only one more tour, though, and a deeply disappointing one at that, before the inevitable could be delayed no longer.

Athers made his first move to step down after the Trent Bridge Test against Australia. His reasoning was straightforward – the Ashes were lost again, he had done a full four-year cycle and it was time someone else had a go. He had been facing the music for a long time and the constant criticism of a press craving change for the sake of it would eventually get through to even the strongest of men. But I do not believe the job had lost its appeal for him, much less that the players had lost any of their huge respect for him; he just felt the time was right. He went home after the game, prepared to think about things but still pretty set in his mind that he should go.

I got on the phone to him to put my opinion across. I told him: 'It's pointless just walking away. You'll be letting the team down.' I assured him that we – the management – were around to help him. I was pretty sure I wasn't getting through, though, and Athers proceeded to tell David Graveney he had resigned. Grav rang Ian MacLaurin, doubtless more through protocol than any hope that he might intervene, but this is one determined chairman. Ian contacted Athers at his flat in Didsbury and simply told him that resignation was not acceptable, that he must think again and lead the team out at The Oval. By the time Athers called me back, the deed was done. 'He's a persuasive chap, that Lord MacLaurin,' he said thoughtfully, having encountered a rare being who could break his rigid mind-set.

Naturally, he was glad to be around, at the helm, for the stirring win at The Oval, but at that time I know he regarded it as his last match. He had agreed not to rock the boat before the series ended but that was as far as it went. And so we went through a similar process all over again, only this time it ended up with Atherton and Graveney face to face over a drink at the Hilton Hotel, opposite Lord's, and Grav convincing him that he should at least speak to me on the phone before his resignation was confirmed. Somehow, I managed to put across my passionate belief that he was still so much the best man for the job, allied to my obvious optimism that we could win in the West Indies that winter. He backed down again.

It is true that such indecision is very unlike Atherton but I can only repeat my view that his motivation throughout was to do the right thing by others. I honestly don't think he worried much about all the brickbats hurled his way – sometimes, he seemed to actively encourage them – and I am sure there were others, apart from me, who told him that resignation would come across as a triumph for the section of the press who had been trying for so long to hound him out, in some cases for no better reason than the hope that they might get a more quotable captain. His Dad, Alan, would have counselled him thoroughly, too, and Athers would have listened to a wise man telling him he did not want to be remembered as someone who quit.

From a personal standpoint, I wanted him around because I felt that, together, we had taken the team some way down a long road and it would not be helpful to have him bailing out. Moreover, he was bloody good at the job – better, in fact, than even I had imagined when I first came into the set-up. The players would do anything for him; I knew it would not be in their interests to have a new man in charge at this point. Just as important, I wanted Athers to take the credit if, as I genuinely expected, we managed to win in the Caribbean.

Losing that 1998 series was perhaps my greatest disappointment with England. I felt West Indies were vulnerable and that we were ready to win a big series. I was close to being right on both counts but the record books say we lost 3-1, a harsh judgement on a contest that could have gone either way until we were blown away on a miserable Antiguan afternoon that ended with the captain's third, and this time unequivocal resignation.

Tours of the West Indies do not start until January, which in our case allows more than the usual time for proper rest and preparation. There was some one-day cricket to be played first, in Sharjah, but the idea was that the full tour squad would fly to the West Indies a week earlier than is customary, in order to practice and acclimatise. But the best-laid plans ...

Antigua was our designated practice venue, and theoretically a good one. The West Indies Board had set up a new cricket centre there and when I went out on reconnaissance, during the autumn, I was impressed. Facilities were good – the downside was that the centre was based on a holiday complex complete with the statutory beer bellies, football shirts, gelled-up hair and earrings. I was assured that we would be billetted separately, in nice lakeside villas, and that we would have a fleet of golf buggies at our disposal for getting around the expansive site. At the time, viewing the facilities under a warm sun and deep blue sky, it didn't occur to me that it might rain all week.

I went home satisfied, though not before a trip to the West

Indies Board offices, in the Antiguan capital of St John's, where I asked them what brand of balls they planned to use in the series. To my surprise, though no particular alarm, they brought out a job lot of the balls used in England six or seven years earlier, the seams as big as washing-lines. Without guaranteeing that these would be the balls used, they seemed to have no alternatives to offer, which gave me plenty to think about. Hit the seam with that type of ball and it might do anything. Curtly Ambrose immediately became a big player – but then so did Angus Fraser.

We had selected Angus in the tour party for two reasons. With a pace attack of Caddick, Dean Headley, Ashley Cowan and Chris Silverwood that contained more imponderables than experience, we needed a dependable safeguard. I also felt that Angus had the qualities needed to coach his skills – I had already put his name forward to the Board – and would be invaluable as a leader of the fast bowling pack. Typically, Fraser, while delighted to be given such a chance, saw the winter differently and came straight out and said he was going to get in the side. After looking at those balls, I wholeheartedly agreed.

Fraser is England through and through. The best compliment that has been put his way is the comparison with Alec Bedser and I think it is valid. His bowling will never let you down and is designed to exploit any inconsistency of conditions, while his attitude is a wonderful example to all. He told the other quick bowlers at the start of the tour that they would need to work harder than usual on their fitness to cope with the extreme heat. 'I'm not bowling your overs at five o'clock,' he would say. Strength and stamina was what was required and Fraser led the way, more professional and enthusiastic than some in the team almost ten years his junior.

It always rankled with me when I heard people say, or write, that the modern England team spent too much time working on fitness, because I have never yet seen a sportsman who has not improved himself for being fitter. The criticism also implies that it is one thing or the other, that getting fitter necessarily means spending less time on cricket skills. This is just nonsense. In my time, the players were never sent on mindless runs at the expense of nets and for all the uninformed talk of a press-ups regime, I can confidently say that we did not once have them doing such an exercise. Our physical routines, devised by Wayne and the fitness expert Dean Riddle, were slick and quick, stretching the muscles and honing the mobility. Then, it would be nets for two hours or more. Even there, Fraser was intensely competitive and his jousts with Atherton in a net, two great mates winding each other up in such a way you would think they were sworn enemies, were worth paying admission money to see.

So although Fraser, at 32, was far from being an unknown quantity, I felt smugly confident that he could be our secret weapon. Indeed, as we flew out of London on the first Saturday in January, I felt confident about everything. I fully expected us to win the series and I spent the journey contemplating a week of solid practice. The first inkling that all might not proceed to plan came from landing through thick clouds. Antigua was dotted with deep puddles and it needed only the first cursory inspection of our putative net facilities to realise that the sun needed to shine pretty solidly if we were to get out and practice the following day.

Well, it didn't. We hardly saw the sun, in fact, as my diary of the trip reminds me. This is no ordinary diary but the loose-leaf type we had devised especially for the players and management to fill in with their daily goals, gripes and observations. My gripe for the first three days was one word – rain – and by the time we reached Wednesday with no sign of any settled weather, a decision was taken to ship out early.

The speed and smoothness with which this change of plans was executed was due in no small way to Bob Bennett, the tour manager. Already, though, the difference between Bob and John Barclay, banished by the spectre of Zimbabwe, was being noticed. A Lancashire man, chairman to both Athers and my-self over many years, we thought we knew him backwards but on this tour he became fussy over matters that I considered irrelevant.

Dressing smartly was his big thing. Nothing wrong with that in a team environment, as I have commented on earlier, but such matters should be dealt with in a matter of seconds. Instead, Bob appointed a dress code committee, which contained the always immaculate Stewart and two of the potential rebels in Thorpe and Hussain. I know he was trying to bring them into line but it didn't work and the subject became a running sore between the manager and me. I found it seriously annoying that a team meeting dedicated to preparing a team to beat the West Indies could waste 45 minutes deciding what we were going to wear.

Bob had managed tours before and by all accounts done extremely well but to my mind the problem on this trip was that he was confusing his roles. As chairman of EMAC, it became apparent to me that he felt he was representing the ECB more than managing the players. During the international games, tickets became an issue, because Bob was busying himself ensuring that Board members – county chairmen or employees who were simply out there having a good holiday – were supplied with complimentaries. I felt this distracted him from the more serious business of the tour.

There are few nicer men in the game than Bob Bennett, a family man who just wants everyone to be happy. But when things go wrong, I found he has a tendency to act the mother hen and his insistence on issuing statements after a minor controversy achieved no more than to write the journalists' stories for them. There was a classic example of this in Barbados, when Atherton was caught by a cameraman apparently flashing a V-sign at Philo Wallace, the West Indian opener. Neither the umpires nor the opposition raised any hint of protest but there is a system in place for dealing with any such incidents and it was duly set in motion

– the match referee, sole arbiter of disciplinary affairs, decided there was no case to answer. That should have been the end of the matter but, instead, Bob and Brian Murgatroyd, our media relations officer, were swayed by the demands of the press and wasted time and effort issuing a statement. This, at a time on the third day of the game when our bowlers were responding brilliantly and putting us in a winning position. It soured the mood of the day for no good reason and suggested, I am afraid, that some of those in authority just did not appreciate what Test cricket is all about.

The press will always want to maximise such incidents. I know some of them come under pressure from their offices in London, especially when photographers mischievously wire pictures that stir up some minor controversy, but it should not have been our job to pander to them. Murgatroyd was a great boon in many ways during our years together; he did get things better organised in terms of media conferences and access to players. In my view, though, there were instances of fussing and faffing around just to satisfy sports editors when we would have been better advised rising above it and saying nothing.

My own relations with the press had their ups and downs during my time as coach. On a social basis, I enjoyed the company of a lot of the guys and would happily spend evenings with them. There were some I would not trust professionally, though, and my opinion of them sank to a depressing low when I accepted an invitation to the end of series media party. It was staged in a beach restaurant in Antigua, immediately after the Barbados Test, and I was horrified when one of the press's jokey awards was given to a photographer for 'getting the picture' of Atherton's gesture. The comment was 'we've got him now' and most of the journalists stood up and applauded. It was an awful evening, the language so deplorable in a public restaurant that I think quite a lot of the journalists themselves were taken aback by it. At one point, I left the table to go to the toilet and on my way back I was hailed by an elderly English couple. The man said: 'Your team is a disgrace'. I had to point out to him that the behaviour he was witnessing was not that of cricketers but journalists.

All of this dismay and disillusionment was to come, yet as we prepared for the first Test of the series at Sabina Park my conviction that we could prove a stronger side than West Indies was being bolstered by the divisions in their own camp. Brian Lara had eventually been appointed captain ahead of Courtney Walsh, which had caused outrage in Jamaica and given Walsh cause to wonder if he still wanted to play. If Walsh pulled out, it was assumed that Ambrose would follow, which would have left them in a mess. The uncertainty was all in our favour, though eventually it was greatly to the credit of Walsh that he not only continued playing but pledged his full support to Lara and illustrated it publicly by putting his arm around the new captain as they took the field at Sabina.

Walsh and Ambrose were to bowl magnificently throughout that series, leaving us all to wonder how different it would have been without them, but what is not generally known is that their actions were questioned – not by us but by the ICC referee for the series, former Australian wicket-keeper Barry Jarman. In his report on the tour, Jarman alleged that Walsh threw a big percentage of deliveries and also cited Ambrose as having a suspect action. Nothing came of his remarks but I was astonished by them. In my view, the idiosyncrasy in Walsh's action is in the wrist rather than the elbow, but it provided a sting in the tail of what had been a pretty busy few months for Mr Jarman. He can hardly have imagined, on his flight from Australia to the Caribbean, that almost the first thing he would be required to do was sanction the abandonment of a Test match inside the first hour.

Sabina Park was a disaster waiting to happen. My diary entry for two days prior to the match relates my view that the 'pitch looks the worst ever'. When it came to aligning the stumps with a string, pulled tight wicket to wicket, the impression of ridges and hollows was given full credence, as the string was on the surface in some places and two inches above it in others. It was disgracefully under-prepared and I think both teams knew that batting on it would be a lottery. Abandonment, however, is not something that you ever contemplate.

We had a further distraction on the morning of the game and in hindsight there was a funny side to it. Jack Russell had been pursuing his usual diet of bananas and beans but had somehow eaten something that upset him. Whether it was a rogue baked bean, as was mischievously concluded, he was ashen when we started our warm-up session and he didn't get any better. Eventually, I went across to where he was slumped on the turf and he just shook his head and told me he could not play. I knew how much this would be hurting him but time was short, sympathy had to wait. My priority was to find Mark Butcher, who had not hitherto played a first-class innings on tour, and tell him he was in the side. Not much more than half-an-hour later he had played his innings and was back amongst us – out first ball to one from Walsh that flew from a length.

Within the course of the 61 balls that were bowled before the fight was stopped, Wayne had to run on six times to treat batsmen for blows to the body. It made for x-certificate viewing and the one consolation was that nobody was seriously hurt. Three wickets went down but batting was such a hazardous business that others could have fallen at any time. Safety was the paramount concern as the umpires began to confer with increasing anxiety but there was also the issue of whether this constituted an authentic cricket match. I was convinced it did not. We sensed something was about to happen as the match referee, Jarman, was unusually positioned in a box immediately next to our viewing area. We could see him speaking to Venkat, the umpire, by radio and hear their anxieties unravelling.

Eventually, I knew it would be stopped and just hoped it would happen to prevent an injury rather than because of one.

I thought the captains handled the situation brilliantly. It helped that Atherton and Lara were good friends from their days as young players but Lara had a tremendous weight on his shoulders in his first game as captain and he conducted himself terrifically well. There had to be some sympathy for the crowd, specifically so for the hundreds of England supporters who had invested their savings and their annual holidays to come and watch the game, but I had no doubt that the decision to abandon was correct and inevitable, as the game would have served no purpose. I assumed this was a unanimous view until I heard Geoffrey Boycott sounding off in typically contrary fashion. He was putting it about that cricket must always continue and, characteristically, turned the subject into some self-glorification by bringing up an epic innings he supposedly played against Derbyshire on a brutal pitch at Abbeydale Park some years previously. He might have got away with the reference but someone in the press box looked the game up. 'Who do you reckon the bowlers were?' came the question. 'Michael Holding,' someone ventured. 'Mike Hendrick,' said another. 'Alan Ward,' added a third. But no. The fearsome bowlers ranged against dear Geoffrey that day were Mortensen, Tunnicliffe, Miller and Moir. Enough said!

The tour itinerary now needed another revision, its second inside a month, and it was sensibly decided that an extra Test match would be scheduled to restore the series to its intended five games. This meant we had to play back-to-back Tests at Port of Spain in Trinidad and I don't think anyone who was present through that fortnight will easily forget them. They were gripping, edge-of-the-seat games. We lost the first when we should have won it but won the second when it seldom looked likely. Most people would conclude this was a fair outcome but from my standpoint it was an opportunity missed. To have gone

2-0 ahead in Trinidad, as I felt we could and should have done, would have tested the mental resilience of the West Indies and put such enormous pressure on Lara, whose captaincy was busy and inventive but not to everybody's taste, that he might even have lost the job.

After we had lost the first of the games, by three wickets, I pondered on it overnight then took the unusual step of openly criticising two of my players. Headley and Caddick had simply not performed and there are some occasions when it is more beneficial to say so than to bottle it up. The press were given my opinions. 'They did themselves no justice,' I said. 'Didn't bowl in the right areas . . . have to do better at this level.' Then I sat back to see how the pair of them would respond. The answer came with greatly improved input as we won the next game from an unpromising position – the irony here being that we were seen to victory by a composed innings from Mark Butcher, who had not even been picked for the game.

Butcher would not have played but for a back injury to Adam Hollioake. Probably, he would still have missed out if Mark Ramprakash had not been struck down by flu – cruel timing for a man whose desperation to play had been expressed, earlier in the tour, in a way that was both immature and intemperate. I have mentioned earlier that I was personally in favour of him playing ahead of Hollioake from the outset but that is not the point. The majority decision was otherwise and Ramps took it badly.

I had told all the players that the role of Riddle was not negotiable, that they were to do whatever he asked of them. Dean was experienced and knowledgeable in his field, much in demand in a variety of sports, and he had a decent relationship with the majority of our players. Ramps, however, refused to follow his instructions on a fitness matter, not once but twice. On the second occasion, I went to see him on an official basis in his hotel room and told him that this was unacceptable. It was plainly a response to being omitted from the Test team but it was not the response I wanted to see. I had known Ramps since he was 15 or 16 and this was far from the first time that he had courted disaster through his volatile temperament. He told me he wanted to discuss his position with someone more senior, by which I took him to mean the chairman of selectors. 'Ask who you like,' I said. 'I doubt whether it will be different.' As I left the room he reacted angrily, bashing the door so hard that it broke the hinge.

Ramprakash has still not entirely conquered the demons in his mind, which may help to explain his absence from the tour party to South Africa last winter, but after this torrid start he did buckle down in the Caribbean and finally received his reward with a place in the third Test at Guyana. He took his chance well, too, batting for a long time in a cause that was as good as lost once West Indies had won a vital toss on a sub-standard pitch. What Ramprakash gave us was a technique that coped admirably with pitches of low bounce, because he, unlike so many modern English players brought up on poor pitches, was prepared to do the difficult thing and play forward. He was just as good, though, on the best pitch of the series in Barbados and his wonderful century, made in a partnership of 205 with Thorpe, helped give us a great chance of squaring the series for the second time. We ran that game from start to finish and it was cruel luck that a deluge of rain, quite freakish for Barbados in March, permitted only 18 overs to be bowled on the last day.

Athers believed that was the best all-round cricket the team ever played under his leadership and I can believe it. To raise themselves for another crack in a final Test starting only three days later was always going to be hard work, though, and it became a virtual impossibility when the game started on a damp pitch and we lost another crucial toss.

I had gone down to the ground in St John's at 3 pm on the eve of the match and been reassured on two fronts. The rebuilding of the place and re-turfing of the playing area was as good as complete, which looked highly improbable on our previous visit, and the pitch looked dry and even. It was after I had returned to the hotel that the groundsman decided to give it a sprinkle, just to juice it up, but he was classically caught out when the morning of the game dawned overcast and showery, with no sunshine to dry it out. It made for an uneven contest on the first day and we were always chasing the game from then on.

Still, it should have been saved and we were close to achieving the draw we deserved through a big stand between Hussain and Thorpe when a nonsensical run-out triggered another of our familiarly spectacular collapses. Seven wickets went down for 26 runs, which would have been staggering if it had not happened so often before. It seemed it did not matter who we picked from number eight downwards – they all batted like number elevens at this level.

That evening was among the worst I was to know. Even I was not fully aware of Atherton's plans. He had been in desperately poor form, his footwork becoming indecisive as his confidence diminished, and this was getting him down badly. I don't think he regretted agreeing to lead the tour but for him, as for me, it was a profound disappointment that it should end like this. He stood down with the dignity everyone would expect from him, making a quiet and simple announcement to the boys and then going to tell the press.

The dressing-room was in a state of shock and devastation now. Defeat was bad enough but the resignation of the captain was something else. Fraser was in tears and others were not far from it, myself included, when Ashley Cowan bounced into the room and started some of the noisy, childish banter we had all heard far too often from him already. Even making allowances for his youth and inexperience, Cowan had not made a good impression on this tour and I told him, quietly but firmly, that this was not the time or place to try and be funny. He even looked surprised. It is this that we are up against, a generation of young players who have simply not been brought up in a culture where winning means everything.

CHAPTER SIXTEEN

Doubts About Murali

I shall always be grateful for the chance to coach England and, while it is for others to judge my degree of success, I enjoyed all the challenges involved in developing the management and preparation of players. We had fallen a long way behind the more progressive of our opponents and I like to think that is no longer the case. What I did not enjoy, indeed what gave me increasing misgivings about the job, was the expanding bureaucracy that seemed to hover over the team like a threatening cloud. Through the summer of 1998 this was to become ever more of an issue in my mind and eventually, after a few weeks in which I tasted both the best and the worst that my job could offer, I was to question seriously if it was worth continuing.

The warning signs were illuminated after the Caribbean tour. I had filed my report in the usual way, highlighting action points and recommendations that I suspected would get no further than a filing cabinet at Lord's, but for some reason I never could fathom, I then had to present myself for a de-briefing with EMAC. With the domestic season already underway, this seemed an inconvenience and a waste of time and planted in my mind the seed of a growing conviction that we now had far too many administrators trying to justify their existence.

I was questioned on the tour at great length, going over all the ground I had covered in my report as if some of those present doubted its veracity. Bob Bennett was in the chair but much of the agitating came from Brian Bolus, amusing company but a highly political man who had designs on Bob's position. Ian MacLaurin was there, too, and it was plain that he and Bolus saw eye to eye on virtually nothing, so the mood of the day was unpleasantly antagonistic. Simon Pack went so far as to confide his view that we must never have another meeting like it.

Simon was well meaning and perfectly amenable but his approach to a job of vague definition was too paper-based and complicated. We were making problems for ourselves by confusing a cricket team with a classroom of delinquent kids. My desk at home was increasingly cluttered with paperwork requiring hours at a time – hours I could more profitably have been spending doing what I was employed to do, which was coach cricketers.

One example of this was the new Player Report Forms. The coach had always been required to report individually on players at the end of a tour but now Simon wanted it done in far greater detail. So I was presented with a pile of forms, five pages to each, in which I had to assess not only the essentials of technical competence and mental resilience but a long list of qualities including manner and bearing, integrity, ambition, humour, co-operation, attitude towards sponsors and social conduct. Simon was a military man and he was applying military thoroughness but, in my view, taking it too far. At the same time, I was sensing a waning of genuine support for me from certain people in authority, which was all contributory to a feeling that the job was getting harder rather than easier.

We had to appoint a new captain for the start of the summer and Alec Stewart was the natural choice, not only through his experience and seniority but because the other plausible candidate, Nasser Hussain, still had a little maturing to do. Graham Gooch loyally supported Nasser for captain but both Grav and I felt it was too soon for him and that he would not command as much respect in the dressing-room as Alec. The appointment was a generous one, covering the time through to the end of the 1999 World Cup, but in Atherton's stead we needed security. As a team, we – and by we I mean the selectors and close coaching staff – felt we were going along in the right way but getting the wrong results. The support structure in terms of fitness, coaching and now psychology through Steve Bull, was getting close to my aims but I am sure I was not alone in sensing a gathering momentum of obstructiveness at administration level.

My priority now was to clarify how I should proceed with the new captain and this presented no difficulties. Alec has always been an exemplary team player and his attitude was exactly as I would have expected from him. When we met, I asked him if he envisaged things changing and he replied that we should carry on as before. I assured him that it was now his show and encouraged him to let me know if he saw things he did not agree with, but from the outset our relationship was good. His style was different to Atherton. He gave a lot more team talks, for one thing, and was never ashamed to state the obvious. He was also far more accessible to the press, at least at first, though he seldom gave much away.

South Africa arrived with a big reputation and beat us comfortably in the first two one-day games, before we produced something close to our best form when it was too late. Our one-day cricket was bothering me now. I knew how I wanted the team to play but the dynamism seemed to have evaporated and even the natural attacking players, such as Knight and Brown, were looking to each other to take the lead. There was not much wrong with our Test form in the first game at Edgbaston, though, and a combination of Atherton returning to form and the South African seamers squandering helpful conditions meant that we were in a winning position when – just as in Barbados – rain on the final day deprived us.

We were thrashed at Lord's, where the atmosphere consistently lifts the opposition far more than it does the home team, and to make matters worse Ramprakash landed himself in more trouble. He had copped a bad decision, given out caught off his elbow, but he responded by telling Darrell Hair, the umpire, that he was 'messing with people's careers', which was not clever. Darrell did his job by reporting the incident to the match referee, who imposed a fine and a suspended sentence. Our Board once again exacerbated the situation by responding to journalists' calls for a statement when the incident had already been dealt with, but the affair left me feeling that there must be a better way of handling such flashpoints – a way football, and various other team sports, already employs quite acceptably. If Hair had shown Ramprakash a yellow card after he walked past him and made his remark, everyone would have identified the offence for what it was. The heat and the intrigue and the speculation, all of which is unhelpful to all concerned, would be taken out of all such situations and a player would know, for instance, that two yellow cards in a series added up to a red and a one-match ban. Is that too simplistic, too visual, too radical? I think not.

At Old Trafford, a fortnight later, the roof looked likely to fall in on us. Gary Kirsten made 47 runs in seven innings during the other four Tests but he made 210 here and South Africa amassed an imposing 552 for five. We were bowled out horribly cheaply, then lost Knight and Hussain for nothing as we followed on. At that point, a four-day defeat by an innings was on the cards and I am quite sure the press were preparing to write those obituaries for English cricket again.

They had already been busy, some of them, claiming that the game was in crisis, a reaction to a few damp days in Manchester when the crowds were relatively small and the cricket unpromising. As a keen reader of the game's history, I know that the same doom and gloom was being spread in 1906 and again in the 1930s, when Neville Cardus wrote of the decline of modern batsmanship. The depression returned in the early 1960s, when crowds dwindled and the game was supposedly dying, but along came one-day cricket as a financial salvation. So nothing has altered through the century and I, for one, did not feel I was involved in a sport at risk as we set out to save that Test match from a dire position.

The manner in which we achieved the draw transformed the summer. It could not have happened without Atherton and Stewart, who played magnificently together in a stand of more than 200, but as the fifth afternoon wore on, and Allan Donald kept charging in, wickets fell at regular intervals. The tension was stifling. The longer a team continues in a trough, the more you start to feel that you have to start drawing, let alone winning. I sat restlessly on the balcony, knowing the potential consequences of the result, and alongside me sat Angus Fraser, padded up far earlier than would be normal for a number eleven, wearing his best hangdog expression and grimly repeating: 'I'm going to have to bat here, I can tell.'

And so he did. The ninth wicket fell and Angus trudged out to join Robert Croft, leaving me with the defiant assurance that Donald 'will have to knock me through the stumps'. This was unmissable cricket, a fantastic cameo, with an apparent no-contest between a great fast bowler and a complete rabbit taking on immense significance. It was brilliant theatre, the more so because nobody quite knew how many overs were left. Somehow we survived. Angus was given the benefit of the doubt with two massive lbw shouts, one of which could easily have been given, and suddenly, cricket being the strange game that it is, the South Africans were trooping off looking downcast and we were all hugging each other and preparing for a celebration. We had been within a whisker of going 2-0 down but the series now looked quite different.

We went to Trent Bridge full of confidence and Fraser, having virtually convinced himself he would not be picked, turned from batting hero to bowling hero. He had an unnecessary downer on himself before the game, because in my mind he was always a likely starter, but he bowled superbly at the heart of a pace attack also featuring Cork, who had rediscovered his outswinger with the help of Bob Cottam, and Gough. Cottam as bowling coach was one of the best appointments made in my time and his input with a number of bowlers was invaluable. He never had to do much tinkering with Angus, though, and during that week in Nottingham the old warhorse bowled like a man inspired.

A great game was still perfectly balanced when we started the fourth innings needing 247. In such situations, Atherton is invariably the key figure and that was the case again. He batted heroically. With typical Englishness, the focus of attention was a hotly disputed decision to give him not out when he appeared to glove Donald to the wicket-keeper. Steve Dunne, the independent umpire, must have had some doubt in his mind so he did what was right – and Atherton did what the vast majority of modern Test batsmen would do by staying put. It is that kind of game now, the days of the gentlemanly 'walkers' are gone, and I don't think there can be any complaints about it so long as those who live by the sword are prepared to die by it. In other words, if you get a bad decision, you must walk off without a word – the clever ones, like Steve Waugh, will always do so.

The Atherton decision was highlighted because it came at such a pivotal moment but we could have pointed to a number of instances in the series when South Africans had been similarly reprieved. The umpire in the middle, forced to make an instant judgement, cannot win in these circumstances, which is why I believe it is inevitable and desirable that the use of the third umpire replay system should be extended to catches. There will always be a sound traditional argument for retaining the romance of human error, but modern players will say, time and again, that they want the right decision. Television now offers such intricate and revealing technology that mistakes are identified and laboured, with no intent to humiliate the umpires concerned, so while one will always have a conscience about taking the game further away from its roots, the availability of correct decisions makes it perverse to ignore it.

The immediate effect of this particular decision was to raise Donald to still greater heights of passion. He was incredibly pumped up, the verbals pouring from him like you've never seen, but Atherton simply stared back impassively. Graham Thorpe calls it being 'in the zone'; Andy Moles of Warwickshire likens it to getting in a bubble. Wherever it is, Atherton was there and taking no notice of the clamour going on around him. The confrontation had stirred him, as it always will, and he played one of his finest innings to take us to the win.

We could not wait to get at them again, after that. The setback at Old Trafford had done incalculable damage to the South Africans and we knew we had them on the back foot. This was confirmed when we arrived at Headingley for the final Test and began hearing tales of clashes between players at their practice sessions. This is a good ground for tuning in to the opposition mood, with its dressing-rooms linked by a corridor and its communal viewing area, and Pat Symcox and Brian McMillan, who had played no part in the series to date, were said to be rocking the boat, agitating in the way that those who cannot break into a side often will. Music to our ears. Added to this, it was a ground on which we felt naturally confident and conditions were pure Leeds – cloudy, dank and made for seam bowlers. The draw was a long-odds outsider in my book; we just had to get on the right end of the result.

On the final morning, South Africa needed 34 to win with two wickets left and a stunningly big crowd was pouring in as we concluded out warm-up session on the outfield. The pattern, that summer, had been that we would gather the players around us at this point and either Alec or I would give a short, sharp message for the day, a battle cry. That morning, when we might have been tense and tight, there was an unmistakable confidence,

Players wore smiles. They expected to win. I spoke briefly with Alec and then, to keep the mood light, we called on Matthew Wood, a young Yorkshireman who was our acting twelfth man, to give the team talk. He was a star. He gestured across to the opposition, going through their own routines 100 yards away, and said in his broad accent: 'I want you all to just have a look at South Africa.' He paused for effect, then added: 'Just spoil their day.' Fraser and Gough ensured that we did just that and a series that might have ended in depressing defeat and protracted inquests was instead a cause for national celebration.

The South Africans were not the most gracious of losers. They put across the feeling that they had suffered badly from the umpiring, even though the statistics showed 14 lbws against England and only 13 against them. Some of their side, including the captain, Cronje, were still on about it when England toured South Africa 18 months later – Cronje went so far as to say that the outcome of that series proved they had been the better side in 1998. What nonsense.

This was not, however, the end of the summer. Not by a long chalk. Indeed, I scarcely had time to enjoy the rarity of the plaudits, and a steady stream of nice letters and messages, before I was embroiled in an episode that left me questioning my future. What a fickle game this can be.

Sri Lanka were the second touring side of the summer – a pattern that is henceforth to be repeated every English season unless there is another administrative rethink – and the schedule involved a triangular one-day competition and a single Test match. It is important here to stress the sequence of events. The one-day cricket was played first and our initial game was at Lord's, against a Sri Lankan side I had seen very little of. We won it convincingly but I was alarmed by the bowling actions of two of the Sri Lankans, Muralitharan and Dharmasena.

In my view, both of them breached the laws as they stand, in that they partially straighten their arm in delivery. Because I had seen nothing like it before, I decided to express my concerns through the right channels. I told Simon Pack first, so that he was fully apprised of my intentions, then made a phone call to the offices of the International Cricket Council at Lord's to check the procedure of such matters. I was told I was perfectly at liberty to write a letter to the match referee, Mr Ibrahim, and duly did so, receiving a swift and formal reply noting my comments.

Nothing further occurred until the Test match at The Oval. Sri Lanka had won the triangular tournament, Muralitharan bowling brilliantly in the final back at Lord's, and the last thing we wanted was a Test match pitch to suit him. That, however, is precisely what we got. The directive about pitches states simply that they should be hard and dry with an even covering of grass but The Oval forgot the grass, which was tantamount to giving Sri Lanka a 200-run start. Our strength, and their vulnerability, was pace bowling, and here we had a home game being played on a pitch you might have found in Colombo, slow of pace and supportive to spin. 'It's a dirty pitch,' was the comment of Graham Thorpe of Surrey as we inspected it on the eve of the game. 'It's scruffy and it will turn big.' He was not wrong.

It was a game full of exhilarating batting, pretty to watch for the uncommitted, but we made 445 and still lost easily. Our attack, with a seam bias and only poor Salisbury to bowl slow, was completely neutered and we had nothing with which to stop the Sri Lankan shotmakers.

Muralitharan took seven wickets in our first innings and was to take another nine in our second. It was the performance of a magician but my earlier, officially stated doubts, remained strong. An impression has been given that I got at Murali after the event, a case of sour grapes, but in fact the comments which were to have such repercussions and such cause for deliberation were made at teatime on the fourth day, before he had even started bowling in our second innings. It is also worth saying that I did not initiate the interview or the subject matter.

Brian Murgatroyd asked me to go on television to fill an interval slot with Simon Hughes, of the BBC, and I took that as an instruction. Simon then dug away as a capable journalist would, pressing me on why our spinner seemed to get so little turn when theirs achieved so much. I replied that it was because 'he is very unorthodox'. Simon then referred to the legality of the action and I said if it was legal, then let's all do it. When the camera was switched off, he raised his eyebrows at me and said that had been an interesting comment. I told him it was no more than I believed and we left it at that.

Upstairs in the press box, many of the journalists were watching this as it was transmitted and I knew I could expect to be questioned on the point when I attended a press conference that evening. Naturally, I have thought deeply about this episode and despite the grief that was to come my way, I do not think I would do things differently if I had the chance again. Put in that position, on live television, of course I was conscious that I could not come out and say the bloke throws. I could, however, plant a seed, and in doing so I was only being faithful to the actions I had taken a fortnight earlier.

In the press conference, however, I did something that was not faithful to these actions, or even true. I was pressed by a journalist from the *Daily Mirror* on what I had said. He asked me bluntly if I thought Muralitharan threw and I said: 'I'm not prepared to answer that question.' He asked if my players believed he was a thrower and I gave the same reply. When he then asked if I had anything at all to say on the subject, I responded that anything I did wish to say would be offered through the appropriate channels. The fib was told when the supplementary question asked if I had already contacted the match referee. I said 'no' and I am still not entirely sure why. I suppose I knew that the truthful answer would set the cat among the pigeons in an even bigger way and I just felt I needed to deflect attention from the subject. It was totally wrong – in my view, just about the only thing I did do wrong in the whole, sorry episode. In due course, I was to find out that the chief executive of the Board thought differently.

CHAPTER SEVENTEEN

Treated Like a Naughty Schoolboy

Tim Lamb made me feel like a naughty schoolboy, which I think is precisely what he had in mind. The treatment meted out to me over this episode was humiliating and left me feeling utterly isolated. Basically, the people who liked to portray themselves as caring, supportive employers hung me out to dry, and if the hidden agenda was to force me to resign, they might easily have succeeded.

The strangest part about it was that nothing happened for 36 hours. On the final morning of the Test match at The Oval, Simon Pack did drop into the dressing-room to see me but it was a purely routine matter he wanted to discuss – relating to a tour itinerary, as I recall. My remarks about Muralitharan were not even mentioned. And I did not hear a word from Lamb through that day.

This was, however, the day on which I reacted to Geoffrey Boycott's sniping at me on television by confronting him outside the commentary box. Boycott, who still seemed to resent my jokey written aside about him some time earlier, had made what I considered a pretty offensive remark to the effect that England would be better off if they had a coach 'who could keep his mouth shut'. I saw red. In the circumstances, it may not have been prudent to tackle him in the way I did, but I would repeat that it was not done in front of a lot of people. Rightly or wrongly, it was also a case of being true to my own, passionate belief in the team and the job I was doing. 'If you've got something to say, say it to my face,' I told him. We ended up being matey enough but, inevitably, the tabloid press got a whisper of what had happened.

It was only at this point, more than 36 hours after my television interview with Simon Hughes, that I received a call from Tim Lamb. Conjecture might lead me to believe there was some media pressure behind this, though he would say he had done no more than allow the match to be completed before making his move. The call, anyway, was ostensibly friendly. He asked me to come to London to offer 'a balanced view' of the recent events. We settled on a meeting at the Regents Park Hilton two days later, on Thursday 3 September.

At this point, it is perhaps worth noting that I was contracted as coach through to the end of August 1999 and that we were about to enter the period that would show how far we had come as a team – the Ashes tour to Australia was to start the following month and there was then to be some intensive limited-overs preparation prior to the World Cup, starting in England in May. We had just roused the slumbers of the nation by winning a series against South Africa. Stability, continuity and mutual support were the pre-requisites of continuing to move forward. Or so I thought.

I travelled down to London by train and made a few notes during the journey. I had no clear idea what was awaiting me but I was certainly unprepared for the presence of a woman I had never seen before. She was introduced to me as Lesley Cook, the new personnel officer of the Board. She had apparently only been in the job for a month and I imagine her appointment was one of the measures introduced after the embarrassing sex-discrimination case against the Board brought up, and won, by Theresa Harrild, a former ECB receptionist. I asked Ms Cook who she was there to represent and she said she was present to ensure 'proper procedures were adhered to'. I responded: 'I thought I had just been asked down for an informal chat.' But, already, it was clear that was not the case.

Coffee and biscuits were served in what began as a reasonably congenial atmosphere. Other than the personnel manager, the only people present in a small conference room on the first floor of the hotel were Tim and Simon Pack, and it was Tim who did almost all the talking. He raised no argument with the television interview with Hughes but said he took exception to something I had said at the subsequent press conference. This surprised me, as I always made a point of checking with Brian Murgatroyd after such conferences for his view on anything contentious that might have been said, and he had assured me it went fine. I relayed this to Tim, who said simply that he disagreed. I also pointed out at this stage that my views on the two Sri Lankan bowlers had been lodged officially and asked Simon to confirm this, which he did.

The incident with Boycott was then raised and the newspaper reaction to this had plainly caused some upset. I informed them that the only other person in earshot was a cameraman and that, yes, we had a frank and sharp exchange, as many people have done and would always do with Boycott, but that we had ended up shaking hands and exchanging phone numbers. They were not satisfied. Tim said that an altercation with a commentator in a public place – they would not be shaken from this – had 'demeaned my position'.

After we had talked the thing through, I was asked to leave the room. I had to go and stand on the balcony outside and it felt like being in detention. With huge irony, as things were to turn out, the Sky TV cricket team were having an end-of-season party in the room next door. John Gayleard, the producer who would, in time, offer me a new challenge, hailed me cheerily but I wasn't feeling in my best party mood.

As soon as I was called back into the meeting, it was noticeable that the atmosphere had changed. No smiles, no geniality now. I was like a jockey up before the stewards. Lamb said they had reached a decision and wanted to issue a statement that Richard Peel had put together. Now Peel is the ECB's Director of Corporate Affairs but I had not seen him that day. 'Where is he?' I asked. 'He hasn't been here.' Tim then stunned me by saying that Peel had been asked to put together three different statements to cover all possible outcomes and they had chosen the one most appropriate.

I am not often lost for words but when the statement was read to me my jaw dropped and I felt utterly speechless. It didn't last. 'What are you trying to do to me?' was the first question I asked, because this was a statement designed to leave nobody in any doubt that the England coach was now treading on eggshells, and if he broke one more he was out of work. I could not imagine Bob Woolmer or Geoff Marsh being put in this position by their respective Boards.

There was no shouting but my anger was clear and for a few minutes Tim and I swapped opinions on the matter quite forcibly. 'You cannot possibly treat your employees like this,' I told him, at which point there came the first intervention from Simon Pack. In his usual quiet, measured style, he said: 'I do think it's rather strong, Tim.'

The upshot was that they agreed to rehash the statement and to contact me later in the day for clearance to release it. I left them to get on my train home and I was not far out of London, feeling decidedly gloomy, when a call on my mobile phone revealed a new statement hardly different from the original. I had had enough. 'Just do what you like,' I said, and rang off.

For the record, the statement issued that afternoon read:

'Tim Lamb, chief executive of the ECB, said: "Following his inappropriate comments about the Sri Lankan off-spinner, Muttiah Muralitharan, and his subsequent reported altercation with a television presenter, David Lloyd has been severely reprimanded, warned about his conduct and left in no doubt as to the responsibilities that go with such a high profile position. The matter is now closed and David goes as coach to Dhaka and to Australia with our full support." David Lloyd, England team coach, said: "I am sorry for the offence I have caused. I am glad this whole business is over and I'm looking forward to the Wills International Cup and to the Ashes tour."

I could have taken issue with many things in that short summary – the 'full support' I was allegedly receiving from the Board, the apology I was supposed to have made and my state of mind regarding the winter. On that long train ride north, I felt such a sense of devastation that I was no longer looking forward to the tours ahead. I was not even sure I wanted to take charge of them. I thought back to the Impact management course in the Lake District and the message of unity that it was supposed to transmit. I thought of climbing that telegraph pole and almost laughed at the futility of it.

I made some phone calls to some trusted friends and listened to their views. The following day, I had calls and messages from some of the players and from my staff – people like Wayne Morton and Alec Stewart were particularly supportive, adamant that I should not give in to the pressure and resign. In truth, it did not take me long to decide it would be quite the wrong thing to do, anyway. I am not a man who gives in easily and my driving motivation was still the interest of the players. Plainly, I was still getting on with them, even if relations with the bosses were strained close to breaking point, and I can honestly say I never had cause to regret staying in the job, even if it did, eventually, end in sadness and disappointment.

The official condemnation of me did not, however, end with the public statement. Two days later, I received a letter from Tim

Lamb that was even stronger in the threat department. He did say that he was 'satisfied that in neither incident was it your intention to bring discredit on the ECB' but he stressed his view that I had 'brought the game into disrepute'. The next paragraph twisted the knife. 'There can be no further repetition of incidents of this kind. If there is, then I have to warn you that it could become the subject of a formal disciplinary hearing, which, in turn, could render you liable to dismissal.'

So there it was. Step out of line once more and you are finished. Now, I appreciate that the Board has a very proper responsibility to protect the image of the game and that all its employees need to be aware of this. I also accept that I had received one prior warning, in Zimbabwe. Surely, though, the tenor of this reprimand was out of all proportion to the offence. I had skirted around the edges of a sensitive subject with the media and I had told Geoffrey Boycott what I thought of him at the time. Was this the stuff of sackings? Would the England football manager receive such high-handed treatment? I very much doubt it.

It all left a nasty taste in my mouth, allied to a conviction that the Board was spreading its wings and exerting its powers in misguided directions. They seemed to want a paperwork mountain and a nanny state, when what they should have been focusing on was the gathering of proper support for the national team initiatives we had been pushing for two years.

The Muralitharan affair was not brought to an end there. It raised its head again the following January, when he was called for throwing by umpire Ross Emerson during a one-day international against us in Adelaide. It was an extraordinary, thoroughly unpleasant game in which Arjuna Ranatunga, the Sri Lankan captain, clashed openly with Emerson over the position he had taken up to view Muralithan. Ranatunga believed, wrongly, that he could dictate where the umpire stood; Emerson put him right. Later that day, when one of the floodlights failed, there were veiled and fanciful accusations from the Sri Lankans that we, as a team, were responsible. By the end of the night, I had never seen our players so irate.

Again, there was some outrage in the media, and talk of a witch-hunt by certain umpires, but I happen to know Emerson was far from alone in his views. Four other umpires put their concerns over Muralitharan's action in writing to Peter van der Merwe, the match referee of that series, and I know from his post-tournament report that van der Merwe himself shared their doubts. 'More than suspect' was the phrase he used to describe the action.

The defence, made repeatedly following my comments at The Oval, that he had already been cleared by the ICC just does not stand up. I checked this with the ICC myself and I was told, categorically, that a bowler can never be entirely cleared, as his action could easily regress to the suspect once again. I was also asked by Bob Simpson, who was on the ICC throwing committee, for the film of Murali I had obtained from Sky TV. I would not release it but there is a certain irony in Simpson subsequently agreeing to coach Lancashire where Murali was still the registered overseas player. There was an ongoing investigation into Dharmasena before I even raised my doubts and Murali's action was obviously going to be scrutinised again when so many umpires in Australia questioned it.

I have come to know Murali quite well in the time since all this occurred, as he played for Lancashire, with great success, during the 1999 county season. He is a lovely lad and a magnificent, match-winning bowler. He had had quite enough of all the controversy surrounding him and I don't blame him. The fact remains that he has a quirk in his action but I have become increasingly convinced that we should not be hounding him, and others like him, out of the game but attending to slight reforms of the law. Presently, it states that an umpire shall call no ball if he is 'not entirely satisfied with the absolute fairness of a delivery', which seems to me too open-ended. It further states that a ball is deemed to have been thrown if the bowling arm is straightened 'partially or completely'. Again, too grey. Take out the partial element and I think that Murali would be fine. Just as important, the rest of us would be in a position to study him, Saqlain Mushtaq and other such magical off-spinners on video and imitate their methods. We should be actively developing their concept of finger-spin, which permits the ball to turn away from the right-hander with an off-spinner's action. They can spin it on any surface and disguise which way the ball will go. They are brilliant, but we should liberate them within the laws and then let's all be in on it.

We had no magic spinner to take with us to Australia. Salisbury was left behind, having yet again failed to grasp his chance during the summer. So, too, was Tufnell, a more contentious omission and one that probably spoke of the change of captain. Atherton always wanted Tufnell on tour. Even the previous year, when Philip landed himself in trouble by jumping out of a dressing-room window to avoid taking a mandatory drugs test, the view of Atherton was that it should be sorted out quickly enough for him to tour. Alec was clearly not so adamant and we set off with a party that included two off-spinners in Robert Croft and Peter Such. Croft, the natural first choice, was to lose his place after one disappointing game. Such played twice, taking five second-innings wickets in Sydney and performing in the professional, committed way I would expect from him. Australia, however, were a long way ahead of us in the slow bowling department, which is a hard thing to admit when Shane Warne did not even make his reappearance after injury until the final Test. Stuart MacGill, another leg-spinner, took 27 wickets in four games, underlining once more the greatest omission in our armoury. 'Get yourself a good leggie,' the Australians would advise. My answer was that we were trying, but it was taking a lot of time and effort.

Though we did not possess anyone to bowl wrist-spin on that tour, we did have someone to coach the batsmen in how to play it. Peter Philpott, a man I knew very well from times together in the Lancashire leagues, had already been used within the ECB Development of Excellence programme, lecturing on leg-spin, and I considered him a very able and astute coach. He had coached Warne and MacGill, which is not a bad recommendation. There was a slight resistance to his age, which was above 60, but he proved himself young at heart and I am glad we made use of him, even if the batsmen's performances against MacGill did not suggest they had absorbed too many of his lessons. At the end of the trip, he wrote me a lovely letter, in which he said we had gone about our business in an exemplary way, but they were simply better than us. 'They out-talented you,' he said, and I could not argue with that.

My last tour as England coach was a fantastic experience in all ways other than the result. We could have no cause to quibble about the 3-1 margin but when I spoke, afterwards, to Geoff Marsh and Steve Waugh, they both said we had given them a good shake and that they were relieved to have won the two vital tosses in Adelaide and Sydney. Both men thought we had developed a terrific pace attack, led by Gough, but that our batters were not good enough. Get down to number five and the rest will come quietly, they thought. That disappointed me but I knew it was accurate.

I did not start that tour with any sense of apprehension over my 'yellow card'. To have gone about my business consciously restricted by the thought of an axe poised over my head would have been self-defeating. It did quickly become apparent to me, though, that the media aspect of the job was being increasingly shunted towards the tour manager, who in this case was Graham Gooch. I tackled Brian Murgatroyd on the matter and he denied that he was under instructions to do this. His view was that it was better for all parties if we shared the load, so that the press did not get fed up with me and vice-versa. I took his point and got on with the job but I did feel that on major, match-related issues, I should have been the spokesman rather more often.

There is no criticism of Gooch implied in this. None at all. I am aware that some observers gained an impression that I felt a resentment to him, as if he was intruding on my patch, but that is not the case. Graham was one of my heroes as a player and I am pleased to call him a friend. We got along terrifically well during the tour. I enjoyed his company and his gentle humour and I felt the combination worked well. Graham was an unusual tour manager in that his obvious strengths lay in his vast playing experience. It would have been a very foolish coach who wasted that wisdom, but he never did anything in the nets without first coming to me and checking it presented no conflict. If there was a reservation about him, it was that his enthusiasm and loyalty for certain individuals could sometimes lead to him spending too much time with them, to the perceived exclusion of others. Hussain, naturally enough, received an awful lot of his attention, but this was a minor issue in a generally excellent relationship.

Graham has since copped some unjustified flak and, during the summer of 1999, he lost his place on the selection commit-tee, which I thought was a pointless, knee-jerk reaction to the cry for change that customarily accompanies a bad performance. Mike Gatting was dismissed as a selector at the same time and I felt for them both. It was said that they were responsible for the contentious recall of Graeme Hick against New Zealand, yet at the same time we were being told that the captain had the most prominent say in selection. The message from this scapegoat mentality was 'it's all your fault' and that was complete non-sense. We were all of us responsible, everyone involved, and if England were going through a trough, this was certainly not the best way of correcting it.

I do hope that Gooch's input is not lost to the England team, because he has a great deal to offer. People who work with him will say he is a superb batting coach, that he could write a book on the approach to it all. It is no accident that Gooch was coached by Boycott. Whatever my differences with him, I have no doubts that if the frills and prejudices could be stripped away from Geoffrey and he was given one-on-one responsibilities with our batsmen, he would be a great asset. Sadly, however, you cannot hire the man without his personality and it was clear to me long ago that his confrontational style would count against him in any formal coaching position with England. My passions may sometimes get the better of me but with Geoffrey, I sense, there would only be one way of doing the job and I know from my own experience that does not always sit well with administrators, the media and sundry other groups you have to satisfy in this role. He would say I have been weak for not stamping on players harder. My answer is that if he tried to approach it that way, he would not last six months.

There were some encouraging plus-points from the Australian series. Gough, Headley and Mullally began to look a potent force; Alex Tudor, a wild-card pick, made an impressive start; Hussain really came of age as a Test match batsman and also showed such an improved awareness of the team ethic that there was no longer any reason to doubt his captaincy potential. And we fought well, winning a tremendous victory in Melbourne over Christmas and competing well for most of the game in Sydney. I don't think anyone can justifiably say we picked the wrong teams or approached it in the wrong way. We just weren't quite good enough, and a lot of other sides have had to admit that against Australia.

My tour report made a list of recommendations to the Board, which included pressing ahead with a leg-spin academy and managing players with a cycle of rest, preparation and practice (which meant centrally contracting them). I also suggested, in writing, that we must 'rid ourselves once and for all of the "them and us" situation' that exists between players and ECB management. I expanded upon this in a few sentences on media relations, praising Brian Murgatroyd for his excellent efforts in a difficult area but expressing the players' resentment that a word out of place in the interviews that are often officially arranged for them can bring a ton of condemnation from Lord's. 'To spell it out bluntly,' I wrote, 'there is a view that there is a lack of support from home base'.

This was an increasingly common view in the dressing-room during that tour and one that I shared with the players. Indeed, as early as Christmas, with two Tests still to play, I knew that the next serious talk I had with my employers could be the one that led to my early departure. I was approaching my 52nd birthday with no feeling of support and security in the job I was doing. I still loved the job, and the lifestyle it afforded me, and I was still convinced there was more I could achieve. But in order to do that, I needed to know that I would be backed by the administration over a period of time. I was soon to confirm my suspicion that they were unprepared to give any such guarantee.

CHAPTER EIGHTEEN

Master of My Destiny

In the spring of 1999, life changed in many ways. I became a married man again and a television commentator again. And, after the most dismaying of finales, I ceased to coach the England cricket team. With marriage to Diana came a new home in Cheadle Hulme, a new garden to occupy me, and a golf club just down the road. I was also to be wed, in a sense, to Sky Television, who made me the first and best offer of a new career after coaching. It was to mean watching a great deal more cricket but that would never daunt me. Wall-to-wall cricket is all I have ever known; I really believe I know the game backwards and I over-react terribly when someone questions my facts and opinions – the failings of a passionate man.

There will be those, I know, who contend I was too passionate to run the England team. They will say that I became one-eyed in my public support of the team and that the kettle in my head boiled a few times too often. That's too bad. Those who appointed me to the position knew my personality as well as my record – at least, if they did not, there was something profoundly wrong – and they got me as I am, rather than some sanitised imitation. It amuses me, in hindsight, that some of those who acclaimed my appointment as an emergence from depression into joy and optimism were the very same people who later took such apparent pleasure in lampooning me. I am not alone in this.

It is an English thing, sad and predictable, this perceived compulsion to hound managers, captains and coaches out of office if their teams do not satisfy the hunger for success.

Well, my team, the England team, fell short of that expectation and we all knew it. We also felt that a great deal had been achieved over three years of hard work, a lot of valuable advances initiated and expert, specialist back-up staff put in place. The England team was run more professionally, with greater vision and awareness than before, and if a lot was left undone, much of that could be laid at the doors of the outdated county system and its reluctance to cede priority to the national needs.

But we had not won enough times when it really mattered. I knew that all too well and, while my cricketing instincts urged me to stay on and strive for the substantial gains that would publicly vindicate all my efforts, the pragmatist within was giving me a different message.

I was no longer a young man and I no longer had the security of a lengthy period of notice – the ECB had made sure of this when they scrapped the 12-month rolling aspect of my contract. I was faced with the possibility of being sacked, summarily, after a poor World Cup, and I was intent that this would not happen. Instead, I would dictate my own future.

I knew already that the way was clear for me to return to the commentary boxes and I was comfortable with the idea. Most of my previous experience was in radio, and the BBC were keen for me to return to *Test Match Special*. Realistically, though, they could not offer the commitment to cricket, much less the money, that Sky Television now does routinely. Channel 4's appearance in the market, screening home Test matches live, added a third dimension and they, too, sounded me out informally towards the end of the Australian tour. I listened to everyone and made no promises whatever. The promises I needed lay at the gift of Ian MacLaurin and his Board.

In mid-March, only six weeks before the World Cup squad

was due to gather, I travelled back down to London for an appointment with Lord MacLaurin at his chambers in New College Street, just around the corner from the Houses of Parliament. I have stressed before that, no matter the extenuating circumstances, I always felt confident and supported in the presence of the Board chairman and, although subsequent gossip and rumour was to make me wonder if I had been naive, nothing changed that morning. Ian was charming, attentive and understanding. Far from giving me an impression that he wanted me out, he appeared to be seeking ways to enable me to stay. Before long, though, it became clear to us both that there was no easy way.

I told him that the point of my visit was a need to know where I stood. My contract was due to expire at the end of August and I reasoned that if they had a new coach in mind for the winter tour to South Africa, it would doubtless be thought sensible to bed him in against New Zealand first. Clearly, it would be unsatisfactory all round if, when the World Cup was over, they decided they wanted me to leave within a matter of weeks.

From a self-protection viewpoint, I was twitchy about whether the television jobs currently on offer would still be available at the end of the summer. With my team hat on, I knew that leaving my future unresolved would offer the press an ongoing speculative story that could not fail to distract attention from the real business of trying to win the World Cup. But more than anything, I was tired of all the innuendo, fed up with the rumours that someone – and I kept hearing that it was Brian Bolus – was doing a lot of background lobbying to get me out. I'd had enough of being a pawn in that game and, at 52, I wanted to be the master of my destiny.

I told MacLaurin that I had other job offers to consider. I took the initiative and suggested that the best solution might be for me to leave the job at the end of the World Cup. This was the schedule I had been considering since before Christmas and I had come to believe it made sound sense for my future and peace of mind. The pride and passion that niggled within me wanted to hear MacLaurin reject the solution and instead offer me an extension on my contract, but I do not believe even he was willing or able to do that.

Honourable to the end, Ian assured me that my contract would be paid up fully. He gave an impression of sadness that the mission we had begun together, creating Team England out of the disunity that had gone before, would not now be concluded in the way we had both imagined. He gave absolutely no sense of 'good riddance'; quite the opposite. Both then, as we talked, and in a letter he was to write later that day, he told me that if I ever needed help in any walk of life, I should ring him. I appreciated that, and left Westminster feeling more relief than sadness. A job I cherished would soon be given to someone else but I had come away with my dignity intact and my sense of direction restored. I was in control.

The news was released immediately, with my full blessing – in this instance, there was absolutely nothing to gain by sitting on it. I did a few interviews on the phone and slept soundly. The following morning, at an hour when my telephone has normally not been roused into action, I answered a typically forthright call from John Gayleard of Sky. Like many Australians, Gayleard is not inclined to take 'no', or even 'don't know' for an answer. By the time I rang off, I had agreed to join his commentary team; within minutes, my fax machine was chattering with copies of the contract.

So the long-term was decided. Only the short-term now needed attention but as I turned my sights to the first World Cup cricket event to be staged in this country since 1983, there were clouds on the near horizon. They came from both the way we were playing and the cricketing politics that would prove persistent, unhealthy company right into the tournament. It was not to be the happiest of farewells.

From a playing viewpoint, I was dismayed that our one-day cricket, dynamite at home both in 1996 and 1997, had deteriorated ever since. It has been said that we tinkered too much with the make-up of the team but this was partly a function of overseas tours, on which only a few one-day specialists were traditionally brought, and partly through the justifiable search for a unit who would operate in the way we required.

I was never in doubt as to the way we should approach one-day games. Maximising the first 15 overs, when batting, is the key to success in modern one-day cricket and, even with renowned strikers such as Nick Knight and Ali Brown, we were not doing so often enough. The next essential is to be busy but not reckless in the middle period of 20 or 25 overs, knocking the ball around and, crucially, establishing partnerships so that good players are in, with wickets intact, when the burst of runs in the final ten overs is required.

It is a simple enough philosophy but it was eluding us frequently. Add to this the loss of intensity in our fielding that grieved me so much and it can be seen that I was hopeful, but not exactly confident, as we entered the Cup. In Australia, though we had reached the final of the triangular tournament, we had seldom produced the sort of cricket I wanted to see. Unacceptably often, we were beaten from apparently invincible positions and I came away disappointed by the mental attitude of the players. Too many of them declined to accept responsibility when the going got tough. Such psychological weakness could easily be exposed on a big stage such as the World Cup.

It may sound contrary, having expressed these concerns, but if it had been left to me I would have included Chris Lewis in our World Cup party. I say this with no loss of memory, no blanking out of the idiotic way he let us down at The Oval in 1996. Chris can be infuriating, elusive and unfathomable but I still like him as a cricketer and it is one of my regrets that, like so many others, I was unable to find the key to him. I had an ally in these views in Alec Stewart and we both knew that to express them at the wrong time would be to make certain people's hair stand on end. During the one-day series in Australia, we met up with Chris, who was playing some club cricket in Melbourne, and I suggested he came to talk to Alec and myself after a day-night game. Back at our hotel, it was midnight when we got together, but then midnight is probably a good time for Chris. We told him that we both wanted him in the World Cup squad but that there could be no promises because resistance would be inevitable. I added that I was prepared to back him publicly but that if he stepped out of line just once the idea would be buried. 'I'd turn up in my pyjamas to play for England again,' he said. 'That's part of the problem,' I responded.

It was no surprise to me that the idea of Lewis met what might euphemistically be called a lukewarm response, and for all my enthusiasm he failed to make the final 15. Instead, we approached the tournament with a versatile and durable looking squad, but one that would need inspiration from a few key individuals if we were to go all the way. And that, I knew from simply listening in my local pub, was what the country was beginning to expect, in the same way that English football fans will expect Kevin Keegan's side to win the European Championships, conveniently overlooking the fortuitous back-door route to qualification. It is, in some ways, an endearing trait, this blind faith, but it doesn't half pile on the pressure if things begin to go wrong.

They were going wrong even before we convened for our preparation period. The players decided they were unhappy with their World Cup contracts and the issue became unnecessarily messy. It was no great departure from similar disputes that have littered cricket down the years, but it was especially poor timing and re-emphasised my already stated views that the players were feeling put-upon by unsupportive administrators.

The squad gathered on 2 May at Eastwell Manor in Kent and

it was not long before there was a good deal more to cause anxiety. The attitude of certain players, for one thing. As early as our second evening, some of the lads were expressing private concerns about whingeing in the camp – and this before we had bowled a ball in anger. Two night later, Graham Thorpe refused to attend an official reception with the members of Kent, our county hosts. He had already told us that his back was stiff and he would be unable to throw but this divisive behaviour from a senior player, and one who had erred in this way before, disappointed everyone. David Graveney, who was manager of the World Cup party, arranged to see Thorpe at 8 am the following morning and my solution – extreme but appropriate for one who was making excuses about his fitness even before the competition began – would have been to replace him. Instead, he was fined £1,000.

Our next little problem was with Adam Hollioake. From being the coming man of English cricket, promoted early and with sound reason to lead the one-day team, Adam had slipped back in the pecking order. No longer captain and no longer sure of a place in the team, he could not get by on his justifiable reputation as a strong character and good team man. He needed to produce more, to establish a senior role, and he did not make a good start after our warm-up match against Essex. One disciplinary misdemeanour at the ground was followed by another on the road to Southampton, when, for reasons only he can explain, he stopped to barrack a village game.

The distractions did not end here. I was personally furious over the publication of a report on central contracts for England players, commissioned by the Board and undertaken by a working party chaired by a man named Don Trangmar. All I knew of Mr Trangmar was that he came from Sussex and had been a director of Marks and Spencer; doubtless his business expertise was of some value in compiling the report but I would have thought that those at the coal face of England cricket should have had some input and it staggered me that it could be completed and released without reference to myself and the other full-time England staff.

Kate Hoey, now the Minister of Sport, had originally agreed to sit on this committee and I approached her when we met at a function, raising my concerns about lack of consultation. She told me that she had attended only one meeting before resigning, and that she left uncomfortable with the way it was being run. Angus Fraser was the one player on the committee but I was also told that his was a token presence and that the real decisions were taken by Trangmar and Peter Anderson, the Somerset chief executive.

I had no quibble with the main recommendations to emerge from the report, as it appeared that the contract situation I had been proposing for some time now had the kind of backing that would make it very hard for the counties to resist. My annoyance stemmed from the implicit criticism of management standards around the England team, comments that incriminated both myself and David Graveney. For almost three years, I had been repeating that we needed to manage the players better and that the way to do that was to employ them centrally so that we could directly control the amount of cricket they played and build around it appropriate periods of rest, practice and preparation. Now, here was a chairman I had never met telling us that the problem stemmed from poor management practices. No matter that I recognised this as a sales pitch to sceptical counties, I found it misleading and demeaning. I told Simon Pack as much, when Grav and I went to see him on the matter, and a day or two later I told the Board I was withdrawing from the World Coaching Conference they had set up in Birmingham as a direct form of protest on their findings.

As if this was not enough to lower my self-esteem at a sensitive time, a dinner on 12 May, two days before the World Cup opener, left me feeling devastated and bewildered. We had moved into our London hotel the previous evening and practised on the morning of the 12th at Lord's, where we would start our programme against recently familiar opposition in Sri Lanka. The Board had organised a dinner for senior officials and, for the first time since his appointment as chairman of EMAC, I found myself in a room with Brian Bolus. I decided it was too good an opportunity to waste.

'Bolly' had always amused me as a player and his infectious sense of humour and idiosyncratic laugh made him as easy man in company. Like me, he had taken his cricketing stories onto the dinner speaking circuit and had even come to me, some years previously, asking if I could put any speaking work his way. I fixed him up with a couple of dinners and did not expect any great show of gratification for it. Nor, however, did I expect the kind of back-stabbing which appeared to have been continuing through the winter.

It was the oddest thing, to me, that we had not heard a word from Bolus throughout our time in Australia. His predecessor, Bob Bennett, had made a point of keeping in touch with the team and, even when officially uninvolved, usually came out on tour to watch a couple of Tests. Bob would not interfere but he was constantly available to advise and encourage. We neither saw nor heard from Bolly, other than through a sequence of newspaper articles that only he could have inspired. One tabloid journalist, who made a habit of speaking on the phone to Bolus, wrote at different stages of the winter that I would be (a) sacked after the Ashes Tests; (b) sacked immediately the tour ended; and (c) sacked before the World Cup. This was quite disturbing when I suspected the source of the stories yet was hearing nothing from him myself.

Bolus is nothing if not genial. Hail-fellow-well-met as ever, he reeled only slightly when I did not instantly return the mood. I told him I wanted to sit with him at dinner and, once we were settled, I asked him why there had been no contact between him and the team and gave my view that it questioned the point of having an England management committee at all. He replied that he had been warned against making direct contact, both by Simon Pack and Ian MacLaurin, and told to address his comments and queries through Simon. I found this strange and unsatisfactory, as, if true, it would often lead to the chairman of EMAC receiving outdated or entirely wrong information about what was going on. But I pressed on. 'How far do we go back?' I asked him, rhetorically. 'If there is someone nailing me behind the scenes, I would like to know who it is, and everything I hear is leading me to you. If that's the case, I want to hear it from you. You've known me long enough to owe me that.'

Bolus did not seem remotely nonplussed, far less embarrassed. Instead, he gave one of his conspiratorial winces and, with a tilt of his head to the far end of the table, presided over by Ian MacLaurin, he said: 'It's not me, lad, it's the grocer. He said we should sack you after the World Cup.'

This irreverent reference to the man credited with making Tesco the biggest supermarket chain in the country left me completely confused. It was common knowledge that Bolus and MacLaurin were at loggerheads, scarcely even on speaking terms, and they were unlikely to speak very kindly of each other. The longer I spoke with Bolus that night, the more obvious it became that he did not know all the facts about my resignation and assumed that I had simply jumped ship. This, too, disturbed me. Yet to take Bolus at his word, when he passed the responsibility for wanting me out onto the Board chairman, was to destroy the impression I had built up of MacLaurin over a period of years. An impression, quite simply, that he was a man I could trust. I recognised he would always be prepared to be ruthless – how else could he have achieved so much in business – but credited him with enough human kindness to tell people to their faces if there were hard decisions to be taken. I am not saying I disbelieved Bolus, or his impression of what had happened, but I could not bring myself to accept its implications of betrayal, either.

To this day, I am unsure what to believe but it does not stop me liking MacLaurin and having great respect for him. Bolus, I know, is a backroom agitator, a cricketing politician, and for all that I still like him as a man, he has a great deal of work to do to command the respect of the England players. Through my last weeks as coach, the team made it very plain that there were three people they did not want to see in their dressing-room – Pack, Lamb and Bolus. This was a difficult situation, as these men were all my bosses in different ways, but while the stand-off saddened me, I could understand and empathise with its origins.

The subject of my successor was now hot. Bob Woolmer seemed the natural favourite to me, as he was about to relinquish his position with South Africa. Bolus, however, was against Woolmer and, among a variety of other names being bandied around, he favoured a coalition of Jack Birkenshaw and James Whitaker. I was not against this, and personally believed strongly that the job should go to an Englishman rather than a foreigner.

All of these issues, however, now had to be banished to the recesses of my mind. The World Cup was underway and we started it impressively, beating the holders by eight wickets in a game in which the Sri Lankans were oddly uncompetitive. It was all so one-sided that it passed in a strangely subdued atmosphere, not helped by a thinly populated pavilion, apparently the outcome of MCC members protesting that they had to pay for their tickets. A pity to dampen such an occasion so small-mindedly, I thought, but we had suffered a classic example of MCC small-mindedness earlier that morning. I had taken the players onto the outfield at Lord's for our usual fielding drills and we were just underway when a steward in blazer, tie and bristling jobsworth expression marched across, calling: 'Who is in charge, here?' It was such a ludicrous question but, in schoolboy fashion, I replied: 'I am.' 'Have you had permission to be on here throwing balls at stumps?' he asked, as if this activity was a subject of general disapproval. None of us could quite believe this. Here we were, the eyes of the nation upon us as we started the quest to win a World Cup at our own headquarters, the supreme ground in world cricket, and some chap in a blazer was asking if we had permission to be on the field. Somehow, it made everyone laugh, easing the tension, and the rest of the day proceeded entirely to plan.

By now, we had taken the toughest of selectorial decisions by promoting Hussain to open the innings and leaving out Knight. There were two motivations here: Knight's patchy form and the wish to make the best use of Hussain. Nasser had been accused of selfishness in one-day cricket but I think his problem was more a lack of know-how. He has always been one-paced – hence, in limited overs cricket, he can be an encumbrance if he bats below number three. Without Atherton, who was still suffering with his back condition, I quite liked the idea of him going in first to anchor the innings and he was receptive to it. Knight disagreed with the decision, as any player of spirit should do, and said he would prove us wrong. But I remain convinced it was the right course to have taken, despite the fate about to befall us.

We dispatched Kenya with ease, Hussain doing his confidence at the head of the order a power of good with an unbeaten 88, but then came unstuck against South Africa. This was a huge game for us and it did not pass unnoticed that Tim Lamb chose to attend the FA Cup final instead. There were no excuses, though. We batted very poorly on a dead pitch and never got within hailing distance of a modest target of 226. Now, there was work to do and results elsewhere were to prove as significant as our own.

We beat Zimbabwe easily, yet they had already pipped India, who were now to thrash Sri Lanka. The first real upset of the tournament came with Zimbabwe's win over South Africa, who batted pathetically, and the upshot was that we resumed a rain-interrupted game against India knowing that it was sudden death – win and we go forward, lose and it's all over.

We did not just lose, we surrendered. It was a diabolically inept performance and the worst way my imagination could have conceived for me to end the job – sudden, savage and so very disappointing. I felt the dismay of the nation and I felt for the players whose inadequacies under pressure had been exposed. By the following day, back at home, I even felt a little sorry for myself. As the inquests and aftermaths clicked into gear, I wanted to get away from it all and contemplated taking my first real break from cricket in quite a time. Then I picked up a phone call from John Gayleard and heard the insistent Australian tones telling me I was to join the Sky team immediately. I felt like refusing, begging for compassionate leave, but I think John understood that I was hurting and that what I really needed by way of release was to work. As soon as I walked into the commentary box, I knew he was right. I had a new team to work with now.

CHAPTER NINETEEN

'Nothing Wrong with Saying What You Think'

A change of jobs did not need a change of personality but it did require me to make some rapid adjustments. This came home to me on the eve of the Edgbaston Test against New Zealand at the start of July, the first England game for more than three years in which I had no direct involvement. There were no pangs of regret, no longing to be back amongst it all in the dressing-room, yet only with a last-minute rethink did I avoid doing something I would have regretted.

Sky, my new employers, wanted to make the most of having me around so soon after I had been operating at the sharp end, and their marketing people rang to ask if I would go down to Birmingham a day early for some promotional shots. They wanted to film me at the England nets on Wednesday morning, handing something over to Nasser Hussain. No alarm bells rang. I just agreed, accepted it as being a part of the new job, and on the Tuesday evening I drove south and checked into our city hotel in Birmingham.

Next morning, I got togged up in my new Sky blazer and set off to keep the 9 am appointment at Edgbaston. It was only a short drive; long enough, though, to realise that what I was about to do was totally wrong. I was out of the scene, I had crossed the floor, and posing for pictures with the new captain would portray me as a man who could not let go of the past.

You could say I got cold feet but I think it was more a case of seeing sense. I drove through the gates of Edgbaston, parked the car, then rang Brian Murgatroyd of the ECB on my mobile to tell him the shots were off. I made a similar call to Sky, then started the car again and returned, relieved, to the hotel.

No-one in the England camp had raised any misgivings about the idea but, once I had pulled out, Brian told me he had not thought it was right, either. It was one of the best changes of mind I ever made and it was sufficient to alert me to the different area I had entered. From that moment on, I trod carefully, keeping well away from the familiar team routines. I did not once attend net practice and, if I entered the players' range on the outfield on the morning of a match, I would confine myself to a cheery greeting and keep walking, determined I would not be accused of clinging on to lost authority.

I found it surprisingly easy. After that first, misguided morning, it never once felt strange to be around the team without being part of it. I reasoned that there are millions of people who change jobs every year and I was just one of them. I was in a different camp and, from day one, I had no difficulty saying or writing things as I saw them. I figured I was not setting out to be popular, any more than I had been as coach.

John Gayleard had told me that my essential packing for a trip with the Sky cricket team would include golf clubs and tennis racquet. We'll have fun, he said, and we did; the commentators, along with the producer, tend to rise early for some sporting activity of their own and there is always something sociable going on of an evening. In playing hours, we get serious. People who criticise Sky – and I have found there are plenty of them – would do well to sit back and consider what the coverage is doing to elevate the game. It is technically excellent and more comprehensive in its scope than cricket had ever dreamed of before the advent of satellite television. In a typical week covering county cricket – or Under-19s or women's games – we might go from Manchester to Derby to Canterbury to Hove. And, to take the commercial plug a step further, we never miss a ball.

It's hard work for all involved but the volume of cricket never daunts me – the more the better, as far as I am concerned. If I was born to do anything, it was to talk about cricket and if my natural enthusiasm transmits itself through the nation's satellite dishes, so much the better.

There was a four-Test series to be played against New Zealand and it was certain to suffer, publicly, as an anti-climax after the heady expectations of the World Cup. Before it could even begin, though, I found myself required to comment on the decisions made within the England team and, here, I had mixed feelings. I approved of the captaincy change, questioned the philosophy behind the appointment of a foreign coach – though not the merit of the man selected – and deplored the obsessive new-broom mentality that saw a good man and admirable physiotherapist, in Wayne Morton, needlessly sacrificed.

It is important to say, here, that I had no axe to grind. Eventually, if with a good deal of reluctance, I had taken my own decision to curtail my time as coach. Not everything had run smoothly, and at times I'd had a distinctly rough ride, but life's like that. In moving out, I felt no great sorrow – just occasional irritation when the insensitive administration machine that has developed at Lord's turned out another piece of needling bureaucracy, such as the letter from the personnel manager, Lesley Cook, requesting that I sent back my company Barclaycard 'cut into two pieces' and mobile phone and 'make immediate (underlined) arrangements to return the ECB car to Lord's'. It was dated 10 June, the World Cup had not even reached its semi-final stage and I was being chased as if they felt sure I would scarper with the family silver.

This kind of thing is, to my mind, just an example of poor employer practice but I was beyond getting worked up about it by then – I had a future to consider. Anyway, the postbag was not all threats and reminders. I received a stack of far more welcome and appreciative letters from many of the people I had worked with over the three years – one I especially treasure from Medha Laud, without whose energy and loyalty and humour, the England set-up would have been in a rare mess.

There were even some pleasant things said and written about me in the media when I stepped down, though this again I could regard with a cheerful indifference. In our sporting environment, everyone reads the papers – even if they do not go out of their way to buy them, they are always around the dressing-rooms and hotels – and everyone gets hurt at times. It happened to me on the tour of Zimbabwe and New Zealand, never more so than when some affectedly clever chap from the Guardian got particularly personal and said they should send for the men in white coats. Down the years, I regularly resented things that were written about the team, or about individual players, and occasionally I would even release the frustration by writing impassioned letters to the offending journalists, knowing they would never be posted. I did not, however, share Atherton's view that the press was incidental or could be treated as such and I think I managed to have a lot of fun with the travelling media. Now, suddenly, I was in their camp and it did not even feel strange. I discovered I could look at what was happening to the team – 'my' team until so recently – and do it dispassionately.

Replacing Stewart with Hussain as captain was, I thought, only logical. If I had still been the coach, I would have actively supported such a move. Alec had begun well in the job, with the win over South Africa only 12 months earlier, but things had not worked out for him either in Australia or during the World Cup. Moreover, Nasser had shown distinct signs of maturing. It could be said that this was overdue, and it is certainly true that doubts about his temperament had a good deal to do with him not getting the captaincy when Atherton resigned, but if he now had the mental approach to go with his tactical nous and experience, he deserved a chance.

We had been obliged to take another difficult decision involving Hussain during the World Cup, preferring him to Nick Knight as our opening batsman. Knight had said he would prove us wrong but, despite our failure to progress in the competition, it was undoubtedly the right thing to have done. Hussain had come on leaps and bounds as a one-day player and, to my mind, the charges of selfishness that had often been levelled at him were wide of the mark – his inability at the short game was more a lack of know-how.

Similar disparaging things had been said of his personality, this being held against him whenever the issue of the captaincy was raised, and I can well see why he was portrayed as selfish, having had to cope for three years with his intense, insular and sometimes, yes, self-centred ways. I also came to appreciate, however, that it was all down to desire, to his great ambition to succeed at the highest level. Once I accepted that, and dismissed the temptation to regard it as something more sinister or deliberately disruptive, it was more straightforward to deal with.

Nasser took his time learning to cope with his own personality and there were days when he infuriated me, and others in the team environment. As he became more aware of this, and sensitive to its repercussions, he would come to me and say: 'Keep talking to me, good or bad'. Generally, I did talk, but sometimes I judged that he was best left to stew it out of his system alone.

He is a complex man and he provokes some polarised opinions. Certainly, I know of some folk at his own county, Essex, who could not even understand his promotion to England vice-captain, saying it was beyond them how we could have him in a position of authority. They were entitled to their view, and doubtless held it just as firmly about his elevation to the captaincy. In July of 1999, though, I reckoned the time was right for him and that he would be excellent for England. I have seen nothing since to make me change that view.

Watching my successor as coach appointed was never meant to be easy but I think I observed it without prejudice, and certainly without jealousy. So far as I was aware, Bob Woolmer was always top of the wanted list and, having observed his work over the years and shared some fascinating discussions with him, I considered him the ideal man, one to whom the players were certain to respond. I know the ECB did some scampering around in his direction and I suspect that sending Simon Pack, who is essentially not a cricket man, to do the talking was misguided. But Bob, anyway, decided that the time was not right for him, so soon after ending his contract with South Africa, so the search had to alter its range.

Before long, it became clear that the three candidates were Duncan Fletcher, Jack Birkenshaw and Dave Whatmore, and plain to me that Whatmore – who had a standing offer to return to Sri Lanka after ending his two seasons with Lancashire – was shortlisted only for window-dressing. So it came down to a shrewd Yorkshireman, vastly experienced in the English county system, or a South African with a high reputation. Birkenshaw had an appropriate track record, having worked wonders with limited resources at Leicester, but I suspect he did not get the job because they knew him too well – Fletcher was by far the more glamorous pick, the more obvious shift of direction. And it was a sea change that those in power were evidently seeking.

I did hold an opinion that, in principle, the England coach should be English. I just happen to think it makes a difference, both to the coach himself and the players he is coaching. But it was not my decision and, once I'd said my peace, that was it forgotten. I did not know Fletcher – had never so much as met him during his season-and-a-half with Glamorgan – but I saw no reason to be anything but supportive towards him. We spoke on the phone, quite soon after his appointment, and naturally enough he wanted to pick my brains about certain players. I happily answered his questions and gave him my views but also pointed out that detailed reports on every player, from each tour and home series, were filed in the Board offices at Lord's. Duncan was surprised and grateful. It seems nobody had thought to tell him this.

My main argument with the appointment was that it did not take effect until the summer was over. Inevitably, there would be a vacuum, potentially draining and disorientating for the team at a time when they needed a return of stability. And it seemed so unnecessary. I do not claim to be privy to all the talks but I do feel the situation was not dissimilar to my own in 1996. I was contracted to coach Lancashire that year, just as Duncan was attached to Glamorgan in 1999. Lancashire agreed without demur that I should be seconded to England immediately, while remaining in their employment until the end of the summer, when a longer-term situation would be developed. If Glamorgan were amenable to a comparable arrangement – and I have heard nothing to the contrary – why on earth did nobody at the Board push it through and get the man installed?

Part of my reasoning in leaving the job early – and resolving it before the World Cup even began – was to give the ECB a chance of a fluent handover. The professional thing to do was to have a new man in place for the start of the New Zealand series and it is beyond me that it could not be achieved. Duncan was continuing to toe the party line, saying that his loyalty was to Glamorgan – in my view that was wrong, his loyalty was now to England instead. The compromise of having Graham Gooch as an acting coach, with David Graveney also playing an enhanced role, was just that – a case of applying sticking plaster over the gaps – and it should never have happened. England's poor performance in a series they would have been expected to win stemmed, in part, from this unresolved saga. The players, I am quite sure, were unsettled in precisely the way I had tried to avoid and I think they would have been greatly helped if the accession of Fletcher had been better handled.

If I chafed over this for the players who had been short-changed, I was seriously upset by the treatment of Wayne Morton, who was not only stood down from his role with the senior side but ditched altogether, despite an expressed willingness to work either with the 'A' team or Under-19s. This, I felt, was a shabby way to deal with a man who had put a huge amount of time and effort into improving the fitness, and thereby the fortunes of the England team.

I am a fan of Wayne and have been since we began working together, but I am not blind to his faults. He did not pander to authority and he wasted no time with the niceties of subtlety. Many were the times, as we sat together in meetings with the top brass, when I would put my head in my hands as Wayne launched some loaded tirade. He did not mind who he upset, so long as he got his point across, and naturally this abrasive style did not endear him to some of those in the ivory towers at Lord's. It is also fair to say that there were players who did not care for his methods, who felt he had too much to say and wielded too much authority. This last factor, though, was down to me, because I regarded him as my ideal foil – Wayne could play the nasty, while I did the nice. Cricketers are always seeking attention and sympathy and Wayne, in his no-nonsense way, just got them back on track. Yes, he could get over-enthusiastic at times, but didn't we all? I always trusted him implicitly as a second-in-command and felt that the right players, those who really mattered in the dressing-room, had great respect for him.

Much his most important contribution, though, was the fundamental matter of getting players on the field. England had a justifiably poor reputation for injuries, especially afflicting bowlers, in the early 1990s and while no man alive can guarantee the well-being of his cricketing charges, Wayne was responsible for significantly reducing our soft-tissue injuries and generally raising the levels of fitness in the squad – not by sending them on mindless runs but by developing programmes to suit each individual and creating an atmosphere in which the players were more aware of their fitness responsibilities.

Dean Riddle, who was brought in by Wayne as a specific fitness expert, also played a substantial part in this, though in hindsight I would have used him a little differently. He, too, joined the casualty list, the apparent rush to sweep away all remnants of the past. I was slightly surprised when they didn't sack the scorer, too ... Wayne's case, however, was the worst, because he did not deserve to go and it distressed him greatly. The Board had persuaded him to give up his contract as the Yorkshire physiotherapist, in order to devote himself more fully to England matters, and he had happily gone along with the idea. Early in 1999, he had been approached by Manchester United, a position that most sports physiotherapists must regard as the Holy Grail, but he chose not to pursue it, never suspecting the card that was about to be dealt to him. He was the principal casualty of the craving for fresh faces and, while I understand the motivation, I cannot accept that it was fair.

England won at Edgbaston – we usually do – and lost at Lord's, just as predictably. I could not be surprised by either result. We always knew this group of players were capable of performing and they did so admirably to come from behind in a typically tense, low-scoring game at Edgbaston. The players love it there, they like the smell and the feel of it, the buzz of the pavilion, the rowdier support from the stands. And they enjoy the pitch, fickle though it can be. I was delighted for them but I knew damned well where the next game was, and I knew we were capable of dramatic peaks and troughs.

Nasser is no fool and he made a point of saying, before Lord's, that the players would approach it with a better body language, a more positive and caring image. It didn't work. Lord's is different from Edgbaston, different from everywhere else we play, and for a variety of reasons the mood of the place motivates visiting teams and stifles England. It happens year after year and Nasser found that he had no better answer to it than the previous captains.

He phoned me after that game and asked my opinion of what they should do. I said that if selection was left to me, I would wipe the slate clean and get some youngsters in. You may say this is more simply proposed from the outside but it just seemed the perfect time to experiment, with two Tests remaining before the tour party for South Africa had to be chosen. Nasser clearly felt caught between the devil and the deep blue sea, feeling the instinctive loyalty to the players he had always known and enjoyed having around, yet appreciating the value of change. I told him that if they kept reproducing players from the same circle, plucking them off in turn like kids from a fairground carousel, the public would lose interest. I said that the boys must know there would be changes – a view that was backed up when Mark Ramprakash recalled how he had waited for the Ceefax announcement of the next team with trepidation, aware that there were sure to be sacrifices. The time was right – yet instead of grasping the nettle, they brought Graeme Hick back.

The one sacrifice in this was Aftab Habib, who admittedly had not shown much in the first two games. I believed there was more to it than this, though, and I said as much in my column in the *Daily Telegraph*. Habib and Chris Read, the young wicket-keeper, were those to whom I specifically referred in saying that new players felt 'traumatised' by the atmosphere in the dressing-room. This was not intended as a tabloid 'flier' and nor was it a cheap shot at a dressing-room I had, until recently, inhabited. I had not sought the information about what had gone on – it had come to me, from the team. There were things I could not and would not repeat but I considered it fair to observe that there was a problem in the camp and that it might be inhibiting those new to the scene.

There was a reaction, of course. The team had its viewpoint on what I had written and some of the players doubtless did not like it, but most of the response was fuelled by the media. I was surprised by how extensively and bitingly it was reported upon by other newspapers, some of whom called my criticism vicious and said I had stepped over the line. Yet these guys knew me well enough – did they honestly imagine I would operate with flannel and soft soap now that I was one of them?

The players came round, of course, and perhaps even responded to what I had said. I certainly detected no frost in the air whenever I encountered them, despite the predictable sarcasm of Atherton. Even Caddick, one of the few players I ever elected to criticise in public as a coach, is fine with me now. I can call him a big, gormless lump and make him laugh and he will admit – and has done in print – that he bowled awfully on that tour of the West Indies. Ironically, we were having a drink together during the South African tour last winter when a copy of an interview he had done for the *Mail on Sunday* reached us. 'Lloyd's treatment of me was a disgrace' was the theme. 'What's all this about?' I teased him. 'Wrong end of the stick,' he replied apologetically. 'Well, you did bowl like a drain in Trinidad, didn't you?' I probed. And he agreed. He's a grand lad, we get along great, but he does put his big, clumsy foot in it now and again.

In the course of the 1999 summer, a few of the players wrote or phoned but I was careful not to seek their company too often. When the summer ended with a New Zealand victory at The Oval, I admired the winners and just felt a few more regrets for an England team that could not produce and perform with any degree of consistency.

The reasons put forward are endless but I will concentrate on just a few. Firstly, the amount of cricket. There is not too much Test cricket, and still won't be now that we are playing seven home Tests each summer. Our country is one of few that can sustain such a schedule, because the public appetite for Test cricket remains healthy, despite the mixed fortunes of the national team. The problem in England, as anyone with an ounce of sense acknowledges, is that far too much is demanded of the Test players every time they return to their counties. Central contracts can prove the greatest single step towards resolving this but it will not happen without pain and resistance because county cricket is an entrenched and much-loved part of our culture. I love it myself, and certainly have no wish to contribute to its death, but the plain truth is that it no longer serves as an adequate preparation for the step up to the inter- national game – and unless it can do that, its function becomes peripheral.

Cricket in England is only a part of life, rather than a way of life as it is in India or Pakistan. In Bombay, they will turn out in their thousands just to watch Tendulkar take his bat to the nets. It's not like that here and, alas, never will be, but we can improve our lot, nonetheless.

The pyramid is different, here. Yes, we now have sound sys- tems in place to introduce kids to cricket at junior school, but the base level will always be the clubs. In general – and I know there are admirable exceptions – clubs are not interested in strengthening links with counties, who in turn are often too pre- occupied with their own parish matters to concern themselves greatly with England. So there are no easy steps up the ladder – a sharp contrast to the system in Australia, where any cricketing lad will say, unprompted, that he wants to captain his country. In England, the equivalent boy is more likely to content himself with an ambition to make some runs for his town club.

As international cricket has strengthened and expanded, the domestic first-class competitions have withered around the world. A shame, but this is evolution. Take the case of Glenn McGrath, who already has more than 250 Test wickets and is one of the first names inked into any World XI team sheet. By recent reckoning, he has only played 16 times for his state side, New South Wales – most of our Test players would do that in little more than a summer.

Wasim Akram is forever expounding his philosophies of cricket and he says that if he comes to England to play a Test series, he is not interested in the other games. Darren Gough, meantime, is haring back to Yorkshire, where only his best is acceptable. Any decent racehorse trainer will tell you that good horses are ruined if you run them too often, and this is the fate of many of our best cricketers. It also helps explain why there is an apparent talent drain after the teenage years. We have long had a successful national Under-19 team and people are rightly bewildered about what happens to them afterwards. The answer is that they enter a county system that, for all its wonderful traditions, is simply not structured to encourage the type of mental and technical excellence required at Test level. All too soon, these gifted 19-year-olds are absorbed by the system and soured by it.

The counties have been primarily responsible for the perpetuation of an outdated structure, and for going back to it even when they have previously agreed to change – the dropped and then hastily revived Benson & Hedges Cup being one staggering example. But the situation might have been improved if the elected executives had spoken out more freely. Since succeeding A C Smith as chief executive of the Board, Tim Lamb has seen himself as protecting the interests of the counties who appointed him. Everyone with the England team at heart wants him to bang the table, to move things forward, to say that he is the chief executive and that this is how things should happen. But he has not done it.

Eventually, I am convinced, we will get there, reach out for a system that allows us to compete on level terms with countries who have passed us by. That progress, and the development of the national team itself, is currently being hampered by administration that is both a jumble and a jungle. They will get it right, because they have to. It might take another ten years, and there might be more casualties along the way, but I will be the biggest supporter of whatever it needs to get English cricket back to the top.

I can afford to observe it more dispassionately now, care though I do. My life with Diana is good, my commentary commitments stimulating and my leisure time happily divided between family – daughter Sarah and her three chidren Sam, James and Jasmine, Graham his new son Joseph, and younger sons Steven and Ben – and hobbies – the fishing, the golf, the wine collecting, the days at the races and the pals at the golf club we call 'The Regiment'.

Cricket has given me a wonderful life, and continues to do so. If there were sad and bad times during my years with England, they were greatly outweighed by the days of fulfilment and enjoyment. It's not my nature to bear grudges and I think I emerged from a job with fiercer spotlight than most in the country without any enemies. I certainly emerged with the unchanged philosophy that there is nothing wrong with saying what you think. I have never been one to deal in don't knows.

Index